EDUCATING THE CREATIVE ARTS THERAPIST

EDUCATING THE CREATIVE ARTS THERAPIST

A PROFILE OF THE PROFESSION

By

SHAUN McNIFF, Ph.D.

Professor of Expressive Therapy and Dean
Institute for the Arts and Human Development
Lesley College Graduate School
Cambridge, Massachusetts

CHARLES C THOMAS • PUBLISHER
Springfield • Illinois • U.S.A.

Published and Distributed Throughout the World by

CHARLES C THOMAS • PUBLISHER

2600 South First Street

Springfield, Illinois 62717

© *1986 by* CHARLES C THOMAS • PUBLISHER

ISBN 0-398-05172-0

Library of Congress Catalog Card Number: 85-14747

With THOMAS BOOKS *careful attention is given to all details of manufacturing and
design. It is the Publisher's desire to present books that are satisfactory as to their physical
qualities and artistic possibilities and appropriate for their particular use.* THOMAS
BOOKS *will be true to those laws of quality that assure a good name and good will.*

Printed in the United States of America
Q-R-3

Library of Congress Cataloging in Publication Data

McNiff, Shaun.
    Educating the creative arts therapist.

    Bibliography: p.
    Includes index.
    1. Art therapy — Study and teaching — United States.
    2. Art therapy — Study and teaching.   I. Title.
    RC489.A7M36   1985   616.89'1656   85-14747
    ISBN 0-398-05172-0

ACKNOWLEDGMENTS

I BEGAN THIS BOOK while living in Connemara and serving as a visiting professor at the National University of Ireland, University College Galway. After completing *The Arts and Psychotherapy* (1981), I felt a need to go further with research into the essential elements of the psychotherapeutic and healing process. Throughout all of my work, there is a commitment to articulating universal and cross-cultural elements of creativity and therapeutic practice. Experience has repeatedly shown me that the best routes to the universal are the particulars of life, tangible entities and practical problems shared by a group of people. However, the specific form of my new psychotherapy book kept eluding me, perhaps because I was not applying my insights into the importance of particulars, and the things that structure daily life, to the process of my psychotherapy research.

While I was serving briefly as a visiting professor at the University of New Mexico and working with Howard McConeghey, the form of this book began to take shape. Prior to visiting New Mexico, I had taught an intensive course at Mount Mary College in Milwaukee, and, while flying to Wisconsin, it occurred to me that I should write a book on higher education in the creative arts therapies. I realized that all of my writings of the previous two years, attempting to uncover the essence of psychotherapy, were really about my experiences with training. This revelation allowed me to expand my work within a more tangible context. I needed to write about what I do everyday as a profesor, dean and psychotherapy trainer.

Since this is the first book on higher education in the creative arts therapies, I have not been able to draw on precedents and a conserve of information to either support or criticize. Because I have synthesized data from many different areas, my personal values will inevitably influence what is presented as the profile of the profession. I recognize the unavoidable projection of self and I am curious to see how well the portrayal and presentation of issues holds up in the future. At first I thought that I should try to present information in a way that revealed as little personal bias as possible. I generally attempted to follow this direction but realized that a book must also have a personality together with a distinct voice and authors must take risks, especially if journeying into uncharted territory. Research in the creative arts therapies is in need of a book unto itself. I have only touched upon the subject in this volume and I would like to do more with it in the future.

Paolo Knill has consulted with me on all aspects of this project and continues as my closest research associate. For my cross-cultural work I thank Phillip Speiser in Sweden, Hans Helmut Decker-Voigt in West Germany, Vivien Marcow and Baruch Zadick in Israel, Annette Brederode in Holland and Finland, and Fridolin Henking in Switzerland. Catherine Cobb has also assisted me. In addition to her critical evaluations of the manuscript, she coordinated the data organization and correspondence with the colleges and universities, submitting information used in Chapter 4, "Characteristics of Academic Training Programs." Vincent Ferrini, Truman Nelson and Rudolf Arnheim are always behind my work as guides. Dick Wylie has been the leader of the academic administrative team that I work with and he has supported my scholarship and freedom. Special thanks are given to my children, Liam and Kelsey, for loving and tolerating a father who spends so much time engaged with books and papers. And, of course, none of this research on higher education in the creative arts therapies would be possible without the students and faculty who represent the profession in colleges and universities throughout the United States and the world. Our profession is a dynamic mix of fiercely independent educators who are expressive of a diversity that, when allowed to manifest itself freely, results in a depth and excellence in training.

A final word of thanks is due to Charles C Thomas, Publisher and Payne Thomas, Editor, for believing in the creative arts therapy profession.

CONTENTS

EDUCATING THE CREATIVE ARTS THERAPIST

1. INTRODUCTION

THERE HAVE BEEN remarkable developments in the creative arts therapy profession during the twenty-year period extending from the mid 1960s to the present time. The growth and expansion of the profession has been manifested within institutions of higher education. The creative arts therapies have been establishing a consistent and respected position on the campuses of colleges and universities throughout the United States and the world. In addition to providing decisive statistical information about the presence of the profession, training programs for creative arts therapists have become a significant educational enterprise within many institutions of higher education. Colleges and universities with successful programs in the creative arts therapies have adopted the profession as an essential part of their institutional missions, not only in terms of service to society but also as a vital and contributing component to the schools' academic and fiscal well-being. The increased presence of academic training programs within institutions of higher education has significantly advanced the status of the profession. However, many academic administrators and educators in related fields of the fine arts, psychology, psychiatry, the arts in education and the humanities are unaware of the existence of the creative arts therapy profession and its expanding position within higher education. Creative arts therapists from the different specializations of art therapy, dance therapy, drama therapy, music therapy, poetry therapy, psychodrama and integrated arts therapy are often not informed of what is happening outside of their concentrations. The different specializations have developed their separate national associations and in the case of one specialization there are two national associations. There is also a national organization dealing with all of the arts in therapy as opposed to the more prevalent pattern of organizing around specific media.

The different creative arts therapies have evolved separately from one another in a dynamic and creative manner. The relative absence of controls has allowed the creative process to unfold in relation to professional needs. Institutional and governmental regulation agencies have had little to do with the first stages of the creation of the profession which has been created by individuals and small groups with personal and shared visions. As a result of this pattern there is great diversity within the field. As the profession has matured, national associations have become more prescriptive and controlling and there is a significant change toward national standardization. High standards and the protection of the public are given as primary reasons for this prescriptiveness. These concerns are valid and undisputed, but there are other motives for educational prescriptions which are connected to the vested interests of individuals, institutions and the continuities of power in a profession.

Based on lists of schools provided by the national professional associations in the creative arts therapies in 1984, we have determined that there are at least 137 colleges and universities in the United States involved in the professional training of creative arts therapists at the time of this writing. We know that the association lists are not completely descriptive of all educational opportunities in the profession. Many schools not included on the lists either did not fit association criteria for inclusion or have not submitted information about their programs to the associations. Based on our personal knowledge of the profession, we assume that more than 200 institutions of higher education are either presently offering formal educational opportunities in the creative arts therapies or are actively engaged in designing and implementing programs or individual courses. Our total estimate of institutions of higher education engaged in creative arts therapy education represents variety in terms of the nature of the school's involvement, which may range from large degree programs on the undergraduate and graduate levels to smaller programs. Institutions may offer undergraduate and graduate training or one of the two. Other colleges and universities offer only selected coursework as part of degree programs in related areas. The number of educational institutions involved in the creative arts therapies is expanded when considering extensive continuing education and workshop offerings throughout the United States; independent study projects that undergraduate and graduate students commonly do for credit; together with theses and dissertations on the creative arts therapies within degree programs in related fields.

There are also many non-academic institutes and clinics involved in creative arts therapy education, most of which takes place on the graduate level. As described at a later point in this book, psychodrama education and training has almost exclusively taken place within private institutes. Rather than approving institutions (as the other creative arts therapies have done), psychodrama has been involved in certifying individual trainers. Art therapy has a group of graduate level institute, certificate and clinical training programs which take place outside of higher education. In addition to these formal educational programs, all of the creative arts therapies have a history of individual apprenticeship training.

THE VALUE OF THE CREATIVE ARTS THERAPIES

All forms of training in the creative arts therapies continue to expand rather than decline, even within the present economic climate in society that is not strongly supportive of human services. This can be attributed to the appeal of the profession to potential students and to the proven efficacy of the work of creative arts therapists who are now employed in varied clinical settings throughout the world. Students are drawn to the profession because of the opportunity to fully integrate interests in art and human service on a level of clinical sophistication which has unfortunately not been universally achieved in the closely related field of the arts in education. The creative arts therapies in their most enlightened and liberating forms are indicating a new vision of art in society which suggests the restoration of an ancient and archetypal integration of the creative process with healing. Although the profession has a strong secular identity and a gift for interdependence with the traditions of psychology and psychiatry, there is, in my opinion, a primal and unspoken spiritual motive which accounts for the rise of the creative arts therapies. This spiritual sense of art and its healing power is not at the forefront of the profession's consciousness, because the dominant institutions of the mental health field speak a different language. The arts, however, with unusual skills for adaptation which have been revealed throughout history, have quickly learned how to speak the language of the contemporary mental health context. Creative arts therapists have been respected by the older clinical professions for their flexibility and ingenious assimilation, which has enabled them to think and act within the constructs of a clinical tradition that on the surface may appear to have little relationship to art.

The genius of the creative arts therapy profession results from the integration of two primary elements, art and health, that have not been associated with one another within the institutions of the "civilized" and scientifcally oriented world. If we look to the past and to the healing practices of indigenous cultures, there is considerable evidence that creative expression and healing belong together. In these traditions the religious and philosophical consciousness is integrated with what might be described as more "scientifically" oriented healing practices. The expansion of the creative arts therapy profession can be largely attributed to a primal (and not always conscious) longing for the integration of the essential elements of the healing process. The nature of the synthesis between art and therapy can take many forms. In addition to the inclusion of traditional art forms (e.g. painting, drawing, sculpting, dancing, music making, drama, writing, etc.) into the many different approaches to therapy that presently exist in the world, the process of therapy itself may be perceived as an art. Conceptual and performance art forms of the twentieth century have indicated that there are few limits to what may be considered as artistic action and contemplation. Art may in fact be better suited to depth psychology than any other mode of inquiry.

The current respectability of the creative arts therapies can be attributed to their ability to expand the scope of communication in therapy. Through the arts, all of the senses are engaged as well as action and the body. The arts increase possibilities for interpersonal and intrapersonal understanding, perceptual awareness, cognitive activity and the affirmation of others. Within the emotional and spiritual context, the arts are vehicles of liberation through which the passions are expressed and respected. Religious traditions that engage the entire body and different forms of expression in worship describe how if God wanted them to pray with just words, they they would not have been given the ability to move, sing and make images. The arts speak the language of the soul and have access to emotional conflicts, disturbances and pains that are not reached through conventional psychological language. "Depth" is a characteristic of serious art.

In addition to being constant vehicles of the depth psychology of the human spirit, the arts are pragmatic and can be applied to therapeutic situations where conventional modes of communication are not as effective. Sensory expression is often the only way to reach people who are in severe states of emotional withdrawal, depression or psychic confusion. The arts allow for the ventilation, cathartic release and transformation of aggression and violent emotions. What has been most influential in the use of the arts in mental health programs is their life-affirming qualities and humanistic spirit. Creative action, imagery and various other expressions of the artistic consciousness not only transform individual lives but institutions as well. The arts validate the human spirit that is present within every institutional setting.

THEORY INDIGENOUS TO ART

In addition to adapting art to the theoretical conventions of the mental health field (a vital and necessary activity for the student and therapist), the creative arts therapies can create and rediscover theory that is indigenous to art. Art is the primary process of the profession and its power cannot be fully realized within theoretical systems and approaches to therapy that approach art as an adjunctive mode of operation. The essential dynamics of therapeutic change can be perceived as creative transformation, and the workings of the psyche can be viewed in artistic terms. I discussed the principles of creativity and health with members of the psychology department at Tel Aviv University, and the chairman of clinical psychology spoke of how healthy people have the ability to change imagery and avoid immersion in pathological obsession. He responded favorably to the conceptualization of therapy as art and the fact that the many different types of situations encountered by the therapist require a creative use of personal resources.

Ultimately, it is a matter of personal philosophy as to whether or not therapists perceive their work as art or science, or as an integration of the two. The acceptance of the art of therapy is, however, unavoidable since the process does not satisfy the basic rules of science. Psychotherapy does not follow a consistent logic and experiences cannot be repeated under constant conditions. Change and adaptation prevail.

Many creative arts therapists have either been content to take on secondary and adjunctive roles within mental health systems or have been willing to conceptualize the relationship between art and therapy within the context of conventional psychological constructs. The mainstream of artistic conceptualization within the twentieth century has not been focused on health and therapy. The arts have abandoned their archetypal healing functions. The combination of art and health can enrich every form of therapy, and creativity can become a major health concept. But first, the creative arts therapy profession must realize that it has the ability to take on a primary role within the health field. The world of art needs to become more involved with principles of health, human relationships, community, the professions and social transformation. If we perceive ourselves within adjunctive and secondary roles, we will create this destiny for the profession.

An art therapy educator told me that we need to look at what we are doing in the creative arts therapies, and what is happening within the person, and articulate this directly rather than within the context of theoretical stereotypes. In this respect our conceptualization of the profession can become more empirical and primary rather than derivative. The more we know of different psychological systems, the more we can use them to develop theories that define and express what is actually taking place within the creative arts therapies. People often lean on psychological conventions in order to feel empowered and identified with a particular point of view. However, these systems obscure direct observations and descriptions of what takes place within the creative arts therapy experience.

The major historic principles of twentieth century psychotherapy are based on the position that emotional conflicts can be rationally analyzed, understood and thus cured. Dreams, free associations and other forms of primary language are utilized but within the context of providing material for rational reduction. Art is in this context used as a source of raw material for a "higher" synthesis and is not engaged as a primary form of therapeutic transformation. Rational analysis approaches the soul as a puzzle to be sorted out. Art does not contradict or belittle the role of reason in psychotherapy, but simply adds the dimension of transformation and, by so doing, augments the scope and resources of psychotherapy.

Artistic transformation has the ability to transcend the limits, "knots" and "binds" of rational discourse. Through the arts, problems and conflicts are engaged within the realm of primary, creative process. The experience of artistic transformation, which involves working with the conflict through the body, imagery, sound and physical enactment, involves the person in the action of using the source of disturbance as the energy and motivation for expression. Through artistic transformation, a re-alignment of the psyche takes place at the primary level of the senses. The experience demonstrates to the person how the problem can provoke creative and humanly significant acts. Art therefore affirms, through tangible forms, the transformative and healing powers of the psyche. Through art the soul cures and purifies itself while maintaining vitality. Students and clients involved in the process of artistic expression in therapy often force themselves to find a rational "solution" to their art rather than allowing themselves to find satisfaction and guidance within the context of the art material. Creative arts therapists must find ways to avoid making art subservient to conventional psychological analysis.

Rational analysis does not have this ability to re-structure the inner world, because it operates in another realm. Within therapeutic systems that proceed exclusively through rational discourse, an emotional problem is identified and "transferred" from the context of the emotions and into the context of reason, where therapeutic dialogue takes place. The person is then expected to take the rational explanation and implant it into the emotions. Effective therapists who communicate principally through spoken language are capable of directly engaging the emotions and the mind, body and spirit sensitivities of the client. When talking in therapy proceeds poetically and imaginatively, within a storytelling form, and when the relationship between therapist and client is an expression of the creative process, spoken language becomes artistic transformation. Therapy and art are concerned with transformative change, and the effective therapist is a person who is able to fully engage the creative resources of the environment.

Mature and experienced psychotherapists realize that therapeutic training often places a disproportionate emphasis on rational, problem-solving strategies which overlook the primal process of the therapeutic relationship. As with the training of artists, emphasis needs to be placed on the formation of the person as the vehicle of therapeutic transformation. Medicine has gone deeply into the realm of chemical transformation and drugs, which raises serious ethical and health issues for the mental health field. James Hillman describes how "the creative is an achievement of love . . . . [and] therapy is love itself" (Hillman, 1978, p. 54 & p. 88). Anna Polcino emphasizes the need for personal affirmation in psychotherapy: "While we struggle in lonely silence to restore our spirit, we need strong, unqualifiedly affirming voices. Only those who offer spontaneous and unreserved affirmation can help us in this struggle and give us the courage and strength to return alone to our thoughts and feelings, to discover what we really want to do and with whom we wish to travel on our journey" (Polcino, 1979, p. 9).

Transformative therapeutic engagement occurs within the primary language of the image, the body, and physical enactment. My clinical work in the creative arts therapies has repeatedly demonstrated that when we leave the language of art, we distance ourselves from feeling and separate our souls from the experience. The principal value of the creative arts therapies is their ability to bring about disciplined and profound therapeutic transformation at the primary level of the senses. Analysis and discussion, as well as interpretation, are often essential parts of the therapeutic experience, especially within the context of sharing and clarifying feelings and thoughts. There is a necessary interdependence between thought and action; reasoning and art. As I will discuss in more detail at a later point in this book, the creative arts therapies have done a commendable job at developing competencies within the realm of analytic psychology. I fear that the profession has done so well that it often overlooks its origins in art.

Training in the creative arts therapies cannot avoid involving students in transformative experiences with the artistic process. In reviewing catalog materials from colleges and universities, I was particularly impressed by the philosophy of education expressed by Middeloo (Sociaal Pedagogische Opleidingen), a training center for creative arts therapists in Amersfoort, The Netherlands, which was founded in 1965. The different "branches" of the creative arts therapies are considered by the Dutch school to be part of one profession. The Middeloo program describes how therapists engage clients in whatever material is most suited to the momentary state of the person. The creative process is perceived as giving form to raw materials. The four-year training program involves students in studies of varied materials in the different art forms with the goal of understanding their unique "possibilities." The training program is committed to the belief that training methods are to parallel the methods of professional practice. Students studying to become expert in facilitating the creative experience of clients are involved in their personal creative and transformative process through training. The catalog describes how "uniform requirements of educational goals" are contrary to the processes that the program is engaged with. Students are expected to "define and redefine" their personal goals and make their "own definitions" (Middeloo, 1984). The process of learning is compared to the therapeutic experience of giving form to materials. The Middeloo program is an example of how processes indigenous to art can guide and shape the education of creative arts therapists.

THE PROFESSIONAL CONTEXT

Higher education has distinct levels of achievement, expressed by the term "degree." The creative arts therapy profession should aspire to the highest degree, if it chooses to place itself within the academic context. Lower level expectations will reinforce lower level identity. The "degree" structure may in fact be an inaccurate measure of competence and sophistication, but it is nevertheless the system that the creative arts therapies have chosen to recognize by pursuing training and professional legitimization within higher education. Doctoral level training in the creative arts therapies will inevitably develop in the near future. In addition to offering opportunities for the most advanced forms of academic inquiry, we need advanced training programs to support clinical practice with scholarship, to educate faculty and professional leaders and to increase the prestige of the profession. It will be to our advantage to develop a variety of doctoral study options ranging from more academic to clinical training orientations. Many creative arts therapy clinicians and educators have already been able to earn doctorates in related fields. This book focuses more on the bachelor's degree, master's degree and non-academic training opportunities that presently exist within the profession. Attention will be given to the controversy that now exists as to whether professional entry level training should, or should not, take place at the baccalaureate stage.

The creative arts therapy profession today is comprised of art therapy, dance/movement therapy, drama therapy, expressive therapy, integrated creative arts therapy, music therapy, phototherapy, poetry therapy, videotherapy, and all other art forms as they are applied to the therapeutic process. Psychodrama has recently allied itself with the creative arts therapies, bringing its psychodynamic and artistic sophistication into the profession. The inclusion of psychodrama results from the fact that this specialization shares core philosophical and operational principles with the creative arts therapies (e.g. creativity, action, group work and an emphasis on the transformation of conflict). There are, however, many psychodramatists who have primary identities with psychiatry, psychology, social work and other professions who do not identify with the creative arts therapies. Although the different disciplines have developed separately from one another, with different educational histories, standards and professional identities, there are many forces within the mental health field, within higher education, within the em-

ployment marketplace, within accrediting agencies, and within the specializations themselves, that are encouraging the creative arts therapies to investigate their common identity. Pragmatic rather than idealistic factors are bringing about increased cooperation between the creative arts therapies. Coalitions are being established as a result of mutual development and survival needs. The different specializations are realizing that they have similar purposes and that mutual organization serves the interest of all participants. The influence that is needed to shape the future can be best realized through a collective effort.

In this book the creative arts therapies are referred to as a single profession which like any other complex discipline is composed on varied areas of specialization. The different creative arts therapy modalities are far more similar than they are different. However, within every family group there is diversity and uniqueness. It is my belief that the strongest group encourages the autonomy and the comprehensive definition of its individual members. This respect for diversity is not only recommended for the different specializations within the creative arts therapies but for the different ways of practicing within a particular modality.

Because our profession is so new, scholarship and literature have been largely focused on describing clinical work. Higher education has developed with little study of itself. There has been even less attention given to comparative study of the different creative arts therapy disciplines. Separateness and isolation are strongly enforced by the lack of cohesion and cooperation between the different creative arts therapy specializations. Art, in the generic sense of all media (Kunst), must be unified as an approach to therapy. This unification can be achieved in a manner which respects media competence. As I stated earlier with regard to art and science in psychotherapy, the manner in which a person approaches the process of integration will reflect personal style and philosophy. Some will choose to work with a single art form and others will feel the necessity to work with more than one. What ultimately matters is whether a person will be capable of integrating all of the resources of the self and of the environment for the benefit of the client. Separations of the essential process of art seriously weaken the influence and combined strength of the profession. The basic theory and practice of an integrated approach to the arts is described in *The Arts and Psychotherapy* (McNiff, 1981).

The integration of the arts in therapy involves more than simply taking a selection of courses in the different modalities. Philosophical and operational coherence is required within both the person and the training program. In addition to the different creative arts therapies, the material available for integration includes all of the resources accessible through comprehensive education. Educational processes emphasizing the personal integration of diversity correspond to similar psychotherapeutic principles.

I presented the rationale for a wholistic approach to the arts in therapy during the "Great Debate" on "The place of art in art therapy" at the 1982 national convention of the American Art Therapy Association:

> Both art and healing must draw from all available materials whatever best fits the situation and is most natural and useful to the participants in the process. The practical, open-minded therapist realizes this. However, some professionals feel that they can be empowered only through full mastery of a particular technique or by identification with and knowledge of a particular theory. Emotional stress has little to do with techniques and isolated theories, and everything to do with the totality of life . . . . Art by its nature includes everything imaginable . . . . Art, like therapy, not only includes all of life but certainly the specific elements of gesture, body movement, imagery, sound, words and enactment. These elements complement one another and cannot be separated in either art or life . . . . I do not wish to deny the validity of the extreme position of focusing exclusively on specific elements and materials in therapy. Power lies in focus, concentration, and discipline. I am sure that there are therapists and healers who do profound work by limiting themselves to specific materials like stones or sand. However, I do not think it is wise to take this kind of specialization further by establishing associations, credentials, and education guidelines for stone therapists and sand therapists . . . . Perhaps the problem is that we have become so big that out of a search for intimacy, a sense of belonging or community and economic stability many of us in the helping professions have increasingly specialized and separated one from the other. Time will reveal that these separations have more to do with the needs of therapists than with the needs of clients (McNiff, 1982, pp. 122-123).

The principle rationale for the establishment of the creative arts therapies as a profession was the need to include the arts, the body and the full range of human expressions in the mental health field. In a relatively short time the creative arts therapies have become essential elements of comprehensive mental health programs. The identification of specializations in the different art media appears to have been necessary to conceptualize and develop the first stages of the profession. As the creative arts therapies mature and their place within health services becomes more secure, it is necessary to not only emphasize the commonalities between the different art forms but also the role that creative and non-verbal expression can take within all forms of therapy.

The older professional associations in the creative arts therapies at the present time are exclusively engaged in single-modality training and credentialing. There is little effort being given to how study in more than one art form can benefit the creative arts therapist. Integrated work is becoming increasingly popular and clinically useful in the creative arts therapies. It might be determined that every creative arts therapist is to select a primary concentration and seek credentialing through that modality. This approach will in fact accommodate the majority of creative arts therapists presently in practice. However, it does not resolve all issues of professional standards and education. The full-time drama therapist who is involved for one-third of the week in movement therapy may be as much engaged in that particular specialization as a part-time dance therapist. And how do we approach the issue of creative arts therapsits who also do verbal family therapy and group therapy?

I do not think that it is reasonable for each specific creative arts therapy association to attempt to credential and establish educational standards for every clinician who may desire to use that particular modality. This would result in an unproductive maze of credentialing and excessive control. Our objective should rather be to increasingly involve all of the mental health disciplines in the different creative arts therapies. Within the most conservative credentialing context, it can be argued that each mental health specialization will benefit from increasing their repertoire of communication modalities. Individual schools may desire to integrate other art forms into educational programs in a single creative arts therapy modality. This integration can be achieved without upsetting the autonomous structure of the different creative arts therapy specializations. It is necessary to support those who want to establish a primary identification with a single modality. It is equally important to validate the work of those who specialize in an integrated approach to the arts in therapy (e.g. *Gesamtkunstwerk*).

The application of principles of creativity within varied media is a vital concentration within the creative arts therapies. Rather than creating new credentialing groups and professional associations that will overlap those that presently exist, it is recomended that the coalition of creative arts therapy associations recognize the importance of integrated arts training and develop credentialing procedures within the exisiting family of organizations. At the present time, the American Art Therapy Association, the American Association for Music Therapy, the American

Dance Therapy Association, the American Society of Group Psychotherapy and Psychodrama, the National Association for Drama
Therapy and the National Association for Music Therapy are all exclusively involved with single-modality training standards and professional
registration. As stated earlier, this approach to specialization appears to
be accommodating the needs of the majority of creative arts therapists
who are practicing today. The American Association of Artist-
Therapists is the only creative arts therapy association which registers
integrated creative arts therapists. The creative arts therapy profession
must become more inclusive of all legitimate and serious training and
clinical activities that either presently exist, or will be offered, within the
context of the field. There is a clear, definitive and common identity for
all of the creative arts therapies that centers on the *primary* use of creativity as a process of therapeutic transformation. Attempts to create professional identity through divisions of the media-related parts of creativity
are not sound. The logical extension of this orientation would be the
creation of different groups responsible for separate educational and credentialing criteria for professionals who are allowed to talk in therapy,
those who are qualified to move, etc.

New associations in the creative arts therapies together with new po-
litical and philosophical movements are healthy and essential to vitality.
They are expressions of change and transformation. The mature and secure profession encourages innovation and diversity and makes every effort to be inclusive of variety and differences. The coalition of creative
arts therapy associations should address itself to maintaining the traditions of the different creative arts therapy specializations while also
pushing forward for the most inclusive and high-quality standards for
the integration of art and therapy. Artists, in particular, should be sensitive to these issues.

THE EDUCATIONAL ENVIRONMENT

Now that the profession has so completely attached its destiny to institutions of higher education, it is timely to investigate the principles
upon which this new alliance is based. No single group of prominent institutions in our society has a comparable vested interest in the creative
arts therapies than the increasingly large group of colleges and universities offering training programs. An educator with whom I discussed this

manuscript told me to "make sure we stay around for a while." As a new profession, the creative arts therapies have concerns about their future stability and, hopefully, this book will contribute to their visibility and vitality.

As with many of my peers within the creative arts therapies, I have been extensively involved in program development throughout my academic career. I have observed how through the creation of programs we have created the profession. As a dean, program director and program developer in the United States, Israel and Europe, I have had the opportunity to be involved in the administration of higher education. The intricacies and history of higher education have fascinated me and provided the motivation for this book. Following the general pattern established by the majority of creative arts therapy educators, I have maintained respect for the primacy of clinical practice and experiential teaching. I have also maintained my identity as an artist.

On a broader perspective, I believe that the creative arts therapies are part of a more general problem in higher education where the pressures of vocationalism, credentialing and the narrow vested interests of different groups are creating a crisis in relation to the role of the humanities and the arts in colleges and universities. These problems apply to the creative arts therapies and the educational policies of our national associations. The creative arts therapies must take a significantly stronger position in support of comprehensive education, training in the arts, the humanities and the continuities of culture. There appears to be little creative dialogue and confrontation between creative arts therapy professional associations and institutions of higher education. The national association prescribes and colleges and universities, eager for professional enrollments, follow.

As a creative arts therapy educator said to me during an interview conducted as part of the research for this book, national associations must encourage high standards through inspiration rather than prescription. As a teacher, I have learned that I cannot prescribe my personal values and experience to others. The educator enters into dialogue with students and colleagues, sets an example, provides guidance and support together with criticism, and transmits motivation for achievement and inquiry. It is my hope that this book will offer an antidote, small as it may be, to the educational prescription trend. Humanistic, cultural and free studies in all areas of knowledge are essential to insure the future depth and quality of the profession. Faculty freedom to teach and the institution's responsibility to offer a course of studies consistent with its educational mission are to be encouraged within the creative arts therapies. If the trend toward the prescription of studies continues, the creative arts therapies profession will find itself associated only with those colleges and universities which are willing to follow a detailed curriculum established by an external group.

This study is intended to give an overview of what is happening today in the education of creative arts therapists. In addition to presenting my experiences as an educator and the values which guide my work, I have investigated the work of others. The comparative review of higher education within the creative arts therapies has been illuminating, in that it has enabled me to learn more about the varieties of educational models that are presently operating within the profession. It has been equally revealing to observe the common elements of training present in all educational programs. The research process has involved the review of catalog materials from colleges and universities from throughout the United States and other parts of the world. Interviews with educators have also been conducted in order to increase sensitivity to varied points of view and issues of common concern.

This book was undertaken to give definition to the profession and to begin a common dialogue between all of the creative arts therapies on the subject of educational priorities. Although I have been actively involved in program development and teaching in Israel, Ireland, Switzerland, West Germany, Sweden, Norway, Finland and Holland, the focus of this book has been the comparative review of the training opportunities that exist within the United States. On the basis of my experience, I believe that a comprehensive study of the numerous training programs within the United States is an appropriate starting point for cross-cultural educational studies. The fundamental educational principles that are described in relation to American programs can be applied to training programs that exist within other cultures. Like their American counterparts, creative arts therapy training programs in other cultures seem to benefit through association with institutions of higher education. For example, art therapy training programs in England tend to be affiliated with schools of art, while music therapy training in West Germany is offered within schools of music (the musikhochschule). Because European institutions of higher education are so closely regulated by government, program development in new areas like the creative arts therapies does not take place with the freedom that often characterizes

American higher education. Consequently, non-academic and privately operated training institutes are being created in Europe.

My goal has been to make faculty colleagues in other disciplines, as well as college and university administrators, more aware of the creative arts therapy profession and the roles that they may take in its future development. I am concerned with reaching present and potential students with the goal of articulating educational principles that they are, are not, or could be experiencing. I am committed to engaging practicing therapists and members of national professional associations in the dialogue about educational principles. Creative arts therapy associations have become primary shapers of educational policy and, in this respect, every professional member should become more aware of their individual responsibility and influence. I am most aware of my efforts to speak to my colleagues in the higher education of creative arts therapists. I have tried to address the major issues and challenges for our shared future and what we can learn from our past and present. In addition to supporting one another, we must begin to develop literature on higher education that will assist existing programs together with those of the future.

The chapters of the book dealing with themes that concern all aspects of higher education in the creative arts therapies are complemented with a discussion of principles that have been most useful to me in my work with students. I have made the most constant use of the material in Chapter 8, "An Artistic Theory of Mental Health and Therapy." It is a consolidated version of years of journal writing and ongoing attempts to record the essence of my work. Through these reflections I have been able to develop a theory of training that involves students in the process of creating their unique personal form, or what might be described as their individual professional style. Education is perceived as a process of personal emergence and formation rather than technical acquisition. Emphasis is placed on the training of the person as an instrumentality of therapeutic transformation.

Chapter 11, "Dialogue With Educators," was a new and lively research activity involving a series of interviews. The articulate and inspiring viewpoints of my colleagues validated many of my ideas, corrected others and in some cases simply presented a different point of view.

REFERENCES

Hillman, James: *The Myth of Analysis*. New York, Harper and Row, 1978.

McNiff, Shaun: Working with everything we have. *American Journal of Art Therapy, 21*, 122-123, 1982.

Middeloo: Training program brochure. Amersfoort, The Netherlands, 1984.

Polcino, Anna: *Loneliness: The Genesis of Solitude, Friendship, and Contemplation*. Whitinsville, MA, Affirmation Books, 1979.

2. HISTORIC TRENDS IN AMERICAN HIGHER EDUCATION

THE CREATIVE ARTS therapist can be viewed as the most thoroughly interdisciplinary of twentieth century human service professionals integrating art, science, clinical practice and spiritual transformation. Though relatively small, the creative arts therapy field is an extraordinary example of multidisciplinary integration. The fine arts, psychology and psychiatry have been primary contributors to the creation of the profession. Other influences have come from education and special education, social work, physical therapy, occupational therapy, anthropology, religion, the humanities and interdisciplinary studies of myth, symbol and ritual. The education of the creative arts therapist thus assumes a more recent place on the family tree comprised of related fields. The specific issues of training creative arts therapists cannot be properly understood unless they are perceived in relation to these other fields and the history of their educational programs.

THE TRADITION OF LIBERAL EDUCATION

During the seventeenth and eighteenth centuries in the United States, higher education was closely tied to religion and a relatively uniform "classical" curriculum. The colonial colleges were modeled after English schools and one of their primary purposes was the education of ministers. Education in other professions was done by apprenticeship with the emphasis on practice rather than theoretical inquiry. The Renaissance principles of education have had a far-reaching impact on American liberal education. Although changes and transformations did occur over the centuries, there was a relatively unbroken continuity in the content of liberal education for 450-500 years, from the time of the early Renaissance to the late nineteenth century in America when significant new directions began to emerge in higher education (Ganss, 1954).

With the exception of training programs for clergy, "professional" education was not a significant factor within the first 200 years of American higher education. Learning was directed toward antiquity and its influence on the present. In addition to medical schools, conservatories of music and visual art academies were established during the nineteenth century as specialized institutions, distinct from the liberal arts college.

The liberal arts tradition in America has been described as a religion (Bird, 1975), the efficacy of which rests more with faith (Winter, Mc-Clelland, and Stewart, 1981) than empirical evidence. The liberal tradition is also clearly associated with elitism and class structure. It can be argued that the prominence of graduates of liberal arts institutions has more to do with their sense of entitlement than it does with the specific content of their education. In this respect college can be perceived as an experience in learning that has more to do with acquiring social and interpersonal skills and establishing identity as a person who has something to offer the world. Studies of liberal arts college education reveal that students tend to develop common traits which include increased intellectual orientation, independence, open-mindedness, aesthetic sensitivity and introspection (Feldman and Newcomb, 1969).

Jacobi (1957) describes how the particular qualities of a college's social and physical environment do have a transformative effect on students. Colleges have differing images and traditions of values which are transmitted to students. These environmental factors can be profoundly influential in both liberal and professional education. There is little doubt that distinctive professional images, attitudes and values are established in training programs for creative arts therapists. The internalization of the values and identity of the training program are more likely to hold a stronger influence in the first years of practice. As additional experience is acquired, self-image and attitudes are transformed by the workplace.

In spite of the many differing opinions on the value of liberal education in America, the liberal arts college curriculum continues as the vital core of undergraduate education. The specific content and configuration of liberal studies is constantly being transformed in relation to the needs of the immediate environment. The influence and prestige of the liberal arts tradition is a result of its age and continuity in transmitting the fundamental intellectual principles of western civilization. This life span runs for nearly 600 years in the modern era and for 2,400 years back to the origins of the classical tradition in ancient Greece. The principles of liberal arts education are of significance to the education of creative arts therapists in terms of historic influence on the structure of curriculum in the profession. The content of learning in the creative arts therapies relates strongly to the continuities of culture, the arts, and human behavior, all of which have historically been taught through liberal arts colleges. The liberal tradition since the time of the Greeks and the Renaissance has maintained that scholarship and the improvement of mind, body and spirit are ends in themselves. The development of these attributes contribute to the well-being of the individual and society. Not only are the creative arts therapies an extension of the tradition of liberal education but also they bring the fundamental spirit of this continuity to contemporary health professions. The creative arts in therapy are providing the vehicle for the revival of historically validated principles of mind, body and spirit integration within health professions.

Many creative arts therapy training programs on the undergraduate and graduate levels have been developed within liberal arts institutions. But the most significant connection of liberal education to the training of creative arts therapists is the fact that many of the students entering graduate programs in the profession have received undergraduate training in the liberal arts.

THE FINE ARTS

The fine arts, not present in the early classical programs of study in American colleges, were to prosper in womens' colleges established during the late nineteenth and early twentieth centuries and ultimately work their way into the bastions of traditional education, where they are today vital parts of the educational process for men and women alike. Bennington College, Sarah Lawrence College and Mills College, which took the lead in establishing progressive studies before and after the second world war, were particularly influential in offering high-quality artistic training that approached the standards of conservatories of music and dance and art academies. These colleges were often more innovative than the specialized art schools which had become immersed in their particular traditions. Within liberal education, women were typically more involved with arts oriented academic studies. This was not the case in the specialized fine arts schools which had historically enrolled large numbers of men.

Dance, the most recent of the primary "art forms" to appear in American higher education, was pioneered by women's colleges and female students in coeducational institutions. Only in recent years have men begun to become widely involved in dance studies. Classical theater and literature have always had an esteemed place in the mainstream of American liberal education because of their high status in the classical tradition. Drama, poetry and various other literary forms were actually the primary vehicles for the transmission of classical culture within the western academic tradition. The Greek and Renaissance scholastic traditions placed emphasis on written language and textual resources. The "book" has since been the dominant symbol of western education. Oratory skills were similarly valued in the classical tradition and contribute to the status of literature and theater.

Educational programs for women have been primary contributors to the restoration of the wholistic and classical integration of mind and body, together with sound, the visual image and movement. College level programs in both coeducational and single-sex schools have today reached a point where there are far fewer differences between what men and women study. Creative arts in therapy training programs on both the undergraduate and graduate levels continue to attract many more women than men. Psychodrama is the only specialization where there is a more equal distribution according to the gender of students and professionals. As with the history of higher education, women are therefore largely responsible for the restoration of artistic, wholistic and multisensory forms of communication within psychotherapy and the health professions.

BEGINNINGS OF PROFESSIONAL EDUCATION

Training in the learned professions of law and medicine took place primarily through practically oriented apprenticeships in America until the nineteenth century when the first professional schools were established (Brubacher and Rudy, 1976). Only in the later years of the century did the professions begin to be fully integrated into university systems. It was not until after the Civil War that Harvard's new and idealistic president, Charles W. Eliot, was able to have all of the university's professional schools require the bachelor's degree. This produced a drop in enrollments during the years of transition to the new policy. The relatively recent development of higher education policies for what we perceive today as the most prestigious of our professions is a vitally important factor to take into consideration when dealing with "newer" professions like the creative arts therapies. We tend to think that graduate level programs for medical doctors and lawyers have been in existence from the very first stages of American higher education. It is therefore of value to compare the beginnings of professional education in older disciplines to what we are striving to achieve today in the creative arts therapies.

Most professionals up until 1900 did not have a college education (Brubacher and Rudy, 1976). During the nineteenth century, professional schools of law and medicine began to be incorporated into institutions of higher education. In the twentieth century, professional associations became more active in establishing standards for education and practice, which were integrated into the curricula of professional schools of law and medicine. A similar progression occurred in teacher education. The training of teachers became a feature of higher education in the late nineteenth and early twentieth centuries but this was, for the most part, in "normal" schools and teacher training colleges. Dressel reports that "By 1900, 92 state-supported normal schools, offering two- and three-year courses, had been established. The quality of these institutions was notoriously poor" (1963, p.10). In time, these institutions were to follow the trends in law and medicine and become integrated into university settings. In more recent years, schools of nursing, formerly associated with hospitals, continued the pattern of moving into the university. This integration of all forms of professional training into colleges and universities can be attributed to growing demands for diversified and costly physical and human resources.

The university has also become a symbol of quality and advanced training in the professions. "Every occupational specialty and business or industry finds a degree of prestige associated with the existence in the college or university of a curriculum identified as preparatory to that field, and thus the pressures for expansion continue. Each such curricular expansion further underlines the trend toward a blending of vocational and liberal goals in education" (Dressel, 1963, p. 18). The professions have moved, and are continuing to move, into colleges and universities which have historically been identified as "liberal" centers of learning. As a result, the profession acquires increased social dignity and credibility through association with institutions perceived as cultural learning centers. Contemporary humanists fear that the increasing inclusion of vocational training programs within colleges and universities may ultimately destroy the continuities of liberal education and culture. It therefore seems essential for the professions to continuously evaluate how the principles of liberal education, embodied by the university environment, can contribute to their training program.

Conservatories of music and schools of art have similarly affiliated with universities during the nineteenth and twentieth centuries. Many have become totally incorporated into universities, while others have maintained their independent status and have affiliated for the purpose of granting degrees and offering more comprehensive studies. Clinical psychology, which emerged as a profession in the twentieth century, grew out of university psychology departments. The demand for training in applied psychology, rather than psychological research, has been so great in recent years that independent schools of professional psychology have been established across the country. These schools are not replacing university training programs, but their growth has been significant. They offer an example of how the more general pattern in professional training, involving a movement toward the university and away from the specialized training center, can undergo a major reversal.

This movement away from the university can be attributed to the fact that training programs and national association education guidelines have become so specialized that the liberal resources of the university are no longer considered necessary for preparation within the profession of psychology. It would thus appear that the form of American higher education, especially in relation to the professions, is established in relation to the needs of the marketplace. "In the short run, colleges may resist external demands for curricular change. But in the long run the program of the college and the university tends to be modeled to a great extent by the demands of the supporting clientele" (Dressel, 1963, p. 17). At the present time, American higher education can be divided into two sectors: one comprised of well-endowed schools that tend to change slowly and over long periods of time, and the other made up of tuition-driven institutions which must respond quickly to contemporary client demands in order to survive. Within tuition-dependent schools there must be a commitment to innovation, creativity and quality in keeping with the mission of the institution. It is within the tuition- and enrollment-driven schools that creative arts therapy education programs have been developed.

Since the widespread integration of professional training into university environments is a phenomenon that has only begun in the twentieth century in what are considered to be the "older" professions, it would appear that university level training of creative arts therapists will be well established together with other related fields by the end of the century. From the historical perspective of the distant future the creative arts therapies will be an integral part of the first century of comprehensive professional training within universities.

What remains to be seen is whether or not creative arts therapy training will arrive at the well-endowed and "elite" universities, now fully engaged with training in established professions of law, medicine, architecture, engineering, business, religion, education, etc.; whether new educational patterns such as the movement of psychology out of the university will emerge; or whether present conditions will be maintained. A major factor influencing the future will be the inevitable development of Ph.D. level training programs in the creative arts therapies. The prestige that every "occupational specialty" receives through affiliation with a university can be expanded today to refer to the prestige that every profession receives through doctoral level education. The doctorate confers dignity on the profession, trains leaders with credentials equivalent to peers in related fields, supports practical work with research and scholarship, and ultimately brings an emerging profession into line with older fields. Doctoral training in the creative arts therapy field is needed today to achieve these goals. The development of Ph.D. programs may bring highly endowed research universities into active involvement with the profession, because so many of the schools offering bachelor's and master's programs are not presently equipped to sponsor doctoral studies. If major research universities become involved in the creative arts therapies, opportunities for government and privately funded research will grow.

An increasing number of creative arts therapists are going on for studies at the doctoral level in psychology and counseling. They chose these degree programs because of the lack of opportunities for advanced clinical study in the creative arts therapies. These creative arts therapists desire both to develop the highest levels of professional skill and to strengthen their credentials. Doctoral study of this kind will advance not only the individual but also the profession and is therefore highly recommended.

As with many related health and education professions, the doctorate will not be the entry level degree for professional practice in the creative arts therapies within the foreseeable future but will be directed more toward research and the training of leaders and faculty for professional education programs. The present movement toward doctoral education in the creative arts therapies parallels earlier patterns within the arts in education. In the early 1960s art education programs were being encouraged to become more involved with scholarship and research in order to assist the field in making theoretical advances. Elliot Eisner urged art education to expand its research activities and not to rely on other fields for advanced study of the artistic process. He described how " . . . Psychologists, sociologists, philosophers, and the like are not necessarily aware of the problems in art education; many of them care little. Art education, as a field, will have to assume responsibility for preparing theoreticians who are capable of understanding the problems of the field and have the competencies required to inquire into them" (Eisner, 1965, p. 290). Art education created a place within the profession for those whose primary responsibility is to clarify the theoretical dimensions of the field. "One needs more than descriptive data for making value judgments of art; one needs a conception of art itself. Such a conception is evolutionary" (Ibid., p. 283).

PROFESSIONAL EDUCATION IN THE ARTS

The literature on professional education rarely includes the arts and focuses on medicine, law, theology, education, architecture, engineering and, more recently, social work, human service, business, public administration and other related fields. Early American professional education in the arts took place largely through apprenticeship. Because of its association with classical studies and mathematics originating in ancient Greece, music took the lead over the other arts in establishing academic and professional programs in higher education. The theoretical traditions in music composition and history were suitable for inclusion in classically oriented educational institutions. These traditions have also served as obstacles to innovation in music education.

Conservatory education began in Germany in the early nineteenth century and spread to America. The Peabody Institute Academy of Music in Baltimore was founded before the Civil War but did not open until 1868. The New England Conservatory was also established in the 1860s. Oberlin's department of music, established in the 1830s, was transformed into the first conservatory within a college (Ackerman, 1973, p. 229). Yale created the first university-affiliated school for the visual arts in 1866. The school was independent from the college and offered non-degree studies (Ibid., p. 231). In the late nineteenth and early twentieth centuries, professional schools of visual art and music continued to be created both independent from, and in affiliation with, established colleges. Because of the professional orientation of studies, diplomas were routinely awarded rather than academic degrees. The diploma is today still a respected credential for professional artists.

Another trend in professional training in the arts concerns the development of arts in education programs in public schools. In 1838 the Boston School Committee included music in the curriculum of the public schools as "a regular subject" meeting criteria for intellectual, moral and physical education. Music instructors were hired and a need for teacher training was thus created (Mark, 1978). The visual arts were first introduced to Massachusetts public schools in response to the need for commercial art skills created by the rapid development of textile, shoe and leather industries. The Massachusetts College of Art was established in 1873 as a normal school to train teachers of industrial drawing and design. Most of the early art and music schools were coeducational. Early art education was product oriented and lacked free expression.

Art educators report that the progressive education movement taking place in the United States during the 1920s introduced concerns for self-expression and creativity into the schools. The writings of Dewey inspired these trends (Eisner, 1965, p. 303). Margaret Naumburg, a pioneer in both art education and art therapy, published *The Child and the World* in 1928. Her sister, Florence Cane, who would eventually write the influential book, *The Artist in Each of Us* (1951), published "Art—The Child's Birthright" in the journal, *Childhood Education*, in 1931. The psychotherapeutic work of Naumburg grew out of her earlier experience in progressive education and art. The writings of Viktor Lowenfeld, a refugee from Austria who arrived in America before the Second World War (*The Nature of Creative Activity*, 1939 and *Creative and Mental Growth*, 1947) were to have a major impact on the development of the art education field as well as art therapy. Early art education studies (when they were concerned with the fundamental nature of the art experience, the relationship between art and life and the impact of art on emotional well-being) were closely related to the interests of creative arts therapists. As art education moved toward standard methods and away from the individual (a course never recommended by many arts educators), an impetus was given to the establishment of the art therapy profession.

The present dilemma of art education is that it is often separated from the mainstream needs and practices of American education. The arts in most public schools are perceived as "special subjects" and they are rarely integrated into the entirety of the school curriculum. Consequently, arts educators are often the first to be let go in times of fiscal austerity. These developments in the arts in education should be carefully studied by the creative arts therapy profession. Adjunctive or secondary roles within health systems should be discouraged in planning for the future. Art and education, as well as art and therapy, need not be separated in any way. Teachers and therapists using the arts as principal modes of expression can take on necessary and primary roles within their places of work. Arts educators interested in relating to the whole person through the creative process have in recent years become increasingly involved with the arts in psychotherapy profession. This is an advantage to mental health and a tragic loss to education which must rethink the place of art in the school experience, making it a primary vs. secondary mode of learning.

Education ought to be equally concerned with the lack of attention given to dance and drama in elementary and secondary schools. Music and art education have been so concerned with their separate domains that the generic interests of creative expresssion in public education have been increasingly losing ground in recent years. The music and art education professions have contributed to the negative situation for the arts in the schools by focusing on their different subject areas and not on the more central and primary place of creative expression in all art forms as a basic skill needed in life. The arts in therapy have concentrated more on the person than the medium, which is always in the service of what is best for the individual. The creative arts therapist is trained to adapt the medium to clinical objectives. Teamwork is encouraged in all aspects of mental health service. The successful creative arts therapist has a sophisticated understanding of other mental health disciplines and is capable of providing generic psychotherapeutic services. The arts are introduced only when appropriate to the needs of clients. This clinical adaptability and respect for the necessary interdependence of all mental health services has enabled the creative arts therapies to move toward core status within mental health systems. Exclusive emphasis on a particular media or art form will, as with the arts in education, keep the creative arts therapies on the periphery of mental health systems in adjunctive roles.

Comprehensive skills as well as concentrations are to be encouaged in the education of creative arts therapists. Professional staff in both educational and mental health settings, who are vital to program quality and continuity, are people who understand all aspects of the system's functions and client needs. These generic skills, focused on the ability to adapt media to the needs of clients, are essential to the future growth and influence of the creative art therapies. Exclusive training in a single medium inevitably results in perceiving the client in relation to a particular art form as opposed to a primary emphasis on the total person and the comprehensive goals of the clinical program. Since the majority of creative arts therapy training programs focus exclusively on a single art form in a manner similar to the training of arts educators, it is recommended that consideration be given to the potential future impact of this approach to education and the formation of professional identity. Single-modality concentration will inevitably reinforce adjunctive roles. The present professional image of the arts in mental health is heavily influenced by the older arts education models of separation and specialization which continue to keep the arts on the periphery of public school education.

On the university level the arts have made significant advances toward inclusion as primary components of the total education process. These positive developments are perhaps largely due to the legacy of the liberal tradition of education which is far more influential in the university environment than within the public elementary and secondary school. On the university level, dance, rarely present in nineteenth century and early twentieth century campus offerings, has made strong advances. Contemporary university education with its wide array of choices has provided an atmosphere conducive to the extraordinary growth of arts offerings since the second world war. Students are no longer traveling to Europe en masse for arts education. The reverse is actually taking place as American colleges and universities have established world leadership in all of the arts and attract students from many countries.

The public school curriculum, especially at the elementary level, has been much more narrowly focused and has not provided for maximum growth in the influence of the arts on the total educational process. The arts in education, largely because of rigid certification requirements, remain a bachelor's level entry profession. As a result of these trends, occupationally oriented artists completing university undergraduate and graduate level training programs have been increasingly going on for professional study in the arts and psychotherapy. The negative results of rigid arts in education teacher certification requirements need to be carefully studied by the creative arts therapy profession. As a result of these standards many qualified artists, who are gifted teachers, are not able to work within the schools. The standards themselves are problematic in that they tend to be media specific and do not stress the importance of integrating the arts into the totality of the school experience. It can be argued that they therefore fail on both artistic and educational grounds. The arts educator is often relegated to a middle ground, not completely integrated with either art or education.

The creative arts therapies profession has generally committed itself to full integration with the mental health profession, a wise course for practical employment purposes. However, there is a pervasive estrangement from the personal artistic process that tends to characterize the careers of many creative arts therapists. Personal commitment to the artistic process is an area desiring attention when considering the future evolution of the profession and educational guidelines. It is strongly recommended that the arts in therapy and arts in education fields begin to work closely on the definition of areas of common concern and that there be a concerted effort to maximize future cooperation and planning efforts.

GRADUATE EDUCATION

It is widely accepted that where the American undergraduate curriculum received its primary inspiration from the English college and the liberal arts tradition of Europe, graduate education in the United States was first modeled after German systems of advanced study. During the early and mid nineteenth century, leading American colleges resisted professional specialization. The Yale Report of 1828 put an end to any possible departures from the classical curriculum and recommended a single required program of studies. Professional and practical work were scorned.

At the time of its 1828 report, Yale was "the largest and most influential college in the country" (Schmidt, 1957, p. 54). John McLean, president of Princeton University, expressed the sentiments of the time in saying, "We shall not aim at innovation . . . no chimerical experiments in education have ever had the least countenance here" (Ibid., p. 67). The sentiments of the era were directed toward training "the mental discipline" of the person. The program of studies could be listed briefly and varied little from school to school (Ibid.). The early nineteenth century presents a striking contrast to the current university "catalog" of courses which focuses more on what is offered than on the person. Professional education was not taking place on a "graduate" level and was not at all integrated into the college experience. It was not until the 1970s that law schools, upholders of traditional precedents, universally changed their degrees conferred from the bachelors of law to the doctor of jurisprudence.

Brubacher and Rudy describe how "the impact of German university scholarship upon nineteenth century American higher education is one of the most significant themes in modern intellectual history (Brubacher and Rudy, 1976, p. 174). In the nineteenth century German universities were pre-eminent in the world in terms of creative learning and research because of the way in which they brought the continental tradition of independent scholarship to its highest point of development. This pattern was of course contrary to what was occurring in the United States, where there was an emphasis on a standardized and institutionally controlled curriculum. The German system was based on concepts of "Lernfreiheit" (freedom of learning) and "Lehrfreiheit" (freedom of teaching). This system guaranteed minimal intellectual boundaries for both students and faculty. Today, West German and Swiss university education is available to a small percentage of the population. Throughout Europe, it is assumed that only motivated and talented scholars can properly use the free environment and resources of the university. America has encouraged mass education as an expression of democracy and equal opportunity and has found that the traditions of "free learning" and "free teaching" are not typically supported within large and complex systems of education.

In post Civil War American society, which found itself on the verge of major industrial and scientific development, the German approach to academic work was of vital importance, as it still is today for the most advanced and creative forms of study. As a result of German influence, research, teaching and scholarship began to be integrated into American higher education. In the early nineteenth century, American colleges were considered more like preparatory schools in contrast to German universities. The founding of Johns Hopkins University in Baltimore in 1876 as a graduate level institution of higher education was the American turning point toward more advanced university study. Johns Hopkins provided the historic opportunity, according to Abraham Flexner, for scholars to integrate their lives through the unification of research and teaching (Flexner, 1930, pp. 73-74).

Harvard was the first American college to establish a graduate department in 1872, and Yale gave the first Ph.D. in 1861 (Dressel, 1963, p. 8), but it was Johns Hopkins which set the pace for graduate study. Clark University in Worcester, Massachusetts followed Hopkins in 1889 when it was founded as a graduate level institution. Although Harvard established its medical school in 1814, the law school in 1817 and a scientific school in 1847, these programs did not function on the graduate level and were not fully incorporated into the university. The same applied to Yale's theology division (1822), medical school (1823), law school (1824), and scientific school (1854) (Brubacher and Rudy, 1976). The new graduate level university model was continued with the founding of the University of Chicago and the Catholic University of America. Bernard Berelson described how graduate education developed in three types of settings in the late nineteenth century: new universities (e.g. Hopkins, Clark and Chicago), private institutions (e.g. Harvard, Columbia, Yale and Cornell), and public universities (e.g. California, Michigan and Wisconsin). "A graduate school based on the German model was placed on top of an undergraduate college based on the English model, and several people believe that this arrangement has plagued the system ever since" (Berelson, 1960, p. 10).

Scholarly journals and learned societies experienced parallel stages of growth and in a short time the university model took hold throughout the United States as the dominant mode of institutional organization. The number of master's and doctoral degrees conferred in the country have grown consistently since the late nineteenth century as well as increasing tendencies toward specialization. Business, industry and human service institutions have generated the expanding need for trained "specialists" over the past 100 years, but this trend may be reaching a breaking point as expressed in contemporary criticisms of higher education which call for more wholistic and multi-disciplinary approaches to training the whole person. Emphasis has been placed on the mastery of prescribed techniques, the performance of specialized skills and the increasing interests of professional associations in keeping specializations distinct from one another.

These tendencies will in time be complemented by a return to wholistic education as suggested by the Yale Report of 1828 which advocated training the intellect and the person rather than the accumulation of facts. Skills are thus developed that can be applied to many different realms of life. As modern society has grown more complex, the specialist is not as essential as the person who can integrate; see themes emerging across disciplines; facilitate interdependence and cooperation; and make sense out of what can otherwise be perceived as massive fragmentation. It is important for the education of the creative arts therapist to take these issues into account and not simply contribute to an expanding system of isolated specializations. Every effort can be given to the development of specific skills within a wholistic approach to training. Where the Yale Report focused on "intellect" and mental discipline, the arts in therapy profession stresses these qualities but includes the senses and creative expression.

The past 100 years of increased specialization in higher education and the professions is largely due to the dominance of what Berelson refers to as "the scientific approach" to learning which began to affect the entire curriculum.

> The social studies began to turn into the social sciences, literary studies became heavily philological and technical, and philosophy lost psychology to science and started on the positivistic road itself . . . . It is always well to remember that the graduate school came into being under the pressures of science and that it has lived its whole life in an increasingly scientific and technological age. It is no wonder that the major critics of graduate study have come from the humanities and certain parts of the social sciences (Ibid., p. 12).

Government and business have poured money into university graduate divisions for scientific and defense-related research. There have thus been extensive funds given to the university to develop an increasing sophistication in technology. Close relationships have been developed between government, industry and scientifically oriented research universities. During this period, advanced studies in the humanities have fallen off sharply as the university continues to take shape in response to the demands of the marketplace. The professional and social value of degrees from elite liberal arts colleges can be perceived as a major reason for their sustained prosperity within a more general educational environment that has not been supportive of the humanities.

Berelson in 1960 observed strong increases in professional education at the graduate level, which has grown even more dramatically in recent years. He described how traditional academic standards, such as the master's thesis, were being relaxed and how the demand for graduates of doctoral programs was growing but that doctoral graduates were less frequently engaged in academic professions. "Professional fields (other than medicine and law) have constantly increased their programs at the doctoral level and in general have coveted the Ph.D. in preference to setting up their own doctoral degrees, even if that meant conforming to the general standards for the Ph.D. set up by the graduate school for the entire university" (Ibid., p. 320).

The master's degree during this century has been less and less associated with the arts and sciences and has become almost exclusively a professional degree. It might be argued that professional training in medicine and law, both of which now offer doctoral level degrees, the M.D. and J.D., is in many ways comparable to master's level education in other professions. Although law, and particularly medicine, require more years of full-time graduate study to fulfill professional entry level requirements than many other professions, the level of study is not necessarily more advanced. Medicine and law focus on practical training in their basic professional programs and do not require advanced independent research and scholarship. There are thus major inconsistencies in professional training due largely to historical trends, the higher social and economic status of certain professions, and a variety of vested interests. In the ideal realm these differences do not have to exist. It can even be argued that graduate level practical training is not always more sophisticated than bachelor's level experiences. It is generally recognized that the graduate student is a more advanced and independent learner and it is the sophistication of the student that determines the depth of learning.

One of the results of the expansion of graduate level training for all professions is the fact that it does encourage the continuation of liberal, general and preparatory education at the undergraduate level. This may be one of the strongest justifications for graduate education in the professions. The extended system of American education may also be perceived as serving the interests and expansionistic inclinations of the education industry. A major positive outcome of the general extension of years that professionals are required to spend in higher education is the growing awareness that education is ongoing and lifelong. The professions themselves are beginning to give serious consideration to the creation of continuing education programs for their members. The progressive shift of professional education from the undergraduate to graduate level also serves the purpose of supporting the tradition of liberal arts and comprehensive education as a viable preparation for professional practice. As we become increasingly involved in an educational environment in which the four years of traditional preparatory education at the secondary level are being expanded to eight, these years need to be re-evaluated, with goals and opportunities for students more clearly articulated.

In relation to the creative arts therapies, the more time professionals give to liberal and cultural studies, together with artistic training and experimentation, the better prepared they will be for advanced study, research and interpersonal work. The creative arts therapies will benefit from a continuing effort to make their basic entry level requirements consistent with mental health professions which now require graduate level training. Because the creative arts therapy profession is relatively new and still in its formative stages of development, the field should develop a vision of consistent entry level degree recommendations. The image of the profession will ultimately be established according to whether or not it chooses to model itself after fields which require bachelor's level training or those that require graduate education.

What is most unique and remarkable about the widespread development of the creative arts therapy profession throughout the western world is the fact that, unlike all other trends in professional and graduate education, this field has come into being without the existence of jobs over the immediate horizon, without government or industrial funding, and with little high level initiation within systems of higher education. The profession has been created by artists, mental health professionals, educators and students with a vision of uniting the forces of art with those of the healing process.

INTERDISCIPLINARY COOPERATION

The place of the creative arts therapies in contemporary higher education cannot be seen in perspective without considering larger historic trends and the major developments taking place within the relatively brief period of modern professional education. The creation of the "field" of the creative arts therapies is an extension of these patterns. Trends within the whole of professional education must be understood to see where we are today and to make assessments of where we will go in the future. In this chapter I have attempted to reflect upon varied and broad resources in higher education and acknowledge that my review has not gone into depth with particular areas. For example, I have not given a history of psychiatric training in the United States and other parts of the world. I also have not included the educational histories of other countries in the review. Although I have not followed the historic continuities of fields related to the creative arts therapies in detail (a task beyond the limits of this book), I have hopefully encouraged more reflection on the process of educating the creative arts therapist by suggesting how varied and "multi-disciplinary" sources have contributed to what we do today. My "American focus" can serve as a case study of the development of a profession in a particular country. My objective has been to document how varied factors have influenced the creation of training programs in the creative arts therapies and that practices in higher education can be thoroughly understood only by investigating relationships to other professions.

From an historic perspective, the creative arts therapy field is a fascinating subject because of the many different academic, professional and artistic traditions that converge through its creation. Although respect and attention will be given in this study to the different areas of art, dance, drama, music and other specializations in poetry therapy, bibliotherapy, phototherapy, videotherapy, etc., it has always been my inclination to think of them generically as part of the creative arts therapy profession. Since all of the specializations are relatively small and share numerous core elements of philosophy and practice, it is important not to contribute to the excessive specialization of the contemporary professions by creating further separations.

The Carnegie Commission on Higher Education has for many years urged the professions to work more cooperatively and to minimize further fragmentations in resources and services. Edgar Schein in a Carnegie Commission sponsored study of professional education reported in 1972 that professional disciplines have become so specialized that even university professors find it challenging to maintain mastery of sections of their specializations. He described how the "knowledge explosion" has inspired increasing specialization, making wholistic understanding difficult and rare. Integrated and cross-disciplinary education is in this respect a more formidable challenge today than specialized education.

> As specialization increases, it becomes harder for professionals to work together on interdisciplinary teams because greater differentiation of fields and specialization leads to sets of attitudes and concepts that can be easily shared only with fellow practitioners in the same or in a related discipline . . . society is generating problems that require interdisciplinary team efforts for their solution . . . and . . . it has been particularly difficult to launch interdisciplinary efforts in an environment dominated by departments built around disciplinary specialties (Schein, 1972, p. 39).

The extreme trends toward specialization have reached their breaking point in mental health and human service professions. Budget constraints and team-oriented systems have increased the relevance of multidisciplinary training. Special skills are encouraged in the different professions together with the recognition that there are a set of core competencies that every human service professional must have. These include interpersonal and communication skills, the ability to make clinical assessments and act in the best interests of the client, and an informed sense of the basic theories and action methodologies on which the field is established. Each staff member is to function as a contributing professional, capable of understanding the fundamental mission of the field while also making unique contributions to the team effort.

Rigid immersion in the confines of a particular profession makes it difficult for a person to function competently in contemporary health service industries. The creative arts therapies have established credibility in mental health systems as a result of their ability to expand the scope of communication in therapy. The arts have also helped to humanize the mental health field while affirming the life-enhancing qualities of creative expression. What is most significant is the ability that creative arts therapists have demonstrated in taking on primary clinical responsibilities. They have been motivated and astute learners while on the job, immersing themselves in in-service and continuing education, together with supervision, in order to increase their skills and meet clinical responsibilities.

In comparison, a serious weakness of the arts in education profession has been its separatism and lack of involvement in all other areas of the curriculum. In general (and with few exceptions) the arts in education have also tended to stay separate from one another. The major disciplines of music and visual arts education have focused almost exclusively on their speciality and have not been strong advocates for total arts education and the strengthening of dance and drama on a national level. There have been notable exceptions, but on the whole separatism in training, scholarship, professional development, association activity and public image has been far more common than integration within the arts in education. With regard to relations with the other arts, the creative arts therapy field has also done far more to support separation than cooperation.

However, the creative arts therapies profession has been more integrated into the totality of mental health practice than the arts in education field has been with all aspects of teaching. The creative arts therapist has sensed that within mental health systems there is considerable work to be done and that conventional approaches have left a large void in terms of responding to the comprehensive scope of client needs. Individual therapists, training programs and the profession as a whole have moved assertively to respond to this need and the opportunity to create new services. In defense of the arts in education profession it is important to note that there is not a comparable opportunity for program development within public education where roles and responsibilities are rigidly prescribed. Again, this lack of freedom within the education field has contributed to the development of the creative arts therapy profession through a transfer of talent and resoruces. The lack of parochialism which characterizes the relationships between creative arts therapists and other mental health practitioners, together with the respect shown to older professions such as psychiatry and psychology as teaching resources, has increased the esteem of the field within the human service community. Training programs and professional associations, created as a result of the success of artist-practitioners, must not contradict the openness, flexibility and ability to work on an interdisciplinary basis that characterized the work of pioneering professionals who gave credibility to the field and the associations and training programs that subsequently evolved.

Schein, in reviewing the history of American professions, is critical of how there is a typical "tightening of boundaries" that associations justify on the basis of maintaining "high standards." Within the creative arts therapies there are movements in this direction, justified by the need to establish the identity and prestige of the profession. However, the defini-

tion of boundaries can be complemented by the affirmation of the interdependence and flexibility that allowed the creative arts therapy profession to come into existence.

> Most of our major professions are now beginning to recognize that they need
> the ability to work with other professions if they are to respond effectively to
> the problems of a modern complex society. At the same time, the traditional
> model of professional education puts so much stress on the professional as an
> autonomous expert whom the client can trust because of [his] high degree of
> skill and high commitment to a professional ethic that we may well have
> trained out of most of our professionals the attitudes and skills that are
> needed to work in collaboration with others. We have built professional
> schools on a theory of education designed to produce autonomous spe-
> cialists, and we have encouraged the evolution of a set of professional asso-
> ciations and societies that have, on the whole, attempted to tighten rather
> than loosen the boundaries of professions (Ibid., p. 36).

Well-established professional associations and training programs are
symbols of "mature" professions. The creative arts therapies are approaching this status. As the growth process continues, the "conserve" of
knowledge expands and standards become more exclusive, demanding
that entry into the profession be based upon prescribed educational experiences. The profession thus helps to create an affiliated industry of
education and training. The content of study and qualifications for faculty tend to be developed by educators and others already commited to
an established set of standards. Inevitably, those who create standards of
education have strong vested interests in the process. The serving of
vested interests is clearly supported more by the creation of specialized
programs, taught by faculty with specialized credentials, than through
support for interdisciplinary studies.

National association involvement in professional education must be
guided more by open-minded and adaptable concerns for educational
excellence than by the protection of vested interests. Institutions of
higher education are to be given the academic flexibility and freedom
necessary to enable them to creatively fulfill their unique missions
within an atmosphere of open inquiry. "The profession wants and needs
to have some peer-group control over the discovery and spread of new
professional knowledge. Through this control it protects itself and the
public against quackery and facilitates the spread of new professional
discoveries once they have been approved. However, this control also
implies a measure of restriction, a resistance to new ideas or techniques
that might unseat old chieftains or require a radical shift in orientation

or jurisdiction" (Gilb, 1966, pp. 78-79). Schein recommends that professions must respond to rigidifying conservatism and association bureaucratization with educational processes that train "role innovators" as opposed to those who are expected to operate primarily within conventional methods. At the present time all the national associations for the arts in therapy are more intent upon requiring specialized study in their particular modalities than they are in encouraging mutual cooperation with peers committed to other forms of creative expression. Creativity and academic freedom are not valued nearly as much as the need to follow association guidelines. The creative arts therapies need to continue to encourage a "creative" spirit of education and training that will enable the profession to realize its full potential and bring the task of educating therapists into correspondence with the process of creativity.

It is vitally important to refine and expand the influence of particular forms of specialization and to study the unique aspects of each art modality with depth in order to perfect its use in therapy. Variety and differences within the creative arts therapies are to be respected and encouraged. We work best as therapists when permitted to develop individual styles which utilize special personal resources. However, individual forms of specialization need not be excessively institutionalized. In this respect, the strongest group or association is that which establishes unity of purpose while recognizing differences and freedom of learning and practice. The refinement of existing specializations and the creation of new concentrations can be encouraged while supporting cooperation between the different modes of inquiry. With regard to the issue of the interplay between special interests and interdisciplinary cooperation, this study will attempt to define "universal" elements of training shared by all of the creative arts therapies together with characteristics that are unique to each modality.

Our emerging profession has the opportunity to carefully heed the warnings of the Carnegie Commission and move into the future in a way which allows us to freely respond to the complexities of practice. Our national associations may assist us in the process by establishing standards which encourage innovation and multidisciplinary cooperation as well as conserving and respecting the traditions of different specializatons. The creative arts therapies, rather than being fashioned exclusively by the standards of the larger professions of medicine, psychology, education and social work, can follow an innovative course which nevertheless utilizes the best of the older professions and maintains professional respectability and stability.

As the creative arts therapy profession matures in the organizational stage of its development through the presence of established training programs and national associations, it is recommended that the profession maintain its historic commitment to the therapeutic elements of creativity that first gave credibility to the field. The many traditions of professional training, graduate education, the fine arts and the humanities, which provided the rationale and resources for the revitalization of the ancient healing qualities of the arts, need not be eliminated through narrowly defined specialization. It is recommended that the profession continue to develop open, liberal, practical, cooperative and inclusive standards of training which will ultimately produce therapists with better skills in their specialties because they will be better informed, better educated and more equipped as human beings capable of responding creatively to an ever-changing environment comprised of different cultures, values and needs.

Professions that survive with strength and purpose are those that address themselves to meeting essential needs of society rather than the more specialized interests of professionals. Medical doctors have varied specializations but they are fundamentally "medical doctors." The same applies to lawyers and clergy. British psychologists have been critical of the narrow and often irrelevant psychological curriculum traditions that exist in their universities where theoretical and laboratory work is emphasized rather than applied psychology. They are encouraging more training in basic human relations skills together with psychological competencies that can be applied to a broad variety of clinical situations (Bender et al., 1983; Canter and Canter, 1983).

Because professional psychology has historically grown out of the university setting and has been closely associated with specialized scientific study, it appears to be only recently developing the more generic skills orientation that has always been basic to legal and medical education. Law schools have historically resisted pressures to specialize and have maintained a commitment to what might be referred to as the liberal arts of jurisprudence. Legal training is, however, becoming increasingly sensitive to its lack of clinical and practical training and the need to draw other disciplines into the study of law. The creative arts therapy profession can benefit from careful study of these continuities of practical and academic study in other professions.

Since the establishment of the creative arts therapies came about through the combination of varied disciplines, it is essential to maintain interdisciplinary study in our training programs. We cannot separate ourselves from these origins. The present, and for the most part universal, orientation of college and university programs in the creative arts therapies toward practical training, guided by theoretical inquiry, is to be commended and continued into the future. The strength of our educational programs lies in a commitment to individualized learning, careful and personalized supervision, an insistence on small classes, the integration of theory and practice and interdependence with other mental health professions. The profession is typically insistent on quality and this may be due to the fact that nothing can be taken for granted within a developing field highly sensitive to how it is perceived both internally and externally. However, more emphasis needs to be placed on the arts themselves, in danger of being de-emphasized because of the strong and justifiable pressures that we feel to establish clinical recognition. Undergraduate and graduate programs are encouraged to integrate the humanities, social sciences and physical sciences into their studies. On the master's level, it is not always possible to provide extensive coursework in these varied areas, but faculty may advise broad reading, admissions standards can encourage the acceptance of students from varied backgrounds, and the leaders of colleges and universities can support interdisciplinary study.

Cooperation and the definition of areas of mutual identity between the various creative arts therapies is to be emphasized. If professional associations and academic programs do not undertake this logical and practical course, external forces will bring it about. Universities, consumers, employers, government, accrediting agencies and other professions will, through their increasing recognition of the value of creative expression in health services, stimulate an eventual integration of the creative arts therapies which will share resources while respecting the integrity of the distinct art forms.

REFERENCES

Ackerman, James: The arts in higher education. In Kaysen, Carl (Ed.): *Content and Context: Essays on College Education*. New York, McGraw-Hill, 1973.
Bender, M.P. et al.: Professional development and the training requirements of psychologists working in special services and other community settings. *Bulletin of the*

British Psychological Society, 36, 233-236, 1983.

Berelson, Bernard: *Graduate Education in the United States.* New York, McGraw-Hill, 1960.

Bird, C.: *The Case Against College.* New York, McKay, 1975.

Brubacher, John and Rudy, Willis: *Higher Education in Transition: A History of American Colleges and Universities, 1636-1976.* New York, Harper and Row, 1976.

Cane, Florence. *The Artist in Each of Us.* New York, Pantheon, 1951.

Cane, Florence: Art—the child's birthright. *Childhood Education, 7,* 482-485, 1931.

Canter, Sandra and Canter, David: Professional growth and psychological education. *Bulletin of the British Psychological Society, 36,* 283-287, 1983.

Dressel, Paul: *The Undergraduate Curriculum in Higher Education.* Washington, D.C., The Center for Applied Research in Education, Inc., 1963.

Eisner, Elliot: Graduate study and the preparation of scholars in art education. In Hastie, W.R. (Ed.): *Art Education.* Chicago, The National Society for the Study of Education, 1965.

Eisner, Elliot: American education and the future of art education. In Hastie, W.R. (Ed.): *Art Education.* Chicago, The National Society for the Study of Education, 1965.

Feldman, K.A. and Newcomb, T.M.: *The Impact of College on Students.* San Francisco, Jossey-Bass, 1969.

Flexner, Abraham: *Universities: American, English, German.* New York, Oxford Univ. Pr., 1930.

Ganss, George: *Saint Ignatius' Idea of a Jesuit University.* Milwaukee, Marquette Univ. Pr., 1954.

Gilb, Corinne: *Hidden Hierarchies.* New York, Harper and Row, 1966.

Grigg, Charles: *Graduate Education.* New York, The Center for Applied Research in Education, 1965.

Hastie, W.R.: The Education of an Art Teacher. In Hastie, W.R. (Ed.): *Art Education.* Chicago, The National Society for the Study of Education, 1965.

Jacobi, P.: *Changing Values in College.* New York, Harper and Row, 1957.

Keel, John: Art Education, 1940-64. In Hastie, W.R. (Ed.): *Art Education.* Chicago, The National Society for the Study of Education, 1965.

Lowenfeld, Viktor: *The Nature of Creative Activity.* New York, Harcourt, Brace, 1939.

Lowenfeld, Viktor: *Creative and Mental Growth.* New York, Macmillan, 1947.

Mark, Michael: *Contemporary Music Education.* New York, Schirmer, 1978.

Mayhew, Lewis and Ford, Patrick: *Reform in Graduate and Professional Education.* San Francisco, Jossey-Bass, 1974.

Naumburg, Margaret: *The Child and the World.* New York, Harcourt, Brace, 1928.

Schein, Edgar: *Professional Education: Some New Directions.* New York, McGraw-Hill, 1972.

Schmidt, George: *The Liberal Arts College: A Chapter in American Cultural History.* New Brunswick, N.J., Rutgers Univ. Pr., 1957.

Winter, David; McClelland, David; and Stewart, Abigail: *A New Case for the Liberal Arts College.* San Francisco, Jossey-Bass, 1981.

3. DEFINITION OF THE PROFESSION THROUGH EDUCATION

T HE CREATIVE ARTS therapies trace their origins to late nineteenth and early twentieth century practices within the mental health field. For example, "phototherapists" speak of how "in 1852 Dr. Hugh Diamond presented a series of photographs of the [insane] to a London audience. Those portraits apparently represented the first systematic use of photography in psychiatry" (Krauss and Fryrear, 1983, p. 3). In 1923 *Bildnerei der Geisteskranken* (Artistry of the Mentally Ill) was published in Berlin by psychiatrist Hans Prinzhorn. The writings of Sigmund Freud, Carl Jung and Otto Rank have contributed significantly to the emergence of the creative arts therapies. Psychiatry has maintained a continuing interest in the creative process, with psychoanalytic literature in particular carrying on the traditions of Freud's investigations of art. Theater and enactment were linked to psychotherapy by J.L. Moreno, M.D., who applied his experience between 1921 and 1923 with the Viennese Theatre of Spontaneity to the mental health field. Moreno first became interested in a "theatre without spectators" in which every person both acts and participates. After he immigrated to the United States in 1925, Moreno's work evolved into the practice of psychodrama which is the application of the process of the theatre of life and personal emotion to psychotherapy.

THE FIRST TRAINING PROGRAMS

Major developments in the higher education of art therapists, dance therapists and integrated creative arts therapists took place in the late 1960s and the 1970s. During that period most of the existing graduate level programs in the United States were developed. Formal training for drama therapists is undergoing more recent development in the United States. The first college and university training programs in music therapy were established during the 1940s and 1950s and program development continued throughout the 1960s. As with dance and art, educational opportunities for music therapists grew significantly during the 1970s.

Single courses in art therapy were offered in a few institutions of higher education during the 1950s and 1960s. Some of these were taught by Margaret Naumburg, who did so much through her books and clinical work during the 1940s and 1950s to establish the profession with dignity. Art therapy was given a tremendous professional boost through the founding in 1961 of the *Bulletin of Art Therapy* by Elinor Ulman. The Bulletin, now the *American Journal of Art Therapy*, provided a vital and sustained forum for communication and scholarship for art therapists throughout the United States. Through its articles, listings of published literature and constant announcements of what was happening in the specialization around the world, art therapy was given considerable resource material for higher education and professional development. The journal helped to give substance and credibility to the profession as a whole while offering inspiration to isolated art therapy pioneers. The creation of high-quality journals and the development of a profession are intimately connected. As with art therapy, the growth of educational programs in other specializations has been similarly associated with the development of journals and published literature.

All of the creative arts therapies have grown from the early work of people described by the various traditions of art therapy, dance therapy, music therapy, poetry thrapy, theater therapy and psychodrama as "pioneers." These people became involved in their work in many different ways. Variety and multiplicity characterize the beginning of the profession. Although there were influential mental health professionals who used the arts in their work in the late nineteenth and early twentieth centuries, what is of primary importance to the profession is the movement toward the creation of a discipline unto itself, focused on the use of artistic expression in therapy. The pioneers in the creative arts therapies may have had differing professional and educational backgrounds, but they were all characterized by a total commitment to the healing power of the creative process as a primary mode of therapeutic transformation.

The profession originated in public and private hospitals, clinics, research institutes, schools for children, centers for the handicapped and wherever else human services were provided. The pioneer might have been an artist, dancer, musician, actor or poet intent upon bringing art to people in need, or a person with parallel but separate life experiences in the arts and a particular human service profession (e.g. education, social work, clinical psychology, the ministry or medicine). Early creative arts therapists adopted a variety of theoretical perspectives for the integration of art into mental health services. Theoretical orientations extended from remedial, occupational and rehabilitation therapies to psychodynamic principles and the inclusion of the artistic process into psychoanalysis. J.L. Moreno was unique in that he not only introduced a method utilizing the creative process in psychotherapy but developed a comprehensive theory of personality based on the principles of creativity and spontaneity. Rather than adapting the creative process to existing therapeutic practices, Moreno did the reverse. His experimental work with groups and action-oriented therapeutic principles anticipated the latter popularity of approaches to enactment in psychotherapy. A multiplicity of theoretical orientations and methods still characterizes the creative arts in therapy field and results in a corresponding variety in training programs.

As with the history of education in other professions, the first training opportunities in the creative arts therapies were offered through apprenticeships. However, where apprenticeship education went on for long periods of time in medicine and law as the primary form of training, its place within the twentieth century history of the arts in therapy was relatively brief. People interested in receiving training would associate themselves with the early practitioners and work along with them. Education was essentially supervision. Other educational opportunities within the particular clinical setting would typically be included into the training of the creative arts therapist. If the apprenticeship occurred within a psychiatric training hospital or clinic, then the educational resources for the motivated learner could be vast. Psychiatric education programs have generally opened their training sessions to other staff and students. Thus, the first stages of apprenticeship education in the creative arts therapies involved multidisciplinary education with psychiatry, social work, psychology, occupational therapy, special education and other professions. Many aspects of the apprenticeship origins of the creative arts therapies have continued in training programs established within institutions of higher education. As with the apprenticeship, practical training through the practicum and internship are the basis of creative arts therapy education. Clinical training experiences also guarantee a continuation of cooperation with other mental health disciplines which are present within the clinical site.

ACADEMIC ORGANIZATION

University and college programs grew out of these first apprenticeships. Many different developmental patterns occurred. The educational programs were sponsored by existing departments and schools within an institution of higher education on both the graduate and undergraduate levels. Universities and colleges often began programs by first offering courses in a particular creative arts therapy subject area through a department of music, art or dance; psychology; education; or general studies. If the course established itself within the curriculum of the school, this would typically be the first step toward developing a program. Often the progression would involve a second step of offering a concentration in music therapy through a department of music or music education; art therapy through art education; and so forth. Early program development was largely connected to the personalities and influence of the educational pioneers in the profession. They were comprised of faculty members in related fields such as psychology, the arts and the arts in education who persuaded their institutions to create training programs; and professionals working within the region of the college or university who proposed educational programs which were ultimately accepted and implemented.

Program development typically took place through the sponsorship of an existing university department. This trend continues today, after the profession has generally established itself within many institutions of higher education. In most colleges and universities it is infrequent to find creative arts therapy programs being given full departmental or divisional status. This is largely due to their small size and the tendency to divide programs according to specializations in a particular art form. Therefore, a music therapy program offered through a department of music might have no relationship whatsoever to an art therapy program in the same university associated with the school of art or art education. It is the unique qualities of a particular institution's departmental organization of the fine arts which will determine whether or not the creative arts therapies will have any relationship to one another. This is typically a matter of chance rather than planning within the profession. If the college or university encourages ties and cooperation between the arts and the creative arts therapies, then they will occur. Institutions of higher education have significant leverage with regard to this issue, since professional associations have been more intent on separation than cooperation.

These patterns of university organization are not unique to the creative arts therapy field. The arts in education have been similarly separated because of pre-existing academic and departmental structures of institutions of higher education. Although there may be profound similarities between the various creative arts therapy modalities, the departmental separations within colleges and universities tend to separate them from one another. Budgetary, faculty and curriculum distinctions thus work their way into the practice of the work and the definition of the profession. Most of the present separations between the creative arts therapy specializations are largely a result of historic trends in the education of artists and arts educators. Our system of higher education not only tends to separate music, visual art, dance and theater departments within the same institution, but each art form has a long and rich tradition of separate, independent academies. Specialized colleges of music and visual art have also established therapeutic training programs in their particular modality.

This fragmentation of the arts is far from Richard Wagner's concept of "Gesamtkunstwerk," which called for the natural integration of all art forms. Jacques Dalcroze, in Geneva, similarly encouraged the integration of different forms of creative expression and his work combining music and movement has had a large impact on European educational institutions. The division of the creative arts therapies is further complicated by the even greater distance that often separates the arts from departments of psychology and social sciences on university campuses. At the same time, these separations between the arts and human sciences, as described in the previous chapter, have been useful in that they have forced the creative arts therapies to work at interdependence, the development of multidisciplinary skills and establishing links to other fields of knowledge.

Approaches to training which encourage cooperation between the different creative arts therapy specializations have been established at institutions of higher education which did not previously have arts departments. The Hahnemann University of Health Sciences in 1967 began training art therapists on the master's level and, based upon the successful development of that specialization, later introduced dance therapy and music therapy programs. Although degree programs in the three specializations are distinct from one another, they are coordinated through a unified "creative arts in therapy program." The creative arts in therapy are part of the Department of Mental Health Sciences in the graduate school. The program brochure describes how:

> In September, 1974, the Department of Mental Health Sciences of Hahne-mann University, Philadelphia, Pennsylvania, began a two year graduate training program for art, dance/movement, and music therapists culminating in a Masters of Creative Arts in Therapy degree (MCAT). The uniqueness of the MCAT lies in the training for the first time anywhere of all three nonverbal disciplines in a medical school setting using a common conceptual framework and core curriculum as well as specialized didactic and practicum training for each discipline (Hahnemann, 1984).

In March of 1974 the Lesley College Graduate School in establishing its program in expressive therapy offered the first fully integrated graduate program in the arts and psychotherapy. Studies were made available to students in the various therapeutic modalities of dance, drama, literature, music, poetry and the visual arts. Each student pursues an individualized and integrated course of study while also being allowed to specialize in a particular art modality. The Lesley program offers graduate degree studies in psychodrama which had previously been taught in non-academic institutes and workshops. In its brochure the Lesley program describes how its purpose is "the full integration of art and the creative process into education, mental health and all other human services institutions" (Lesley, 1984). Studies are available today at Lesley which expand the creative arts therapies to the treatment of physical illness. As the program grew in size, it received full divisional status within the graduate school with its own dean and faculty. The Lesley College Graduate School places primary emphasis on training human service professionals and educators, and the creative arts therapy program was its first offering in the arts. As with Hahnemann, Lesley did not have to deal with vested academic interests in the arts and departmental structures which make cooperation difficult at other colleges and universities.

The concentration of faculty, student, institutional and community resources in a cooperative effort between the various art forms can ironically allow for increased specialization and the pursuit of individual interests within a more diversified curriculum. Academic and financial practicality is also ensured through a common core of clinical studies within these programs. Administrative overlap is limited through the concentration of all creative arts therapy training resources in a single program. This contrasts to the possibility of specialized creative arts therapy programs being offered at the same academic institution through different departments with little to no coordination.

Other schools, tied to older arts traditions, have been able to bring about cooperation between the arts in therapy. Pratt Institute, a specialized school with a long history in training visual artists, offered one of the first master's degree programs in art therapy. This program was expanded to include a concentration in movement and dance therapy and now offers the M.P.S. degree in creative arts therapy. In addition to specializations in art therapy and dance therapy, Pratt has a concentration in creative arts therapy in special education. The Department of Expressive Therapy at the University of Louisville, although concentrating on art therapy master's degree training, provides opportunities for study in the other creative arts therapies. The Louisville program is based on philosophical premises that engage the entire continuum of human expression in all modalities. More recently, established graduate programs in the creative arts therapies are giving consideration to combining resources in the different creative arts therapy specializations. Goucher College has created master's degree programs in both art therapy and dance therapy. Hofstra University places emphasis on the integration of art therapy, dance therapy, drama therapy, music therapy and poetry therapy in its master's program in creative arts therapy. Programs at these different institutions demonstrate the potential for creating opportunities for interdisciplinary study within educational programs for creative arts therapists.

UNDERGRADUATE AND GRADUATE EDUCATION

Although there are a variety of graduate program structures in the creative arts therapies, there is a general consistency in academic standards. There are, however, historic differences within the creative arts therapy profession as to whether the bachelor's or master's degree is to be considered the entry level credential for clinical practice. Because of its seniority in the creative arts therapy field, the music therapy specialization was established prior to the era in the mental health field when master's level education became a common feature. Music therapy credentialing was developed on a parallel basis with bachelor's level mental health professions such as occupational therapy and teacher education. It also appears that virtually all of the numerous music therapy training programs in the United States are part of music departments which have a strong focus on undergraduate studies. This majority orientation is now written into national association education and registration guidelines which reinforce the pattern of training.

Art therapy and dance therapy education grew dramatically during the 1970s, which was a time when the master's degree took on new importance as a credential in the human services. Mental health systems were becoming increasingly complex and diversified and the society was moving toward higher levels of professional training. The American Art Therapy Association and the American Dance Therapy Association have since recommended the master's degree as the basic clinical credential. Bachelor's level study in the creative arts therapies is encouraged by the art and dance therapy associations but as preparation for graduate training. Although the music therapy specialization through its national associations supports graduate study, it has maintained its recognition of the bachelor's degree as the basic credential for professional practice. There are music therapy educators and practitioners who believe that all therapists should be educated at the graduate level. However, at the present time they are in a minority position.

There are thus major discrepancies between the educational and professional credentialing standards of different elements of the creative arts therapy field. Also, where the specializations of art therapy, dance therapy, music therapy and, more recently, the emerging specialization of drama therapy have tied training to academic institutions, psychodrama education has largely taken place outside academia. Doctor Moreno established his personal training center in Beacon, New York and, as a result of his "role modeling" and its subsequent impact on professional credentialing, similar non-academic training centers have been created in other parts of the country. Psychodramatists have historically received their academic credentials in other fields and have then gone on for psychodramatic training which is generally carried out on a level equivalent to advanced graduate study.

As a group, psychodramatists are highly credentialed with most practitioners holding master's and doctoral degrees. 1979 statistics indicated that over 50 percent of all psychodramatists held M.D. or Ph.D. degrees, while 6 percent had only the bachelor's degree. The fact that psychodrama training generally takes place in non-academic institutions presents an interesting issue in terms of future planning in creative arts therapy education. The advanced professional level of psychodramatic education challenges, rather than undermines, training and education standards in the other creative arts therapies. Groups interested in limiting the "proliferation" of academic degrees and new professional specializations might prefer the psychodrama approach which maintains older mental health professional training programs (e.g. medicine, psychology, social work) while providing extracurricular study in the psychodrama specialization.

One of the most pressing issues today in creative arts therapy education is the discrepancy between the national association guidelines for music therapy training and the educational standards of the other creative arts therapy specializations. Virtually all creative arts therapy educators in specializations other than music therapy believe that bachelor's level standards will contribute to the continuing perception of the creative arts therapies as adjunctive and secondary forms of professional service. They believe that bachelor's degree standards negatively affect the efforts of those who desire to increase the "psychotherapeutic" respectability of the profession. If the creative arts therapy specializations are perceived as different professions, then the bachelor's level standards in music therapy could simply be viewed as different from, and perhaps lower than, the graduate level standards in art therapy, dance therapy, drama therapy and psychodrama. However, the logical conclusion of those outside the different specializations is that there is a profound similarity to the application of all of the arts to mental health service and that there are numerous practical and professional reasons for reinforcing the image of the various specializations as part of a single profession. Major inconsistencies in educational standards between the different specializations will therefore not serve the long-term interests of the profession.

As we note in the following chapter, it is not productive to label music therapy's education standards as less than those of other creative arts therapy specializations. It is essential to approach the problem of inconsistencies in educational standards with attitudes of respect for the different specializations and an openness to their unique strengths. Our review of music therapy educational materials from many different institutions of higher education revealed that training in the specialization tends to be well organized and committed to standards of excellence. Music therapists have distinguished themselves in professional practice for many years throughout the United States and no doubt have extensive evidence to validate their approach to training. The following section of this chapter indicates that music therapy educational programs have much to offer the other creative arts therapies in relation to the integration of the therapist's artistic identity with professional practice.

There are critics of American higher education who assert that the number of years a professional spends in school will not necessarily improve competence. We acknowledge that there is considerable truth to this position. We are more concerned with a coherent image for the creative arts therapy profession with regard to educational standards that is consistent with contemporary facts of mental health practice. From an educational perspective we feel that a highly prescribed professional program at the bachelor's level can *severely* limit opportunities for comprehensive education. Bachelor's level standards are clearly not appropriate if the creative arts therapy profession's educational standards are to include: comprehensive education, professional artistic training, in-depth clinical training on a level comparable to other major mental health disciplines, and the integration of these different educational experiences into the practice of the creative arts therapies.

A possible solution to the problem presented by the discrepancy in educational entry level training in the creative arts therapies would be to distinguish the primary psychotherapeutic use of the arts from more educational, recreational, remedial and specific problem-solving approaches where bachelor's level training is not necessarily inappropriate. There are few authorities that will disagree that psychotherapeutic training must be done on the graduate level and demands many years of advanced training and supervision. Distinctions between different forms of therapy could resolve much of the inconsistency that characterizes contemporary creative arts therapy education.

There are in fact few bachelor's level programs that would present themselves as training psychotherapists. Perhaps largely because of its bachelor's level education policies, the music therapy profession does not tend to give itself a psychotherapeutic image. Our review of undergraduate program descriptions in the creative arts therapies revealed that few offered opportunities for the full integration of practicum and classroom experiences. Graduate level training programs in art therapy, dance therapy and psychodrama are becoming increasingly psychotherapeutic in their orientation. Creative arts therapists do in fact work with varied clinical populations which may necessitate the use of both remedial and psychotherapeutic skills. Art therapy, dance therapy and psychodrama have resolved the situation simply by stating that professional training takes place on the graduate level and that undergraduate education is to be of a preparatory nature. Because of the complicated issues that characterize the inconsistencies in the educational standards of the different creative arts therapy specializations, it may not be possible to make this simple distinction between undergraduate and graduate education in the near future. An interim solution might be to make the distinction between graduate level psychotherapeutic training in music therapy and undergraduate educational, remedial, recreational and specific problem-solving approaches to training. However, we noted that many graduate programs in music therapy do not have a clear psychotherapeutic orientation. They appear to offer more advanced study in the general approaches to music therapy offered at the undergraduate level.

In its 1984 catalog, DePaul University defined music therapy as "a unique synthesis of musical teaching techniques and contemporary behavioral theory." If music therapy is defined in this way, then bachelor's level standards are valid. Neither this definition nor the present music therapy education guidelines of the National Association for Music Therapy address issues related to psychotherapeutic training and practice. Schools affiliated with the smaller American Association for Music Therapy appear to be more oriented to graduate level psychotherapeutic education for music therapists.

It could be an important first step toward consistency in educational standards between the different creative arts therapies, if all of the specializations can come to an agreement on the specific therapeutic skills and roles that are addressed within both baccalaureate and graduate programs.

If a change to graduate level training in music therapy is made, the academic and financial interests of colleges offering bachelor's level programs could be threatened if they do not have the capability to offer graduate studies. Major educational changes in established professions are not made easily. Perhaps the impetus to change in music therapy education will have to come from outside the specialization, from employers desiring more advanced training equivalent to the other creative arts therapy specializations, from government, credentialing agencies, third-party insurance payers and a possible negative trend in job opportunities for bachelor's degree graduates.

MUSIC THERAPY

Music was the first of the creative arts therapies to offer university level training in the United States. According to The National Association for Music Therapy, the first formal college training for music therapists was offered in 1944 and by 1950 "a few universities" had established degree programs. Feder and Feder (1981) describe the leadership role that the Veterans Administration hospitals took after the Second World War in developing music therapy based on medically oriented research which investigated the ability of music to bring about physiological changes and stress reduction. In comparing the historical development of music therapy to art therapy and dance therapy, Feder and Feder state that "Research in music therapy has tended to center in the areas of specific problems, such as autism, behavior disorders, mental retardation, and physical disorders. In contrast with research in art therapy or dance/movement therapy, research in music therapy tends to be more rigorously 'scientific' (probably one reason for the heavy behavioristic orientation in music therapy) and to develop narrow bodies of findings in specific areas on a pragmatic basis" (Ibid., p. 116).

Master's thesis topics at the University of Kansas and Florida State University during the 1950s included the following: "A Study of the Influence of Familiar Hymns on Moods and Associations: Potential Applications in Music Therapy" (Burns, 1958); "A Study of the Vascular Changes in the Capillaries as Effected by Music" (Sears, M., 1954); and "Postural Response to Recorded Music" (Sears, W., 1951). In 1968, E. Thayer Gaston of the University of Kansas edited *Music in Therapy* which is a collection of papers giving definition to the music therapy specialization. Contributors discussed the following topics: "The Use of Music Therapy with Retarded Patients"; "Improvised Music as Therapy for Autistic Children"; "The Psychiatric Approach and Music Therapy"; "The Drum Corps as a Treatment Medium"; and "Music Therapy for the Severely Retarded" (Gaston, 1968). Highly influential publications in the music therapy specialization have included the writings of Nordoff and Robbins (*Music Therapy in Special Education* and *Therapy in Music for Handicapped Children*) and Juliette Alvin (*Music Therapy for the Autistic Child* and *Music Therapy for the Handicapped Child*). The major published books in music therapy of the 1960s and 1970s thus deal consistently with themes of music and special education, multiple handicaps, autism and physiological medicine. Within the music therapy specialization today, behavioral theories, which involve musical stimulation in behavior change, are widely respected.

In 1945 Isadore Coriat published a paper in the *Psychoanalytic Review* attempting to relate music therapy to dynamic psychology. However, it would appear that music has not had the close association to psychotherapeutic practice that has characterized the development of visual art therapy, dance/movement therapy, psychodrama and dramatic enactment therapy. This is an important factor of history which accounts for the way in which the contemporary creative arts therapy specializations relate to one another. There appear to be significant differences between therapists who work psychotherapeutically and those who are more concerned with the remediation of defined problems. Rather than create further separations between the various specializations, it is important to approach the situation with attitudes of mutual cooperation.

There is a tendency for more psychotherapeutically oriented creative arts therapists to look negatively upon the historical association of music therapy with bachelor's level training. This is unfortunate, and the developmental patterns of the various creative arts therapy specializations can be viewed more positively and with the attitude that all of these different therapeutic applications of the artistic process are vital to the progression of the field. The research and experiences of music therapists have much to contribute to the other creative arts therapies and vice versa. For example, art, dance and drama therapists who work with the multiply handicapped can benefit from an understanding of the pioneering contributions of music therapists to this population which include research into the therapeutic use of rhythm and non-verbal communication. The contemporary creative arts therapies are also becoming increasingly involved in the treatment of physical illnesses. Again, there is much to be learned from music therapy research on the physiological effects of musical expression and listening. Music therapy educators proudly emphasize the long history of their specialization in medically oriented research.

The September 1984 issue of the American Art Therapy Association Newsletter, in commenting on proposals for the national conference, described how the association received "an unprecedented number focusing on art therapy with the elderly, physically handicapped and medically ill. This suggests important developments in the breadth and diversity of our field" (AATA, 1984). Art therapy research into physical illness can in turn benefit music therapy. Recent music therapy practices show great interest in the use of imagery for purposes of relaxation and healing. This is an example of the fundamental interdependence of visual imagery and sound in the therapeutic process. Arts in psychotherapy journals, as well as national conference programs, are also presenting an increasing amount of cooperative studies between the arts. This interdependence must be encouraged in our programs of higher education.

There are issues of historic separation and disagreement which complicate the cooperative process. Music therapy again offers an illustration. The National Association for Music Therapy, established in 1950 and previously based in Lawrence, Kansas, was apparently not meeting the needs of all music therapists in the United States and in 1971 the Urban Federation for Music Therapists was incorporated in New York. The Urban Federation has since changed its name to the American Association for Music Therapy. There are now two national associations in music therapy, both involved in separate credentialing processes and educational approval systems.

However, in reviewing recent materials on music therapy education, we saw many indications of increasing cooperation between the two associations. For example, graduate level programs in music therapy often list credentials by either of the two associations as a prerequisite for admission. We have also been informed that the two groups are now working cooperatively on professional credentialing procedures which will include a single national qualifying examination.

In its 1984 publication on career opportunities in music therapy, the National Association for Music Therapy maintains its bachelor's level professional orientation together with its concern for handicapped children. "Handicapped children comprise a large contingent of those now receiving music therapy. They may be mentally retarded, emotionally disturbed, or cerebral palsied; crippled, blind, or deaf; deprived and/or disadvantaged; or they may have multiple disabilities. Children with learning problems also profit greatly from music therapy. The therapist's professional skills are utilized in a wide variety of treatment and educational settings" (NAMT, 1984). The Urban Federation for Music Therapists felt the need for educational and professional standards that would address the problems of therapists working within the complex sociological environments of American cities. The new association has maintained the traditional music therapy orientation to bachelor's level training.

The National Association for Music Therapy places heavy emphasis on traditional music education and directs undergraduate programs to require that 45 percent to 50 percent of all studies be in music and that 20 percent to 30 percent of the curriculum be focused on "Music therapy, psychology, sociology and anthropology . . . general studies, 20 percent to 25 percent; electives approximately 5 percent" (NAMT, 1984). In light of the various problems that have been presented concerning education in music therapy in comparison to the other creative arts therapies and the implications of bachelor's level professional standards, the fact that the National Association for Music Therapy requires that so little of the undergraduate program be in the music therapy area raises serious concerns. The 20 percent to 30 percent requirement also has to be distributed between music therapy, psychology, sociology and anthropology. This amounts to approximately one year or less of undergraduate study. However, the music therapy credentialing process does require a six-month clinical internship in addition to the regular requirements for the bachelor's degree.

The discrepancies between music therapy and the graduate level standards of the other creative arts therapies are significant. The graduate programs in the other creative arts therapies characteristically average two years of intense study and an average of approximately 49 to 50 credits in creative arts therapies and related graduate level psychotherapeutic studies. It would appear that the undergraduate standards of the music therapy profession cannot be considered appropriate for psychotherapeutic training and should clearly state this to avoid confusion. This is especially significant due to the fact that undergraduate social science studies, essential for admission into graduate programs in the other creative arts therapies, are included in the relatively small percentage of studies designated for music therapy. The music therapy specialization should distinguish credits taken in music therapy from those in the social sciences so that a clear statement of the association's criteria for clinical training is given. Specific competencies required of the music therapist should also be listed together with a clear articulation of the outcomes of the educational experience.

The American Association for Music Therapy does present a comprehensive list of competencies required for music therapy practice, many of which do not seem possible to develop on the basis of bachelor's level study. The music therapy associations and educational programs must describe what kind of therapists they are training in their undergraduate professional programs. The response that they are training "music therapists" is not sufficient in light of the realities of today's mental health field. The music therapy specialization must deal with what their bachelor's level graduates are prepared to do and what they are not prepared to do in terms of professional service. And most importantly, the music therapy specialization must take a clear position on how their bachelor's level entry requirements compare to the graduate level requirements of the other creative arts therapies. It must be noted that the other creative arts therapy specializations have not adequately defined professional roles in relation to the many dimensions of "therapy." We want to clearly state that this is not a problem that is unique to music therapy. However, inconsistencies between undergraduate and graduate level training orientations bring the issue of defining what we mean by "therapy" to the forefront.

The close affiliation of music therapy training with the formal study of music also distinguishes the specialization from the other creative arts therapies. Although music study cannot substitute for clinical training, the support the music therapy profession gives to artistic training is important. It can be argued that art therapy, dance therapy and drama therapy might consider placing more emphasis on artistic competency and incorporating it into the clinical training program as recommended by the music therapy associations. Art therapy and dance therapy, which are more oriented to master's level training, would state that two-year graduate programs demand more clinical emphasis, lacking in music therapy requirements, and that artistic skills are prerequisites for admission. The therapist thus develops as an artist in undergraduate school, through previous graduate study in the fine arts, or in other forms of professional training. Where music therapy is weak in clinical training and requirements for advanced psychotherapeutic study, the profession is strong in its support for the therapist's artistic identity, an issue that the other creative arts therapy associations have yet to address.

Music therapy has also been unique in that it requires schools applying for training program approval to be accredited by the National Association of Schools of Music. This joint approval process clearly supports artistic standards, but the requirement also adds a high level of prescribed study at the undergraduate level and little flexibility for program innovation in music therapy. The art therapy specialization has not entered into a similar joint accreditation relationship with the comparable association for schools of art because of the potential loss of freedom in terms of the content of studies and limits placed on the types of schools that can offer training programs. The affiliation of music therapy with the National Association of Schools of Music appears to have had a profound impact on the profession. Virtually every school, with occasional exceptions, offering "approved" music therapy training appears to be much more oriented to music than to clinical practice. In comparison, art therapy and dance therapy are not so strongly tied to a single training environment. Programs within departments of art and dance are common in undergraduate schools but not on the graduate level. Graduate programs in art therapy and dance therapy have been primarily developed within educational environments where there is more emphasis on the integration of artistic and clinical training. If there is an imbalance in art therapy and dance therapy graduate education, it is in the direction of more emphasis on clinical training.

Music therapy is also distinguished from the other creative arts therapies in terms of the classical orientation to music training that still exists today in many institutions of higher education and conservatories. James Ackerman, in a Carnegie Commission study on the place of the arts in higher education, described how abstract theoretical traditions in music allowed it to become widely established in American colleges during the nineteenth century as opposed to the other arts which never enjoyed similar "academic" respectability. Music, according to the Carnegie Commission report, also provides more employment possibilities in both teaching and performance. Ackerman is critical of the tradition of teaching music theory which he perceives as lacking vitality and innovation and which is excessively tied to fixed sources of knowledge. "Probably because of its more secure position in the academy and in society, education in music seems to the outsider to be the most rigidified, the least disposed to self-examination and change, and the most closely linked to the torpid institutions that control the public performance of music" (Ackerman, 1973, p. 239).

Professional association guidelines and institutions of higher education appear to have developed music therapy training within the formal tradition that Ackerman describes. This may account for why music therapy has not been as visible within the mainstream of twentieth century psychotherapeutic innovations as dramatic enactment, visual imagery and bodily expression. The present situation of music in psychotherapy is not at all due to the essential nature of the medium. Within indigenous healing traditions music plays a primary role and it is always integrated with movement, enactment, dreaming, spiritual discovery and the total environment. We also believe that music therapy has tremendous psychotherapeutic potential that is not being realized. There is a need for the development of a depth psychology of music in relation to therapy.

The National Association for Music Therapy in their published materials lists only those schools that are approved by that association. This contrasts to the art therapy and dance therapy associations which list all educational opportunities, both those which applied to the association for approval and were approved, and those that did not apply. According to the 1984 education publication of the National Association for Music Therapy, seventeen colleges and universities offered association-approved master's degree programs: Catholic University of America, Duquesne University, Florida State University, Hahnemann University, Loyola University, Michigan State University, Radford University, Southern Methodist University, Texas Woman's University, University of Georgia, University of Kansas, University of Miami, University of Minnesota, University of Missouri-Kansas City, University of the Pacific, University of Wisconsin-Milwaukee, and Western Michigan University. Seventy-one colleges and universities offered approved bachelor's degree and only one school offered a graduate degree without a bachelor's program at the same institution.

The music therapy specialization is further distinguished from art therapy and dance therapy in that the National Association for Music Therapy also lists six institutions offering doctoral study in music therapy (i.e. Florida State University, Michigan State University, University of Georgia, University of Kansas, University of Minnesota, and Texas Woman's University). Opportunities therefore exist at a number of institutions for doctoral research. This can be attributed to the academic seniority of music therapy in relation to the other creative arts therapies and to the fact that music therapy education programs have been developed in universities offering doctoral level studies. Similar involvement on the Ph.D. level can be anticipated in the other creative arts therapies in the coming years.

In 1974 the National Association for Music Therapy listed thirty-two undergraduate programs and seven master's programs. In the ten-year period between 1974 and 1984 the number of programs more than doubled.

In 1984 the American Association for Music Therapy listed three graduate degree programs (i.e. Hahnemann University, New York University, and Temple University) and four undergraduate schools. Like the National Association for Music Therapy, only schools that applied for approval and were approved by the association were listed.

DANCE THERAPY

Both art therapy and dance therapy graduate training, initiated in the late 1960s and early 1970s, developed with the conviction that professional education in the creative arts therapies was to take place on the master's level. Both the art and dance therapy associations perceive undergraduate studies as "preparatory" and their education standards deal only with graduate education. The American Dance Therapy Association was founded in 1966 and the first graduate level training programs dedicated exclusively to dance therapy were established in the early 1970s. In 1971 Hunter College established a master's degree program with support from the National Institute of Mental Health. Both New York University and UCLA had previously offered dance therapy coursework and opportunities for graduate level dance therapy concentrations. In 1984, according to the American Dance Therapy Association, there were eleven colleges and universities offering graduate degree programs in dance therapy (i.e. Antioch New England, Antioch San Francisco, Columbia College of Chicago, John F. Kennedy University, Goucher College, Hahnemann University, Hunter College, Lesley College, New York University, Pratt Institute, and the University of California at Los Angeles). There were four other schools offering graduate coursework and twelve institutions where undergraduate "preparation" was offered (ADTA, 1984).

The American Dance Therapy Association approves only master's degree programs with a major emphasis in dance therapy. In the 1984 list of educational programs, seven of the eleven master's degree programs had applied for and received approval. Undergraduate programs are not approved by the association, but only schools offering courses at accredited schools and taught by a dance therapist registered by the association were listed. The same criteria apply to the listing of all graduate level coursework. Therefore, dance therapy training opportunities at colleges and universities that are taught by a professional who is not registered by the American Dance Therapy Association were not listed. The American Art Therapy Association formerly required that courses credited toward registration as an art therapist be taught by a registered art therapist. On the basis of advice received from legal counsel, the association dropped this requirement and now requires that courses be taught by a "professionally qualified art therapist." For the purpose of assessing educational quality, a primary criteria should not be whether the prospective faculty member belongs to a particular association and has received their endorsement. Assessments of faculty and program quality should be made exclusively on the basis of the unique credentials of the people and institutions involved. Educational listings based on whether or not people are registered with the particular association would appear to serve the interests of the association more than the profession as a whole which will benefit from comprehensive information as to all dance therapy educational opportunities.

Dance therapy received its artistic inspiration and early identity from the work of Marion Chace at St. Elizabeth's Hospital in Washington, D.C. As the specialization developed, it has become closely associated with the movement analysis system of Rudolf Laban, which, according to the teacher of Laban movement analysis, is best utilized in cooperation with other disciplines. In addition to movement analysis and observation skills, specialized dance therapy training conventionally includes study in human anatomy and kinesiology. Dance therapy educators are at the present time exploring varied approaches to the process of movement observation and the evaluation of non-verbal expression. In these early years of its professonal development, dance therapy, like music therapy, has focused largely on the particular medium and scientifically oriented coursework which heightens specialized knowledge. American Dance Therapy Association educational guidelines do not recommend study in the historic dance-related fields of theater, music and the visual arts. Dance has historically been the most recently defined of these art forms within western society. It grew out of theater and music. Dance therapists will state that movement is the oldest and most primal form of human expression and this point is not disputed. However, what is being described here is the development of dance as a contemporary fine arts discipline.

Dance therapists universally use music in their work and typically do not receive advanced training in the medium. Dance therapy sessions engage participants in the enactment of emotions and the visual perception of the body in space. Historically, dance has been keenly aware of the dramatic and sculptural qualities of movement. These areas suggest possibilities for cooperation with the other creative arts therapies. Video playback and phototherapy also have much to offer dance therapy as again demonstrated by the artistic history of the dance medium and its rich collaboration with film, photography and video.

Largely bypassed by the early psychodynamic systems of therapy in the twentieth century, the body is being actively engaged in contemporary psychotherapy, a trend which supports the expansion of the clinical applications of dance therapy. Dance therapists are adapting their work to the body oriented theories of Wilhelm Reich and Alexander Lowen. J.L. Moreno can be perceived as the first major twentieth century theorist to engage interpersonal enactment with the whole body in psychotherapy. Other enactment therapies have followed. Al Pesso, a dancer by training, created psycho-motor therapy, which, interestingly enough, seems to attract little attention within the American dance therapy community and receives much more serious consideration in the Netherlands. Psycho-motor therapy is based on principles of movement enactment. There are also the contributions of the Feldenkrais system, the Alexander technique and Barbara Mettler. These, and many more approaches to movement are advancing society's understanding of the need to engage the entire body in health systems. There are also the increasing western interests in yoga, Chinese movement meditations, wholistic health, indigenous healing traditions, the revived respect for ethnic dance forms, physical training, running and recreational dance. All of these trends are supporting the growth of movement therapies. Dance therapy in this respect enjoys a unique contemporary potential for development.

In dance therapy as well as the other creative arts therapies, program size and enrollments have a primary influence on curriculum and the content of studies. Most programs tend to admit from fifteen to twenty graduate students each year. These graduate programs are generally specialized on a single art modality and do not involve academic and administrative coordination with other creative arts therapies. Programs are designed so that the group of students entering at the same time take all of their courses together. Choice and elective offerings are minimized. Concurrent with this organizational pattern in many creative arts therapy master's programs, national professional associations are becoming more prescriptive about what is to be offered within an "approved" training program. This process encourages the progressive standardization of the curriculum. Choice and variety are eliminated as issues because of the significance attached to having a program approved by a national professional association. Standardization thus tends to be encouraged more than the expression of differences. Academic freedom and the autonomy of institutions of higher education are gradually being sacrificed in the interest of the professional stamp of approval which is considered by most schools as an essential element in attracting students.

Larger programs with many resources, varied course offerings, flexible educational philosophies and cooperative academic and administrative coordination with other creative arts therapies and related mental health professional training programs within the same school, do not have their strengths recognized by national association education guidelines. Varied and innovative studies are typically considered to be outside of the boundaries of the association's education requirements. All professions tend to be alike in their inherent tendency to construct narrow boundaries around academic inquiry and performance. In this respect, they work contrary to the principles of comprehensive education. But it must be realized that these boundaries are what give definition and a sense of purpose to professions.

James Hillman describes how "A field—painting, mysticism, medicine—even when fertilized with *knowledge* from other fields, generally requires a sacrifice of creativity elsewhere. The field objectified in the opus responds and determines the gestalt of the creative force. The creative is shaped by both the general limits of the field and the specific limits of the opus into which it flows" (Hillman, 1978, p. 20). According to Hillman, the opus in psychology is the psyche and soul of the self and other people. Psychotherapeutic professions dealing with the creative process do not lend themselves to containment within narrow boundaries.

Dance therapy has through its high standards for movement and theoretical training furthered the trend toward graduate level and advanced study in the creative arts therapies. Dance and movement therapists have also made historic contributions toward the integration of mind and body in psychotherapy. The dance therapist is typically an intelligent, inspired and dedicated advocate for wholistic approaches to treatment within mental health services. As the field progresses toward higher levels of study, this potential to engage the whole body in psychotherapy will be taken further. Research and training will benefit from investigations into how movement is interdependent with other forms of life. All of the creative arts therapies must be cautious about their tendencies to become exclusively engaged with the "pure" qualities of their medium and to further separate themselves by specializing in a particular concentration according to a prescribed course of studies.

The specializaton process is not without value within the context of clinical work, research and institutional identity. People are in this respect left with the choice as to whether or not they want to become involved with a specialization or a particular way of offering services. Freedom and personal choice are of vital importance within the context of professional service and professional education. However, national associations and other institutions responsible for establishing guidelines for professional education must avoid narrow boundaries and personal bias. They must be respectful of variety, choice, differences, innovation and creativity which always involves divergent modes of operation. By so doing, they will historically increase the power of the profession and its ability to engage a wider audience.

ART THERAPY

As with related specializations of dance therapy and music therapy, art therapy has continued the professional separation of art forms established by earlier patterns in arts education and fine arts training in both the United States and Europe. However, art therapy training guidelines established by the American Art Therapy Association do not require a prescribed series of artistic or scientific studies focused exclusively on the visual art medium. Requiring a particular system or course of studies results in an omission of other systems and courses. The education guidelines of the American Art Therapy Association allow for considerable flexibility and the creation of different program identities in curriculum and theoretical orientation. The association recommends that a majority of graduate courses be in art therapy, but it does not require a specific set of studies according to particular theoretical systems.

The American Art Therapy Association was established in 1969. According to the association's published list of educational opportunities (AATA, 1982) (the 1982 list was being distributed when information was requested in 1984), master's degree programs in art therapy were offered at twenty colleges and universities: Antioch University West, San Francisco; College of Notre Dame, California; Eastern Virginia Medical School; Emporia State University; The George Washington University; Goucher College; Hahnemann University; Hofstra University; Indiana University of Pennsylvania; Lesley College; Lindenwood College for Individualized Education; Loyola Marymount University; Marywood College; New York University; Pratt Institute; State University College at Buffalo; University of Illinois at Chicago; University of Louisville; Vermont College of Norwich University; and Wright State University.

Five graduate programs offering master's degrees in art education, art and counseling with a major emphasis in art therapy were listed (i.e. California College of Arts and Crafts; California State University at Los Angeles; College of New Rochelle; University of Bridgeport; and University of New Mexico). Art therapy training institutes offering degrees through affiliated colleges were also listed (e.g. the Toronto Art Therapy Institute with Beacon College and International College), together with schools offering other forms of art therapy coursework.

The American Art Therapy Association approves only master's degree programs with a major emphasis in art therapy. Undergraduate programs are not approved. In the list received from the association in 1984, ten of the master's degree programs had applied for and received approval from the association. The association's list is inclusive of all educational opportunities in the specialization and does not require regional accreditation or other exclusionary criteria for the purpose of qualifying for listing. The American Art Therapy Association also lists Canadian, British and Dutch training programs.

As a result of its inclusive policies, the American Art Therapy Association has encouraged a wide variety of training options. In addition to graduate degree study, the association lists forty undergraduate colleges offering preparatory courses and programs of study. The majority of these colleges do not offer graduate degree programs. This pattern of not having undergraduate and graduate study in the same institution contrasts sharply to the music therapy specialization.

Art therapy is unique among the creative arts therapies, in that it has a long tradition of formal training programs within settings other than institutions of higher education together with non-degree programs within colleges and universities. The 1982 list of art therapy training programs refers to three categories of non-degree education: "graduate level certificate programs," "clinical training programs," and "institute programs."

The clinical training programs are generally a continuation of the apprenticeship system and they are typically based in treatment facilities. The American Art Therapy Association standards for registration and the association's educational guidelines continue to recognize various forms of non-degree training for professional credentialing and, therefore, these programs continue as viable alternatives. The dance therapy and music therapy associations do not recognize non-degree programs in their education materials. Psychodrama offers another distinct contrast in that, historically, most training has taken place on a non-degree basis in clinical settings and psychodrama institutes. The 1982 American Art Therapy Association education publication lists six clinical training programs (Art Studio, Incorporated, Cleveland; Bethesda Hospital Association, Ohio; Carrier Foundation, New Jersey; Harding Hospital, Ohio; Milwaukee Psychiatric Hospital; and Temple University).

The art therapy association has historically been committed to considering the individual apprenticeship with a professional art therapist as a form of preparation for clinical practice. This support for diversity in training opportunities has been largely due to two factors: (1) respect for tradition and the various education models that contributed to the development of the profession; and (2) recognition that there are many regions within the United States and other parts of the world where people do not have access to master's degree training programs.

There do not appear to be clear differences between the categories of "graduate level certificate programs" and "institute programs" as presented by the association. These categories seem to be generally interchangeable. Within both, there are groupings of academic institutions and private training centers. Institutions of higher education tend to become involved with institute and certificate training as an alternative to master's degree study. This is often because the institution chooses not to or is not authorized to offer master's degree studies in art therapy but wishes to provide what might be considered somewhat comparable graduate training. The American Art Therapy Association has historically supported these alternatives and recognizes the many contingencies that must be faced within different regions and institutions. The association's policy has consistently been one of supporting quality higher education in varied forms. Six graduate level certificate programs are listed by the art therapy association (i.e. Atlanta Art Therapy Institute; Mount Mary College; School of the Art Institute of Chicago; State University College at Buffalo; Toronto Art Therapy Institute; and University of London, Goldsmiths' College) and six institute programs (i.e. Eagle Rock Trail Art Therapy Institute, California; Institute for Expressive Analysis, New York; Institute for Sociotherapy, New York; New School for Social Research; Pittsburg State University; Saint Louis Institute of Art Psychotherapy). We are aware of only one certificate program established since the publication of the art therapy education listings (i.e. The Thomas Merton Institute in Milwaukee).

In summary, there are significantly more institutions involved in art therapy training on the master's level than in dance therapy and music therapy. Many more opportunities exist for undergraduate study in art therapy than dance therapy. Music therapy has more undergraduate programs of study than both art therapy and dance therapy. Both art therapy and music therapy have many schools throughout the United States involved in training programs, with music therapy offering slightly more formal degree programs. Within the art therapy specialization, there are far more alternatives for training within both academic and non-academic settings. Dance therapy and music therapy associations, by contrast, only support training within degree programs, with the two music therapy associations only listing approved programs. The creative arts therapies profession as a whole presents a wide diversity of training alternatives and different standards for professional credentialing. It might be argued by some that the situation with regard to educational guidelines is inconsistent, haphazard, confusing and supportive of many vested interests. It is imperative for the various specializations to begin to work cooperatively to construct mutually supportive and consistent educational guidelines that will increase the credibility of the profession and strengthen its position in terms of external review. Coordinated guidelines can contain the best of all the different educational approaches and demonstrate a movement toward mutual coherence. The historic approach of the American Art Therapy Association to education can be used as a model for integration because of the way in which the association is able to maintain high standards while also supporting a variety of different approaches to training.

POETRY THERAPY

Poetry therapy, though organized on the national level through the Association for Poetry Therapy, has not been active in establishing formal training programs within institutions of higher education. The history of the contemporary use of poetry in therapy is considered to have begun with the efforts of Eli Greifer, a lawyer, pharmacist and poet, who in 1959 began a poetry therapy group at the Mental Hygiene Clinic of the Cumberland Hospital in Brooklyn. Greifer cooperated with the psychiatrist, Jack Leedy, who became a leading advocate of poetry therapy and author on the subject. On the West Coast, Arthur Lerner, who holds Ph.D. degrees in both literature and psychology, directs the Poetry Therapy Institute in Encino, California, which offers private professional training. Gilbert Schloss, at the Institute for Sociotherapy in New York, has integrated poetry with psychodrama in training groups.

In 1974, Lesley College, through its expressive therapy master's program, provided a graduate degree concentration in poetry and the expressive use of language in therapy. Self-directed graduate programs, such as Goddard College and the Union Graduate School, have provided the opportunity for in-depth independent programs of study in the creative use of language, poetry and literature in therapy. Poetry therapy is a considerably small professional specialization when compared to the other creative arts therapies and it has not developed comparable educational industries and national association educational activities. Individual courses have been given at various academic institutions in the past and continue to be offered. Closely related to poetry therapy is the practice of bibliotherapy, which involves the therapeutic use of literature. As with poetry therapy there has not, to our knowledge, been much activity in the development of formal training programs for bibliotherapists.

Small specializations involving the therapeutic application of poetry, literature, creative language and other media, such as photography and video, are essential to the development of the creative arts therapy profession and deserve significant attention. Within an educational environment which gives attention to all art forms, these smaller specializations can flourish. The future strength of the creative arts therapy field will be dependent upon the extent to which it can harness and integrate the resources of all forms of artistic expression into a coherent professional image. The isolation of small specializations such as poetry therapy, phototherapy and bibliotherapy works against the interests of the whole.

James Hillman describes all psychology as a poetic process. Hillman's psychological writings offer an example of how literary and poetic thought can become primary psychological and therapeutic processes. Rather than simply adapting "poems" to conventional psyhology, the creative arts therapies might consider the poetic dimensions of thought and expression. Depth psychology reveals the poetic origins of consciousness.

ARTIST/THERAPISTS

In 1978, the American Association of Artist/Therapists was established in the state of New York to represent the interests of all of the creative arts therapies within a single organization. The association addresses itself to all aspects of the creative process in therapy and does not focus exclusively on a particular medium. The artistic process, in its many forms, is considered to be the primary element of therapy. Psychotherapy, according to the association, is perceived as art and the therapist who functions creatively is considered to be an artist. The association has expanded the conceptual and practical limits of art in relation to therapy as suggested by Otto Rank, who described psychotherapy as one of the ultimate forms of artistic activity. The association's founder, Steve Ross, writes that, "Artist/therapists recognize that they are their own best instrument. . . . (They) continually invent their method, according to their and their client's unique personalities" (Ross, 1984). The association maintains its commitment "to promote the general recognition of the process of therapy as practiced by artists" (AAAT, 1984). The American Association of Artist/Therapists and the affiliated International Association of Artist/Therapists have raised vital issues such as the definition of art in relation to psychotherapy. Members include psychotherapists with doctoral degrees and others who have master's degrees in related fields or what the association describes as "significant accomplishments in the arts." The association supports many alternative vehicles for training and offers courses through its office in New York and its annual national conference.

The American Association of Artist/Therapists applies the artistic process to all aspects of psychotherapy and addresses itself to the identity of the psychotherapists as an artist. The primary concern of the association is the complete integration of artistic and psychotherapeutic processes. Rather than applying "art" to therapy, the two are perceived as elements of a single process. Potentially, the core ideas of this association can relate to all forms of psychotherapeutic training. In this respect, the American Association of Artist/Therapists differs from the other creative arts therapy specializations and their national associations. The association does not deal with the isolation of different specializations but rather with the universal aspects of all psychotherapeutic practices. Rather than treating "art" as a separate discipline within the larger psychotherapeutic context, all psychotherapy is perceived as art. The ideas presented by the American Association of Artist/Therapists are in agreement with the pervasive contemporary attitude that the skillful and effective practice of psychotherapy is an art. The association presents a challenge to the creative arts therapy field in terms of the need for the profession to begin to clearly define what it means by the use of "art" and creativity in therapy. The ancient history of the philosophy of art suggests that simple and universally agreed upon definitions of art are nonexistent. Artists have insisted that there need be no boundaries between art and life. When asked to define art, Picasso replied with a question asking what is not art.

The American Association of Artist/Therapists has raised fundamental issues that have not been addressed by the other creative arts therapy associations. Dialogue between the different groups is essential. As art therapy, dance therapy, drama therapy, music therapy and other smaller creative arts therapies have developed, they have defined themselves through the different physical materials of art modalities. The specializations have prospered as a result of this focus and their ability to introduce new and tangible modes of communication into therapy. The artist/therapist association has contributed to the evolution of the creative arts therapies by raising philosophical issues as to the nature of art and therapy. Rather than threatening the more "material" oriented specializations, the artist/therapist "idea" expands the creative arts therapies with the notion that all therapy can be perceived as art.

DRAMA THERAPY

Because psychodrama deals with a specific theory and methodology of theater and therapy, other traditions and ways of using drama in human relations have joined together to establish the specialization of drama therapy. The National Association of Drama Therapy was established in 1979, making it the most recently organized of the creative arts therapy specializations. The application of drama to therapy and education has been established in Great Britain in a more comprehensive fashion. Fleshman and Fryrear in *The Arts in Therapy* maintain that "Great Britain has taken the lead in the development of drama therapy" (Fleshman and Fryrear, 1981, p. 116). Peter Slade, who began his work in England in the 1920s, is considered to be responsible for providing the impetus for the development of child drama and drama therapy. Brian Way has in the past twenty years become the major British ambassador on child drama and constantly tours throughout the United States training teachers.

Sue Jennings, the British drama therapist, published *Remedial Drama* in 1974 and has been actively engaged in drama therapy practice and training in Europe throughout the 1970s and 1980s. The work of Jennings has had a major impact on the development of the drama therapy specialization.

In describing its orientation to training, the National Association for Drama Therapy states that "Drama therapists are trained in theatre arts, psychology and psychotherapy. Training in theatre includes improvisation, role-playing, puppetry, mime and theatrical production" (NADT, 1984). Varied theater practices and theoretical approaches are possible within the context of drama therapy. Child psychotherapy, often synonymous with "play therapy" (Axline, 1947 and Moustakas, 1953), has historically found dramatic play with toys, animals, puppets, art materials and other objects to be a primary mode of communication. Play therapists have made major contributions to the theoretical and practical application of the creative process to psychotherapy, although their work is not typically considered to be part of the creative arts therapy field. The history of child psychotherapy demonstrates how important it is to encourage multi-disciplinary training and practice within the mental health professions.

The National Association for Drama Therapy lists three graduate programs (i.e. Antioch University, San Francisco; Lesley College; and

New York University) and two undergraduate programs (i.e. Eastern Montana College and William Paterson College, New Jersey). Undergraduate courses are also listed as being offered at Avila College in Kansas and at Loyola University in New Orleans.

In keeping with art therapy, dance therapy and psychodrama, the drama therapy association encourages professional training at the graduate level. "While an individual may be registered as a drama therapist with a minimum of a Bachelor's degree, this does not present the optimum degree of formal training, particularly in regard to clinical theory. Additional coursework and supervised experience, beyond the Bachelor's degree, is necessary to meet the requirements for registry. Although undergraduate programs in drama therapy cannot serve, in and of themselves, to prepare students for professional practice, they can introduce students to the core concepts of drama therapy, provide a strong background of skill, experience and comfort in drama/theatre, and give them a general understanding of psychological and social processes" (Portner and Irwin, 1983).

As with the American Art Therapy Association, the National Association for Drama Therapy does not require specific courses of study but, rather, recommends varied studies in drama/theater, behavioral sciences, drama therapy, and psychotherapy. Drama therapy also approaches professional registration through a flexible "point" system similar to the one used by the American Art Therapy Association. As a new and developing specialization, drama therapy encourages different forms of training. Points are presently given toward registration for undergraudate study. In the past, the American Art Therapy Association also gave points toward registration for undergraduate study but eventually stopped the practice in the late 1970s. Given the position of the National Association for Drama Therapy on the preparatory nature of undergraduate education and the need to encourage graduate study, it will probably only be a matter of time before the association follows the course of the art therapy association in not awarding points toward registration for bachelor's level training. In their early years of development, the art therapy and drama therapy associations found it necessary to recognize all forms of study in relation to professional registration, since the first priority was the building of a professional identity and empowering the relatively small number of people who began to establish clinical programs throughout the country. As the specialization grows and graduate training programs become established, then the association tends to move toward attaching exclusive professional training status to master's level study. There is typically a period of transition during which pioneering practitioners who do not meet the new criteria are "grandfathered and grandmothered" into professional registration.

PSYCHODRAMA

Psychodrama is unique among the creative arts therapies in that it does not approve training programs but rather approves individual trainers. Psychodramatists certified as trainers by the American Society for Group Psychotherapy and Psychodrama can offer professional level education in private institutes and training groups. Training can also take place in institutions of higher education, but, with the exception of graduate level psychodrama training first initiated at Lesley College in 1974, education continues to take place outside of colleges and universities. What is significant about the history of psychodrama training is its ability to grow and prosper without the credentialing status of higher education. This is largely due to the depth, sophistication and wide practical application of the theoretical writings of J.L. Moreno.

Psychodramatists typically receive graduate education in other mental health fields, although distinguished contemporary practitioners have been previously educated in the arts, religion and the humanities. Psychodrama thus continues to maintain a strong interdisciplinary orientation. Because so many people have come to psychodrama from social work, medicine, psychology and other professions, psychodramatists do not always think of their method as a primary form of professional identification. However, a significant number of practitioners do consider psychodrama as their primary professional identity. As a result of the growth of mental health services during the past twenty years, an increasingly large number of people have been hired to work as psychodramatists within clinics and hospitals. St. Elizabeth's Hospital in Washington, D.C. has taken a primary role in education and professional role development through its psychodrama unit and advanced graduate level training positions. The training experience in psychodrama thus takes place within the context of what can be described as apprenticeships with board certified trainers.

The American Board of Examiners in Psychodrama, Sociometry and Group Psychotherapy was incorporated in 1975 for the purpose of establishing national standards and certification procedures. This board is a legally separate organization from the professional membership association, the American Society of Group Psychotherapy and Psychodrama which was founded in 1942, making it the oldest American creative arts therapy national association. This separation of certification from membership is a legally necessary course of action that all of the creative arts therapy professional societies will ultimately have to follow. The Board of Examiners certifies two levels of professionals. The first is "practitioner" and the second, and more advanced certification, is "trainer, educator, practitioner." In 1984, the Board of Examiners listed the names of one hundred and six people certified as a trainer, educator, practitioner. These people are working in the United States, Australia, Canada, England, France and West Germany. The board also reported that in 1984 there were thirty-four training institutes operating in the United States, Australia, Canada, England and West Germany. Twenty-eight of these institutes were in the United States.

The first professional level for psychodrama practice is the "practitioner." In the case of psychodrama, educational recommendations are interchangeable with certification standards. Education requirements are simple and straightforward:

1. A minimum of 780 hours of training with one or more board certified trainer, educator, practitioners.
2. One (additional) year of supervised clinical experience.
3. A graduate degree from an accredited university, in a field relevant to a candidate's area of practice, or an acceptable equivalent to a graduate degree (knowledge of the following areas is expected: human growth and development; theories of personality; abnormal behavior-psychopathology; methods of psychotherapy; social systems) (American Board of Examiners PSGP, 1984).

Psychodrama has, in keeping with art therapy and dance therapy, established the master's degree as the entry level academic credential. However, what is unique and intriguing about psychodrama is that the graduate degree is typically in a "related field" (i.e. social work, psychology, medicine, creative arts therapies, etc.). The Board of Examiners does not require the degree to be in psychodrama or even to involve psychodrama studies. Psychodrama has a system and history of training and certification which has resulted in distinctly different educational patterns than the other creative arts therapies. The present system is so established, both professionally and economically, that it is not likely to change within the immediate future.

Although psychodrama training takes place largely outside of higher education, psychodrama as a specialization has a much higher percentage of practitioners with advanced degrees than any of the other creative arts therapy specializations. In 1979 the American Society of Group Psychotherapy and Psychodrama gave the following statistic on degrees held by members: "M.D. 21%; Ph.D. 32%; M.S.W. 17%; Master's 22%; Bachelor's 6%; Other 2% (American Psychiatric Association, 1980). The American Art Therapy Association, a master's degree oriented profession, presented the following statistics in 1979 of degrees held by members: "Bachelor's 14%; Master's 80%; Doctorate 4%; Other 2%" (Ibid.).

The psychodrama statistics on degrees held by members reveal that the practice of requiring degrees in a particular creative art therapy specialization does not necessarily produce a more highly educated professional group. These statistics are of vital importance to an investigation of the more generic issues related to education in the creative arts therapies and plans for future cooperation between the specializations.

The model of the psychodrama association is particularly relevant to the situation where mental health professionals with advanced training wish to become educated as creative arts therapists. Only psychodrama has a clear and efficient course of studies for them to follow. In the case of the music therapy specialization, the person with a Ph.D. in clinical psychology would have to return to undergraduate school in order to meet association guidelines for training. Future coordination and creative planning would allow the different associations to work together, carefully studying what is best about their various training models, with the goal of establishing more consistent educational standards. The educational histories of the different specializations and the present educational realities can be respected while exploring how the various creative arts therapy specializations can be brought into a closer relationship with one another. Psychodrama policies can help the other specializations deal more effectively with experienced psychotherapists, many of whom have doctorates, who wish to receive training.

Another feature of psychodrama which is unique among the creative arts therapies is the fact that certification standards do not require any prerequisite training in drama and other theater related arts. The powerful therapeutic theater that takes place within psychodramatic enactments would indicate that this policy is justified. Interestingly enough, teachers of theater, actors and others interested in the dramatic art form often become involved in psychodrama to deepen their understanding of the pure nature of the medium. Psychodramatists do receive drama training but within the context of psychodramatic education and practice. This aspect of psychodrama, perhaps more than any other of its unique features, calls into question some of the primary educational principles of the other creative arts therapies, especially since psychodramatists hold the highest level of academic degrees within the creative arts therapies. This contribution of psychodrama to our understanding of how media-related expertise is developed has come about largely because of the history of psychodrama training taking place outside of higher education. If training programs were historically developed in academic institutions in relation to a theater department, then drama courses would surely have been required. The history of music therapy education developed in this way, through departments of music, and that specialization presents the most pronounced contrast to psychodrama in training procedures and levels of degrees held by professionals.

Psychodrama is also distinguished among the creative arts therapies by the original insights of its creator, J.L. Moreno, who conceived of therapeutic theatrical forms that were fully integrated with life and not constrained by what he referred to as the "conserve" of dramatic tradition, which according to Moreno limited creative expression. The theoretically radical and innovative origins of psychodrama again contrast to other creative arts therapy specializations that were developed in close association to both artistic and clinical "conserves." It can be proposed that the conceptual and operational sophistication and creativity of the psychodramatic process have been responsible for involving so many mental health professionals who hold advanced degrees in other areas. There has not been a comparable engagement of psychotherapists from other disciplines in creative therapy specializations attached to more traditional forms of artistic and clinical process.

Typically, what people believe to be necessary in terms of professional education results from the sense that the proper way to proceed is the traditional way. Moreno, however, went contrary to the theatrical, educational and clinical traditions. Creative arts therapy programs might benefit from media training being fully integrated with therapeutic functions as opposed to separating the two. Psychodrama education offers evidence of how there can be a full integration of form and function in media training. Psychodrama also offers a vital and challenging image of art to the world of theater and the arts, the therapeutic power of which results from the complete integration of art and life. There are few examples in western society of such a successful and complete synthesis. Artists in many cultures, concerned about the irrelevance of art in everyday life, have yearned for such a dynamic and aesthetically pure union between art and the depths of a person's existence.

The psychodrama training model does not negate what can be learned and applied from drama training and the closely related Eastern European experimental theater traditions of Stanislavski and Grotowski. These learning experiences are recognized as valuable. What is unique to psychodrama is the clear statement that these experiences are not required as prerequisites for training. Music therapy training guidelines again offer the most striking contrast, in that they prescribe a large and specific list of music courses which are to be taken at the undergraduate level. Art therapy, dance therapy and drama therapy have been more liberal and have not required specific courses, but there is a clear tradition in these specializations encouraging separate studies in the particular medium. Continuing education and experience in arts media are of vital importance for all creative arts therapists, including psychodramatists. What psychodrama educational models present for consideraton is whether or not this training need be required by professional associations and educational programs. The issue is made even more intriguing by the fact that psychodrama is the only creative arts therapy specialization which has profoundly affected the practice of the art form from which it is derived, as well as the more general practice of individual, group and family psychotherapy.

J.L. Moreno felt "that it was foolish to consider making psychodrama a career" (Buchanan, 1980, p. 48). He perceived it as a way of life. However, as the practice of psychodrama became increasingly influential, it has gradually taken on a professional identity. The continuing success and respectability of the psychodrama section of St. Elizabeth's Hospital, one of the oldest continuing creative arts therapy clinical programs in the United States, has contributed to the movement toward professionalism. The creation of specific job descriptions and clinical programs for psychodramatists inevitably furthers career possibilities within the specialization. The same applies to the development and growth of training programs and employment opportunities for psychodrama educators.

With regard to future cooperation between the creative arts therapies, Peter Rowan, an Executive Council member of the American Society of Group Psychotherapy and Psychodrama, spoke of how 30 percent to 40 percent of all psychodramatists are not in favor of being perceived as part of the creative arts therapies because of the low educational and professional levels that they see characterizing certain specializations. He also feels that third-party payment eligibility, sought after by many creative arts therapists, might negatively affect all of the specializations because of government's historic tendency to require a standardized curriculum as is presently the case with psychology and social work. Rowan feels that third-party payment eligibility may be the worst possible thing that can happen to psychodrama and the creative therapies (Rowan, 1984). Negative results can be avoided if the creative arts therapies maintain standards of educational freedom and variety while acquiring the benefits of third-party payments for the profession.

The present time appears to be a critical period in the historic development of the creative arts therapies. The specializations are moving closer together for purposes of legislative cooperation on issues of common concern, yet educational standards are highly inconsistent. Psychodramatists, who do not want to be grouped together with the creative arts therapies, are joined by people involved with art therapy, dance therapy, drama therapy and music therapy who feel that these disciplines should maintain separate and different identities together with autonomous educational and professional standards. Issues such as third-party payments and job development are encouraging specializations to work closely with one another. Third-party payers will not be able to accept the present inconsistencies in educational and professional standards that characterize the profession today. Large bureaucracies will not recognize tiny professional specializations for third-party payment when these groups can be logically consolidated with closely related disciplines. Distinctions will have to be clearly made between the objectives of both undergraduate and graduate studies. Standards for graduate level psychotherapeutic training must be established and differentiated from educational and remedial training opportunities offered on the undergraduate level. It is time for the different specializations to independently initiate their own efforts to anticipate these future problems and to design creative responses which will meet the needs for clearly defined and universally accepted educational standards while also protecting the diversity and uniqueness of training styles that presently characterize the profession.

INDEPENDENT STUDY

During the late 1960s and 1970s many conventional American college and university campuses offered options for individualized and independent study coursework in subjects of the student's choice. The educational options listed by the various creative arts therapy associations describe either structured programs or regular courses. Individual and independent courses of study do not appear on these lists. Thousands of students have either prepared themselves for graduate study or professional work through coursework of this kind. Independent study has been used on campuses throughout the United States as a vehicle for addressing the wide variety of students' academic interests which may extend beyond the limits of regular faculty and curriculum resources. With the guidance of a faculty advisor, who may not always be expert in the particular field of inquiry, the student goes about researching and mastering a designated body of knowledge. Through independent study, the creative arts therapies have appeared as part of the academic experience in many schools which do not offer formal studies in the field.

In addition to individual courses of study, entire graduate and undergraduate programs in the creative arts therapies have been created through independent study structures. All of the creative arts therapies have been included. The independent study system has not only expanded the range of academic inquiry within higher education, but it has, in the case of the creative arts therapies, served to integrate the apprenticeship model with higher education. Independent study credit is often given to students for practical work and supervision that they receive through field experience with an experienced creative arts therapist. Goddard College flourished during the 1970s as a center for independent study in the creative arts therapies. Degree programs could be developed on both the master's and bachelor's level. Many creative arts therapists received their master's degrees through Goddard. The college gave them the opportunity to continue in their professional work as creative arts therapists and to integrate their jobs into the master's program. The Goddard program was national in scope and provided people in isolated geographic regions with the opportunity to pursue degree studies. Each student worked with a core faculty member who was typically an educational generalist. The core faculty advisor then helped the student in choosing a "field faculty" advisor who was typically a person outside the Goddard community who offered expertise in the student's field of interest. Although Goddard was a leading educator of creative arts therapists during the 1970s, the role of the college in the profession has never been formally recognized by the various professional organizations because the school did not offer a single, structured program of studies which fit the educational guidelines of the associations.

Independent study and research in the creative arts therapies has also taken place on the doctoral level. Dennis White of the University of Houston reported that in the thirty-year period from 1944 to 1974, eighty-five doctoral dissertations directed toward art therapy were completed at forty-eight universities (White, 1977). The appearance of these art therapy related doctorates is extremely significant when considering that they were produced within institutions that did not have formal doctoral programs in art therapy. Doctoral research of this kind can be considered as another form of independent study which does not fit into the existing educational guidelines of the various creative arts therapy professional associations. There is surely similar data to be discovered on dissertations related to other creative arts therapy specializations that have been completed within universities without formal degree programs. It is intriguing to observe how American higher education, especially in institutions encouraging liberal and experimental learning, has accommodated needs for independent study in the creative arts therapies. This reality of educational history continues to be unaddressed by the training guidelines of the various creative arts therapy specializations.

DOCTORAL STUDY

As mentioned previously, the National Association for Music Therapy lists six universities with doctoral programs in music therapy. The 1982 American Art Therapy Association educational listings include two schools which report offering doctoral studies (i.e. New York University, D.A. in art therapy; and the University of Maryland at College Park, Ph.D. in art therapy research). The Lesley College Graduate School plans to offer Ph.D. studies in all of the creative arts therapies with an emphasis on leadership, higher education and artistically oriented research. At the present time, Lesley provides the opportunity for post-master's study through its Certificate of Advanced Graduate Studies (C.A.G.S.) and its post-doctoral fellows program. The National Association of Drama Therapy lists a doctoral program concentration at New York University in drama therapy which is offered through the Department of Educational Theatre.

The Union Graduate School Ph.D. program, offered by the Union for Experimenting Colleges and Universities, has been particularly active in educating creative art therapists. In 1964 the Union for Experimenting Colleges and Universities was established in Yellow Springs, Ohio in close relationship to Antioch College, which was one of many experimentally oriented institutions making up the original academic organization. Other members have included Bard, Chicago State, Franconia College, Friends World College, Goddard, Governors State University, Hofstra, Loretto Heights, University of Massachusetts School of Education, University of the Pacific, Pitzer, Shaw University, Skidmore, Stephens, Webster, and the University of Wisconsin-Green Bay.

The Union Graduate School Ph.D. program is based on principles of self-directed study. Time intensive residencies within the Union community are combined with independent study and the program allows students to take courses at other universities. The flexible and student-centered model, emphasizing creativity and the development of new settings for learning, has provided a timely resource to the emerging creative arts therapy profession in need of expanded opportunities for doctoral study. Edgar Schein of the Massachusetts Institute of Technology, in his study on professional education, sponsored by the Carnegie Commission on Higher Education reported that:

> Perhaps the most advanced model of an inter university independent study is the Union Graduate School doctoral program. Students in this program are expected to do a major portion of their study outside of any formal curriculum by concentrating on independent reading and research; but they may also take courses at any university in the world . . . . They are encouraged to study as apprentices to distinguished leaders in their field or in some highly educative social situation such as an under developed country, inner city or planned community . . . . In place of the Ph.D. dissertation, the student normally completes a 'project demonstrating excellence,' which may take the form of traditional research, the publishing of a book, the design and implementation of a significant social change, or the creation of a substantial piece of art, music or literature (Schein, 1972, pp. 105-106).

Admission to the Union Graduate School has historically emphasized the applicant's ability to present a program of study which is not possible within a conventional Ph.D. program. The Union thus found itself working with many creative arts therapists without specifically planning a doctoral program in the profession. The various creative arts therapy professional associations have not given serious consideration to the situation where the individual student creates the program of learning in cooperation with faculty consultants. National association guidelines have rather focused on the more conventional process of creating structured and fixed programs of study for students. Because of its student-centered policies of self-directed study, creative arts therapy doctoral students within the Union Graduate School have had the freedom to pursue a wide range of studies, impossible within any other academic institution.

The recent history of self-directed graduate programs in the United States indicates that they serve as indicators of major educational needs not being met by other institutions of higher education. With the extensive development of master's and bachelor's degree programs of study in the creative arts therapies during the 1970s, there has been a corresponding need created for Ph.D. study which will inevitably be the next major growth area in creative arts therapy education. Advanced study is needed to train the leaders of the profession and to support the field with research and scholarship.

A comparable situation can be observed in the arts in education. Once the profession became established within colleges and universities, many opportunities for doctoral study were created. In his study of art therapy doctoral dissertations, Dennis White describes how:

> If the intensity of this interest remains constant, or increases, and the number of certified master's level degree programs continues to expand, the requirement for doctoral programs specifically staffed and directed toward art therapy education may be expected to increase. The need for such programs will become increasingly acute as individuals acquire the master's degree and prepare to seek out institutional settings where additional advanced work may be pursued. Another pressure which can be expected to support the development toward advanced programs in art therapy will come from the institutions themselves. As universities and colleges begin to appropriately respond to pressures generated from the community for advanced study with respect to art therapy, the institutions will in turn generate a need for such programs as they seek to acquire qualified professionals to fill those instructional positions necessary to support their newly created degree programs (White, 1977, pp. 3-4).

SUMMARY

Each of the creative arts therapy specializations has a distinct history with regard to higher education. Although the different specializations have developed at similar times in our society and in response to similar needs and opportunities within the health-related fields, there has been little cooperation and direct sharing between them in relation to education. The suggestion that the various specializations of the creative arts therapies are one professional group is considered by many to be an unacceptable statement, so vested are the interests of the different concentrations. These separations are supported by the educational history of fine arts education in western society and by the closely related profession of the arts in education. Differences, rather than similarities, have been consistently stressed. However, it must be recognized that these differences are largely due to the specific visions of pioneering people which allowed the different creative arts therapy specializations to come to prominence. The specialized interests are thus often extensions of the personalities and life experiences of the people who helped to create the field.

Education within the creative arts therapies has become a multimillion dollar industry. The people who tend to make the standards for education within professional associations are often the people who are engaged with educational programs in one capacity or another. Heavily prescribed studies rather than flexibility and innovation are clearly advocated in the educational guidelines of some professional associations. These trends will utltimately eliminate the open space that allowed the specializations to be created. As the creative arts therapy field grows, opportunities for creative innovation and further professional definition, together with the expansion of clinical and conceptual models, must be encouraged.

The Council of Graduate Schools in the United States in its statement on the master's degree described how:

> The scope of knowledge today is so complex and is growing so rapidly that the mature scholar as well as the graduate student must select a particular field and almost certainly, a specialty within that field in order to make an effective contribution . . . . A program may be offered by a department specializing in the particular field, or sometimes, if the program is interdisciplinary, by a specifically authorized committee or group of professors, each of whom is competent in the particular field or closely related ones (The Council of Graduate Schools in the U.S., 1976, p. 3).

In its policy statement, the council describes how the number and variety of master's degrees awarded in the United States has surpassed the growth of bachelor's degrees. In keeping with the Carnegie Comission on Higher Education's articulation of the contemporary need to complement the growing trend toward specialization with interdisciplinary study and cooperation, The Council of Graduate Schools in the United States recommends that "the number of names used for mater's degrees and specialty designations be held to an absolute minimum" (Ibid., p. 6). The council reports that in 1976 there were in excess of three hundred different titles used for master's degrees. The creative arts therapies have contributed to this increase in titles due to the fact that master's degrees are currently offered in each of the specializations, and even within the same specialty areas degree titles will vary.

The encouragement of future cooperation between the creative arts therapy specializations is not intended to discourage or oppose specialized study. To the contrary, cooperation and the sharing of resources can take the specialization process even further in terms of research, scholarship and academic studies that will increase our understanding of the different art modalities.

There have been recent expressions of cooperation between the creative arts therapies on the national level which suggest significant potential for future professional development. In 1978 the Maurice Falk Medical Fund, in cooperation with the American Psychiatric Association, sponsored a coalition meeting in Washington, D.C. involving the various creative arts therapy national associations. In 1978 the President's Commission on Mental Health appointed a task panel to deal with "the Role of the Arts and Therapy and Environment." The coalition established at the Falk Fund conference grew into the Legislative Alliance of Creative Arts Therapies which is made up of representatives of the governing boards of the American Art Therapy Association, the American Dance Therapy Association, the National Association for Music Therapy and the Federation of Trainers and Training Programs in Psychodrama. The alliance coordinates activities of common concern for all of the associations with regard to legislative issues and developments in government. These activities follow the establishment by the Veterans Administration and the Office of Personnel Management of civil service job descriptions for "creative arts therapists." The federal job description refers to the creative arts therapies as a generic professional category rather than listing each of the specializations. Recognition of the creative arts therapies was also given in the Mental Health Systems Act of the federal government. The National Committee Arts for the Handicapped has prospered since the 1970s and receives federal and regional funding. The programs of the national committee deal with all art forms in an integrated manner and serve as another indicator of the importance for cooperation and consolidation between the creative arts therapy specializations.

Recent literature on innovative trends in the mental health fields is consistently recognizing the creative arts therapies as a profession. Clinics and training programs are finding that interdisciplinary skills are far more practical than single specializations. When we requested information on the dance therapy program at John F. Kennedy University, we received a letter stating, "We have just terminated our dance/movement program as it existed in order to combine it with other non verbal therapies to give our students a broader and more marketable training" (JFK Univ., 1984).

People outside the particular specializations tend to perceive the creative arts as inherently connected. In light of these realities, it will be in the interest of the various creative arts therapy national associations to support consortium and coalition structures which will guarantee cooperation together with recognition of the integrity of the different specializations. The consortium structure can respect differences while encouraging the definition of commonalities. An administrative structure can be created which will allow the associations to work together on vital issues of education, research, credentialing, licensure, third-party payments, relations with government and obtaining support within the private sector. Overlap in national office facilities, administrative staff and other costs can be trimmed.

The lack of consistency in basic principles of practice and education must be a goal for future planning. A more coherent image of the profession and the different specializations can be presented to the public as well as to experts trying to determine exactly what is going on in the education of creative arts therapists and in their professional practice. The unified effort will ultimately bring increased status to the profession. Cooperative evaluation and planning cannot help but serve the interests of the different specializations if they approach the process openly and with a desire to learn from the experiences of colleagues. Through a unified planning effort, the best of all educational structures and opportunities can be spread throughout the profession. Difficult problems such as the differences that presently exist between the specializations with regard to entry level education, theories of practice, professional definition, the encouragement of interdisciplinary or exclusive specialization studies, the place of personal artistic training, non-academic versus academic training, etc., can begin to be addressed within a shared forum. The more established professions of law and medicine demonstrate how variety and specialization can be achieved while maintaining an integrated professional identity. However, there are potential problems within the creative arts therapies of too much central organization and standardization in the creation of education guidelines that need to be watched carefully. The consortium idea offers a way to have both coordination and variety.

Current studies of higher education and the professions indicate that there are endless possibilities for future specializations. Already we have not only the separation of the different creative arts therapies, but also separate organizations within the same art form in music therapy. Drama therapy is developing as a new specialization, distinct from psychodrama. There are also the poetry therapists, the video therapists, bibliotherapists, phototherapists and other art forms that may in the future develop therapeutic systems. Ultimately, the establishment of completely separate specializations with different organizational and educational structures will reach a breaking point. Colleges and universities offering studies in all specializations will be unable to maintain relations with the many associations claiming to have jurisdiction over educational practices. The profession must become more enlightened with regard to educational planning. The continuing practice of creating a multiplicity of association fiefdoms is not appropriate to contemporary professional education. These practices have been allowed to continue because the different specializations have been able to develop completely unto themselves with virtually no outside interference.

Cooperation should not interfere with the creative vitality of the profession but only eliminate unreasonable, inefficient and restrictive practices. Rather than rigid standardization, it is recommended that future coalition efforts be directed toward the coordination of variety and the definition of universal elements of clinical practice and training. Within a cooperative arrangement, short-term and easily achieved objectives may be identified as well as more difficult, complex and long-term goals. The most immediate problem is the lack of agreement on the role of undergraduate training. Closely related to this problem are differences as to when specialization should take place, the value of liberal education on the undergraduate level, and the need for requiring graduate training for professional practice.

Critics of graduate and professional education in the United States identify many problems facing training for all of the professions. These problems include: competition for clientele; the addition of new knowledge to the curriculum; over-emphasis on a standardized, required course of studies attempting to produce uniformity; professor centered learning as opposed to structuring training around the experience of the learner; not enough emphasis on practice and clinical training; the negative human effects of trends toward quantification in research and the evaluation of professional efficacy; the distinctly American tendency to solve problems by adding new courses and new specialization; distancing from rigorous study of the humanities; the offering of too many different kinds of degrees; and a lack of emphasis on creativity and independent study (Mayhew and Ford, 1974).

Criticism has also been directed toward the seemingly endless differentiation that takes place within a profession as it expands in response to demand. Social work has responded to this situation by creating levels of professional qualification. Others have continuously lengthened the number of years of study. "The most prestigious professions have been those who could keep their aspirants longest in school before formally admitting them to professional school, then longest in professional school itself, and then longest in postgraduate apprenticeship — and all this without a break. The situation is most nearly approached in medicine" (Hughes, 1973, p. 288). Professions in high demand develop educational industries that continue to grow in relation to the need for, and popularity of, the profession. This has all taken place without evidence documenting that there is any relationship between length of study and professional efficacy (Mayhew and Ford, 1974, p. 27).

Professional schools have been criticized for their lack of experimentation, innovation and creativity. "Professional schools have usually been content to codify and pass on conventional lore to insure that their graduates are fully accepted both by the profession and by the licensing agencies" (Ibid., p. 17).

Creative arts therapy training programs have avoided many of the problems that older professions face and have substituted creative alternatives largely because the first educational programs were closely associated with contemporary clinical practice. In the area of the integration of practical work with theoretical learning, all of the creative arts therapies have developed educational approaches that can be emulated by older professions. Creativity, independent study opportunities, interdependence with larger mental health disciplines and a reasonable length of study also seem to characterize education in the creative arts therapies. However, as other professions have matured there is typically an increased involvement of national associations and licensing bodies in setting standards for education. This generally results in movements toward standardization and uniformity; an over-emphasis on the same required courses in programs throughout the country; the development of curricula by national associations as opposed to having studies be designed by institutions of higher education and faculty-student evaluations of individual needs; an increasing distance from the humanities; and the offering of a wide variety of degrees. Although interdependent relations are successfully established with psychiatry, psychology and other major sources of power within the mental health field, there is virtually no encouragement by national associations of inter-specialization study between the various creative arts therapies.

The following chapter will describe characteristics of the training programs in the creative arts therapies and provide a comparative analysis of all educational opportunities presently available within the profession.

REFERENCES

Ackerman, James: The arts in higher education. In Kaysen, Carl (Ed.): *Content and Context: Essays on College Education.*, New York, McGraw-Hill, 1973.

Alvin, Juliette: *Music Therapy for the Autistic Child.* London, Oxford U Pr, 1978.

Alvin, Juliette: *Music Therapy for the Handicapped Child.* London, Oxford U Pr, 1976.

American Association of Artist/Therapists: Public information brochure. New York, AAAT, 1984.

American Art Therapy Association: *AATA Newsletter, 14*:3, 1984.

American Art Therapy Association: Art therapy education listings. Reston, Virginia, AATA, 1982.

American Association for Music Therapy: Manual on AAMT approval of educational programs in music therapy. Springfield, N.J., AAMT, 1984.

American Association for Music Therapy: List of educational programs. Springfield, N.J., AAMT, 1984.

American Board of Examiners in Psychodrama, Sociometry and Group Psychotherapy: Certification standards. New York, ABEPSGP, 1984.

American Dance Therapy Association: Educational opportunities in dance/ movement therapy. Columbia, Maryland, ADTA, 1984.

American Psychiatric Association: *The Use of the Creative Arts in Therapy*. Washington, D.C., APA, 1980.

Axline, Virginia: *Play Therapy*. Boston, Houghton Mifflin, 1947.

Buchanan, Dale: Psychodrama: An overview of the first 58 years. In American Psychiatric Association: *The Use of the Creative Arts in Therapy*. Washington, D.C., APA, 1980.

Burns, Robert Franklin: A study of the influence of familiar hymns on moods and associations: Potential application in music therapy. Master's thesis, Florida State University, 1958.

Coriat, Isadore: Some aspects of a psychoanalytic interpretation of music. *Psychoanalytic Review, 32*, 408-418, 1945.

Council of Graduate Schools in the United States: *The Masters Degree: A Policy Statement*. Washington, D.C., 1976.

Feder, Elaine and Feder, Bernard: *The Expressive Arts Therapies*. Englewood Cliffs, N.J., Prentice-Hall, 1981.

Fleshman, Bob and Fryrear, Jerry: *The Arts in Therapy*. Chicago, Nelson-Hall, 1981.

Gaston, E. Thayer (Ed.): *Music in Therapy*. New York, Macmillan, 1968.

Hahnemann University: Masters of creative arts in therapy program brochure. Philadelphia, 1984.

Hillman, James: *The Myth of Analysis: Three Essays in Archetypal Psychology*. New York, Harper and Row, 1978.

Hughes, Everett: Higher education and the professions. In Kaysen, Carl (Ed.): *Content and Context*. New York, McGraw-Hill, 1973.

Jennings, Sue: *Remedial Drama*. New York, Theatre Art Books, 1974.

John F. Kennedy University: Admissions letter. Orinda, CA, Sept. 20, 1984.

Krauss, David and Fryrear, Jerry: *Phototherapy in Mental Health*. Charles C. Thomas, Springfield, IL, 1983.

Lesley College Graduate School: Institute for the Arts and Human Development brochure. Cambridge, MA, 1984.

Mayhew, Lewis and Ford, Patrick: *Reform in Graduate and Professional Education*. San Francisco, Jossey-Bass, 1974.

Moreno, J.L.: *The Theatre of Spontaneity*. Beacon, NY, Beacon House, 1973.

Moustakas, Clark: *Children in Play Therapy*. New York, McGraw-Hill, 1953.

National Association for Drama Therapy: General information brochure. New Haven, NADT, 1984.

National Association for Music Therapy: A career in music therapy. Washington, D.C., NAMT, 1984.

Nordoff, Paul and Robbins, Clive: *Music Therapy in Special Education*. New York, John Day, 1971.

Nordoff, Paul and Robbins, Clive: *Therapy in Music for Handicapped Children*. New York, St. Martin, 1971.

Portner, Elaine and Irwin, Eleanor: *Education and Training in Drama Therapy: A Survey of Programs*. New Haven, National Association for Drama Therapy, 1983.

Ross, Steve: *Artist/therapist: Bringing order out of chaos*. New York, American Association of Artist/Therapists, 1984.

Rowan, Peter: *Private conversation*. Cambridge, MA, 1984.

Schein, Edgar: *Professional Education*. New York, McGraw-Hill, 1972.

Sears, Margaret: A study of the vascular changes in the capillaries as effected by music. Master's thesis, University of Kansas, 1954.

Sears, William: Postural response to recorded music. Master's thesis, University of Kansas, 1951.

Slade, Peter: *Child Drama*. London, U London Pr, 1954.

Way, Brian: *Development Through Drama*. New York, Barnes and Noble, 1969.

White, Dennis: Art therapy related doctoral dissertations, 1893-1974. Unpublished paper, Univ. of Houston, 1977.

4. CHARACTERISTICS OF ACADEMIC TRAINING PROGRAMS

IN ORDER TO gather information to be used as a basis for the identification of characteristics of academic training programs, letters were sent to all graduate and undergraduate schools listed by the various creative arts therapy associations. After reviewing these lists in 1984-1985 we requested brochures, catalogs and other materials describing the course of study at 143 institutions of higher education (see Appendix). We discovered from our mailing that 6 of the institutions listed by the various associations no longer offered training programs. Based on the information that we have received and the lists of national professional associations, we assume that at the present time there are at least 137 institutions of higher education involved in varying forms of creative arts therapy education, 111 of which offer undergraduate training, 59 that offer graduate education, and 33 schools that offer both graduate and undergraduate education. We know that there are colleges and universities involved with education in the creative arts therapies that are not recorded on the national association lists. Omissions are regretted, especially since we have been committed to reviewing all available materials on higher education in the profession. Based on our experience in this study, we urge colleges and universities to submit information on their programs to national creative arts therapy professional associations and we encourage the associations to update their lists as often as possible. We also encourage associations to follow the example of the American Art Therapy Association in listing all educational opportunities in the field and not just those that are approved by the association.

At the time of this writing, 110 colleges and universities have responded to our request for information, including the 6 schools that no longer offer programs. This gives us a total of 104 institutions that have submitted information about their programs. Twenty-three percent of the schools we wrote to have not replied with catalog materials. We telephoned many institutions as a follow-up procedure after our first mailing.

We believe that the information we have received is descriptive of the major educational activities within the creative arts therapy profession at the present time. All of the institutions that we perceive as prominent within the profession have responded. Schools that did not respond include institutions that offer occasional courses in the creative arts therapies which are not integrated into programs of study. However, it does appear that these schools have offered creative arts therapy courses in the past and it is likely that most will continue to do so in the future in one capacity or another. It also appeared that a number of schools were undergoing curriculum, faculty and administrative changes at the time of our request for information.

We have attempted to base our assessments of higher education in the creative arts therapies on a review of all educational opportunities available at the present time. Small and newly created programs were given careful consideration together with more established programs. It is perhaps true that the fundamental characteristics of higher education in the creative arts therapies can be best determined by reviewing program materials from a smaller and select group of colleges and universities which: clearly present their programs of study in catalog materials; have maintained a training program for a considerable number of years; and enroll and graduate a consistent number of students over this period of time. From our review of program materials, it was clear that all schools did not meet these minimum criteria. However, since the creative arts therapies are an emerging profession, we felt it important to review and evaluate every available educational program. Wherever possible, we distinguish between exceptional cases and general trends as best represented by the core of colleges and universities which offer stable and clearly presented programs of study.

All information presented in this chapter is based on the most complete data we were able to receive. Our totals should be approached as approximate figures. The information is to be considered as giving an indication of characteristics and patterns in the education of creative arts therapists and not as definitive data. Statistics in higher education are subject to great fluctuation over time. Our purpose in gathering information was to investigate how creative arts therapists were being educated within the United States during the time of this study. The desired outcome is a descriptive rather than a statistical statement. Statistics about creative arts therapy education, although useful, are not the primary objective of this study, since quantitative information will become obsolete within a brief period of time. Descriptive statements, interpreted with a concern for the future and an understanding of the past, will hopefully have a continuing relevance to the educational process. We have approached the information on different programs with the goal of determining how it reveals essential subject matter and educational patterns which underly all programs. Attention has also been given to programmatic differences and unique qualities.

It is apparent from a review of curriculum and program structures on the master's and undergraduate levels, that programs are far more similar than different. The majority of programs tend to be small on the graduate level, enrolling twenty new students or less each year. All master's degree programs appear to require two years of study. Practicum learning and various other forms of clinical experience are emphasized in all graduate programs together with psychological skills needed to establish an interdependence with other mental health disciplines. The integration of practical training with theoretical learning is stressed on both the graduate and undergraduate levels. Master's programs consistently require previous experience in the arts together with psychological competencies for admission. Virtually all master's programs require a thesis or independent research project which is carried out during the second year of study.

Undergraduate programs are typically offered through fine arts departments. Personal artistic training as part of the curriculum, perhaps as a result of this relationship to arts departments, is far more common in bachelor's progams. Master's level programs appear to be more autonomous and often have their own directors and department heads. On both the master's and bachelor's levels the majority of programs are highly specialized and do not offer opportunities for study in more than one creative arts therapy modality. However, we have observed that there is an increased movement toward interdisciplinary study, in that a number of schools have recently begun to offer courses in other creative arts therapy modalities. Some of the larger training programs in the field, graduating a significant percentage of the professionals employed in the creative arts therapies, do offer studies in more than one creative arts therapy modality. On the undergraduate level, there is a cooperative relationship between fine arts and psychology departments. In master's programs, psychological skills are typically taught within the creative arts therapy program, although opportunities exist for study outside the program. Small graduate programs are more apt to rely on the resources of other departments within the college or university, whereas large programs tend to offer the total curriculum within the program.

Virtually all programs design curriculum in response to the education guidelines of national professional associations. Conformity appears to be more highly valued than divergence. However, master's degree programs vary in terms of the title of the degree granted. Both master's and bachelor's programs offer opportunities for practical work with varied clinical populations. Course offerings are far more similar than different. Each of the creative arts therapy specializations has a cluster of core courses which are offered in different programs.

TYPES OF SCHOOLS

College and university training programs in the creative arts therapies are offered throughout the United States. We have based our percentages of the types of institutions involved in the higher education of creative arts therapists on a review of the 137 schools that we have included in this study. The categories that we used to distinguish institutions were: public university or college; private university; private liberal arts college; and specialty schools (e.g. fine arts, education, medicine, external degree, experimental). The following percentages apply to institutions offering degree programs in all of the creative arts therapies:

> public university or college 45%
> private university 18%
> private liberal arts college 26%
> specialty school 11%

Within the art therapy, dance therapy, drama therapy and music therapy specializations, the percentages of the types of institutions were:

> *Art Therapy* (58 schools)
> public university or college 31%
> private university 17%
> private liberal arts college 31%
> specialty school 21%

Dance Therapy (20 schools)

public university or college 30%
private university 25%
private liberal arts college 20%
specialty school 25%

Drama Therapy (7 schools)

public university or college. 14.3%
private university 57.1%
private liberal arts college. 14.3%
specialty school 14.3%

Music Therapy (74 schools)

public university or college 54%
private university 16%
private liberal arts college 26%
specialty school 4%

Percentages are not given for psychodrama because there are so few institutions of higher education offering training in this specialization at the present time.

At the present time, 29 percent of all creative arts therapy professional education takes place at schools with religious affiliations; 44 percent of the private universities and 81 percent of the private liberal arts colleges offering studies in the creative arts therapies have religious affiliations. Catholic institutions of higher education make up 60 percent of the total group of religiously affiliated schools offering training in the creative arts therapies. The other 40 percent is comprised of colleges affiliated with different Protestant denominations (e.g. Baptist, Church of the Brethren, Disciples of Christ, Lutheran, Methodist, Presbyterian and Seventh-Day Adventist).

Only 1 of the 16 Protestant denominational schools offers training in art therapy. Dance therapy and drama therapy training were not offered at these schools according to the information we received. All 16 schools offered training programs in music therapy.

Art therapy was the most common program of study within the Catholic schools; 16 of the 24 institutions (67%) offered programs or coursework in this area. Music therapy followed as the second most common creative arts therapy specialization offered in Catholic schools — 11 institutions (46%). One Catholic school offered studies in drama therapy, one offered coursework in dance therapy, and 4 offered studies in both art therapy and music therapy. The school that offered studies in dance therapy also had programs in art and music, while the school offering studies in drama therapy also had a music therapy program.

The following figures give the percentage of the total educational opportunities in the different creative arts therapy specializations which are offered at religiously oriented institutions of higher education:

art therapy . . . . .29% of all art therapy schools
dance therapy . . . . .5% of all dance therapy schools
drama therapy. . . . . .14.3% of all drama therapy schools
music therapy . . . . .35% of all music therapy schools

---

Educational opportunities in the creative arts therapies are offered by many different kinds of schools. Public universities and colleges offer more programs than any other type of institution (i.e. 61). However, the combined total of private universities (i.e. 25) and private liberal arts colleges (i.e. 36) equals the public total. What may be referred to as the more elite private liberal arts colleges and universities of the United States are not significantly involved in creative arts therapy education at the present time. Although there are exceptions, educational programs have for the most part been developed at enrollment driven institutions. Religiously oriented schools are significantly involved in the creative arts therapies. We saw little influence of spiritual thought and healing practices on the curriculum of the creative arts therapy programs in these schools. The training programs consistently conform to the secular standards of the mental health field and national professional associations in the creative arts therapies. It is recommended that religiously oriented schools explore how their unique spiritual, cultural and historic traditions can be applied to the creative arts therapies and the mental health field as a whole. Theological principles such as sacrament, ritual, sacred dance, symbol, transformation, prayer, meditation, communion, mourning, compassion and celebration are relevant to therapeutic practice. Dance therapy and body oriented training opportunities were conspicuously absent from institutions with religious affiliations.

It is also recommended that creative arts therapy educators support efforts to develop training programs and courses in the more traditional and "elite" colleges and universities of the United States. If these schools are involved in the older professions of law, medicine, the ministry and psychology, then it may be asked, "Why not the creative arts therapies?" It is in the interest of the profession to have training opportunities offered by all sectors of American higher education.

DISTRIBUTION OF UNDERGRADUATE AND GRADUATE PROGRAMS

As stated previously, of the 137 colleges and universities listed by national professional associatons as offering educational opportunities in the creative arts therapies in 1984, 111 are engaged with undergraduate studies, 59 with graduate programs, and 33 with both undergraduate and graduate studies. The following figures describe the distribution of undergraduate and graduate training opportunities in the different specializations:

Art Therapy (58 schools)

Undergraduate	*Graduate*	*Both U & G*
38	32	12

Dance Therapy (20 schools)

Undergraduate	*Graduate*	*Both U & G*
11	14	5

Drama Therapy (7 schools)

Undergraduate	*Graduate*	*Both U & G*
4	3	0

Music Therapy (74 schools)

Undergraduate	*Graduate*	*Both U & G*
72	20	18

Music therapy clearly has the highest percentage (97%) and largest number of schools involved with undergraduate studies. This can be attributed to the bachelor's degree level credentialing standards in the specialization. Music therapy also has the smallest percentage of schools involved with graduate level training. However, because of the fact that there are so many schools involved with music therapy training, the total number of schools offering graduate level studies in music therapy is significantly more than drama therapy and dance therapy.

The art therapy specialization has the largest number of schools engaged with graduate training, and dance therapy has the highest percentage of graduate programs in relation to the total number of schools involved with dance therapy training.

CREATIVE ARTS THERAPY SPECIALIZATIONS WITHIN SCHOOLS

The vast majority of colleges and universities engaged with creative arts therapy education (88%) offer training in only one area of specialization. One hundred and twenty schools offer training in one creative arts therapy modality and 17 schools are engaged with more than one modality; 13 schools offer programs in two areas of specialization; 2 schools offer training in three areas of specialization; 1 school offers studies in four areas of specialization; and 1 school offers training opportunities in the four areas of art therapy, dance therapy, drama therapy and music therapy as well as psychodrama and poetry therapy. It would appear from this information that integration between the different creative arts therapies is not a high priority in the profession. However, it is important to note that many of the largest training programs in the creative arts therapies are among the small group of schools offering programs in more than one area of specialization. Therefore, there may not be such a large imbalance in percentages if figures were determined on the basis of the total number of students involved with higher education in the creative arts therapies as opposed to the total number of schools.

TOTAL GRADUATE CREDIT COUNTS

Graduate programs in the creative arts therapies showed great discrepancies in the total number of credits required for the master's degree. Our review of credit totals is based on information received from schools answering our request for catalog materials. In some of the school catalogs, credit totals were not listed. Based on the information we received, the highest total required for the master's degree was 72 credits and the lowest was 30 credits. The average credit total for 40 graduate programs in art therapy, dance therapy and music therapy was 46.9. The following figures reveal the high and low credit counts for the specializations of art therapy, dance therapy and music therapy. Average credit totals are also given for each specialization.

Art Therapy

high . . . . .68 credits
low . . . . .36 credits
average . . . . .48 credits
(figures based on information from 20 schools)

Dance Therapy

high . . . . .72 credits
low . . . . .36 credits
average . . . . .51 credits
(figures based on information from 11 schools)

Music Therapy

high . . . . .68 credits
low . . . . .30 credits
average . . . . .40 credits
(figures based on information from 9 schools)

DEGREE TITLES

Master's degree programs in the creative arts therapies tend to express independence and variety in their degree titles. The M.A. (master of arts) degree is the most common credential. M.A. degrees are awarded in art therapy; clinical art therapy; dance therapy; expressive therapy; creative arts therapy; psychology with a specialization in art therapy, dance therapy or drama therapy; in art with a specialization in art therapy; in education with a specialization in art therapy; or multidisciplinary studies. A number of music therapy programs grant the M.M. (master of music) degree. Other degrees include the M.C.A.T. (master of creative arts in therapy), M.P.S. (master of professional studies), M.M.E. (master of music education), M.M.T. (master of music therapy), M.S. (master of science), M.A.T. and A.T.M. (master of art therapy).

There is general agreement in the higher education community that the number of different master's degrees should be kept to a minimum. There are advantages to having a single degree title for an entire profession as exemplified by the M.D. degree. A single degree will eliminate confusion and will help the credential to become more "established" and better known. However, at the present time agreement on a single degree title is not a widely discussed issue in the creative arts therapy profession. It is, however, an issue that should be studied from a long-term perspective, with the goal of determining what will be in the best interest of the profession as a whole.

At the bachelor's level, creative arts therapy specializations make use of established degree titles. In art therapy, the B.A. degree appears to be the most common credential given at the undergraduate level. Other schools offer the B.S. in art therapy or the B.F.A. (bachelor of fine arts) in art therapy. Most music therapy undergraduate programs offer the B.A., B.S. or B.M. (bachelor of music). There appears to be a fairly even distribution between the number of schools granting these three degrees in music therapy. A smaller number of schools grant the B.M.E. (bachelor of music education) degree in music therapy.

PREREQUISITES FOR GRADUATE STUDY

All graduate programs require either undergraduate coursework or demonstrated competence in a particular art medium and psychology. A minority of schools requires a minimal number of credits in these areas and specific courses. Many schools require a bachelor's degree in either the fine arts, the arts in education, psychology or the social sciences. Some programs specify a major in the fine arts with a minor in psychology, or vice versa. Several schools require a bachelor's degree from an accredited college or university and do not require a particualr major concentration. Some schools require either a 3.0 or 2.8 cumulative grade point average (G.P.A.).

Dance therapy graduate programs generally do not require a bachelor's degree in dance but do ask for a "strong" or "extensive" dance background or the equivalent of a dance degree. One school requires "intermediate" dance ability. There are creative arts therapy graduate programs which encourage comprehensive undergraduate education in the humanities and a "broad liberal arts and behavioral science background." However, the majority of graduate programs in the creative arts therapies makes no mention of the humanities as a prerequisite for graduate study.

Art therapy programs consistently ask for a portfolio of visual artworks. Dance therapy programs generally require a movement demonstration and assesment, while music therapy programs often request an audition. Most graduate programs appear to require a personal statement, autobiography, letters of reference and interview. Many, but not all, programs require the Graduate Record Examination or the Miller Analogies Test.

One school states that its program is directed toward "mature individuals" and another requires "satisfactory health status." It is assumed that prerequisites of health and maturity are directed toward selecting emotionally stable people who can successfully undergo the pressures of psychotherapeutic training and work. However, caution is advised in creating admissions standards that may appear to be discriminatory. "Satisfactory health status" prerequisites should not discriminate against people with physical handicaps or other problems which do not necessarily impact negatively on personal abilities to work as a creative arts therapist.

Many music therapy graduate programs are directed toward people who have earned bachelor's degrees in music therapy and who have already met educational criteria for music therapy registration. These programs often involve as little as 30 graduate credits and require undergraduate degrees in music therapy or music together with registration prerequisites. Some schools will admit students who do not have undergraduate prerequisites for registration but require that they "fulfill deficiencies." Extra coursework may in some cases be taken concurrently with graduate study. Some schools offer undergraduate "equivalency" training for those who earned their bachelor's degrees in fields other than music therapy. The general tendency of music therapy graduate education appears to be one of requiring extensive undergraduate study in music, music education or music therapy.

The University of Kansas offers a separate tract for those who do not have bachelor's level prerequisites in music or music therapy and who are preparing for entry into the music therapy profession. Most music therapy graduate programs do not tend to display comparable flexibility in admissions requirements. As a whole the music therapy specialization has many more specific prerequisite requirements for graduate admission than art therapy, dance therapy and drama therapy. This may be largely attributed to the fact that the specialization as a whole is geared toward meeting professional entry level and registration requirements at the undergraduate level. Most graduate programs are therefore oriented toward advanced training for the professional music therapist. Since the other creative arts therapy specializations are providing entry level training at the graduate level, they have considerably more freedom as to whom they may admit.

THE HUMANITIES IN UNDERGRADUATE EDUCATION

Undergraduate programs in the creative arts therapies are generally directed toward students who have made early career decisions and who desire to begin vocational studies in college. As stated previously, virtually all educational opportunities in music therapy are directed toward this population. Art therapy, dance therapy, drama therapy and psychodrama are considerably more flexible in terms of undergraduate study and provide many more opportunities to focus on the humanities at the baccalaureate level. Many of the undergraduate programs in the creative arts therapies are in Catholic colleges which have maintained academic requirements in the humanities.

From our review of music therapy undergraduate curriculum materials, we observed that there are considerable differences between schools as to how they approach the humanities and other general education requirements. In many of the schools, music therapy undergraduate studies (outside of music, music therapy and music education) appear to be primarily focused on psychology and human behavior, anatomy, physiology, sociology, anthropology, biology and special education. Psychology and human behavior requirements typically equal those for music therapy. Although music and music history are to be considered as humanities disciplines, music therapy undergraduate curricula in some schools are noticeably weak in more comprehensive studies of history, philosophy, languages, the classics, literature and the other fine arts. There are schools which provide virtually no opportunities for studies in the humanities. We noticed that if a school attempts to include all of the national association requirements for music therapy and other prescribed coursework within the conventional four-year undergraduate credit total, then there is little room left in the curriculum for other studies.

However, we were pleased to see that a number of colleges and universities offering undergraduate music therapy programs have seriously addressed themselves to the importance of comprehensive undergraduate education, including a strong concentration in the humanities. The music therapy undergraduate program at Eastern Montana College offers diversified studies in music, music therapy, psychology and the humanities. We found the Eastern Montana curriculum to be exemplary in its efforts to provide a complete educational experience within the limits of guidelines for professional training established by both the national associations for music therapy and schools of music. The program is clearly distinguished from those undergraduate music therapy programs that require a curriculum composed primarily of music (e.g. piano, choral, aural comprehension, voice, string, conducting, performance, chamber ensemble, theory, orchestration, composition, history, band), music therapy (e.g. introduction, methods and materials, psychophysiological, child, adult, clinical internship) and psychology (e.g. general, abnormal, child and developmental, of music, research methods).

The Eastern Montana College program requires:

48 quarter credits in general education which may include "Oral-written expression such as a library research paper and interpersonal communication; physical education, including two quarters of dance; humanities; science and mathematics including human physiology and anatomy; and social sciences including introductions to sociology, psychology, and philosophy" (EMC, 1984).

27 quarter credits in psychology, special education and behavioral science.

87 quarter credits in music including "Applied music (performance), music history and theory, conducting, instrumentation and arranging, composition, and teaching methods" (Ibid.)

30 quarter credits in music therapy including "psychology of music, its influence on behavior, and its use in therapy" (Ibid.).

6 quarter credits of practical experience in music therapy.

4 quarter credits for a six-month internship at the conclusion of the program which leads to certification as a registered music therapist. (The catalog describes how the 6 credits of practical experience is part of a 34-credit music therapy total. Apparently, this means that the 6 credits of practical experience is part of the 30-credit requirement in music therapy, to which the 4-credit internship is added for a total of 34 credits.)

In reviewing music therapy undergraduate catalog materials, we observed how other schools offered more expansive coursework which will, hopefully, begin to influence music therapy education standards. In addition to attempting to provide students with opportunities for comprehensive education and studies in the humanities, Montclair State College offers several undergraduate courses in art therapy and requires music therapy students to take an introduction to art therapy course. The Meadows School of the Fine Arts at Southern Methodist University requires music therapy undergraduates to take courses in art modalities other than music. At Florida State University, music therapy majors may use dance as a second performance area, and 46 percent of the total degree program involves coursework in liberal studies together with behavioral and natural sciences. Arizona State University requires music therapy majors to take six credits in art, theatre or dance. Temple University provides for six credits of arts electives. Depaul University has a dance therapist teaching "music movement therapy" for music therapy undergraduates. The Maryville college catalog describes how the music therapy undergraduate program is "well supported" by studies in the humanities and other areas. Schools with religious affiliations tended to require studies in religion. A small group of music therapy undergraduate programs require coursework in dance. The University of Miami undergraduate program in music therapy has a requirement in "folk dancing" in addition to a course in "elementary modern dance."

Music therapy undergraduate education is characterized by a heavily prescribed curriculum, although individual schools vary significantly in relation to the degree of choice that is given to students within the total program of studies. Schools that do make significant efforts to increase opportunities for choice and liberal studies are nevertheless restricted by the many requirements established by national professional associations. When schools do attempt to expand opportunities for study in the humanities, mathematics, natural sciences and the other fine arts, the total number of courses in these areas is always far less than required studies in music, music therapy and psychology.

Music therapy educators might consider developing five-year programs of studies that will lead toward both graduate and undergraduate degrees. The additional year of study would not result in a major increase over the present system of education in the profession, which requires a six-month clinical internship after the four years of undergraduate study are completed. Additional credits can be awarded for the six-month internship which might focus on advanced clinical skills, group therapy, family therapy and the creative arts therapies as well as music therapy. A five-year combined bachelor's and master's program would allow for more comprehensive educational opportunities and increased choice at the undergraduate level. This model is not far from present standards in music therapy, which often only require 30 credits for the master's degree.

In our opinion, a six-year program of study, involving thesis work in the final year, is preferable and in line with educational standards in the other creative arts therapies. However, we acknowledge the unique educational history of music therapy which tends to parallel the field of occupational therapy in terms of bachelor's level standards more than it corresponds to the other creative arts therapies. The present approach to bachelor's level professional entry level training clearly restricts necessary educational opportunities in the humanities and other areas of learning. If we assume that the present educational model of music therapy (though different from the other creative arts therapies) does in fact work, then a five-year program of study leading ultimately to the master's degree may be suitable. This model can build upon and expand the present strengths of music therapy undergraduate education while providing opportunities for advanced study as well as a more comprehensive undergraduate education. It is important that creative arts therapy specializations which require master's level credentials do not assume that, because music therapy requires only the bachelor's degree, music therapists are less adequately prepared for professional work. It is more appropriate for all of the specializations to respect their varied and unique educational histories and methods and attempt to work together to reach agreement on more consistent educational standards. We believe that the development of five-year programs can be an important step in this direction.

The major problem that a movement toward five-year programs would present is that there will be schools presently involved in undergraduate education that do not grant master's degrees. As recorded in our information on graduate and undergraduate education in music therapy, the majority of schools involved in music therapy education only offer the bachelor's degree. In reading the literature distributed by these institutions, some noted that they have from 45 to 50 music therapy majors. With such large enrollments at these institutions there may be considerable support for the present system, which will make changes difficult. In lieu of offering master's degrees, colleges that do not have the authorization to grant graduate degrees may either grant a graduate level certificate, as many schools do within the art therapy specialization, or affiliate with another institution for the purpose of providing opportunities for graduate credits and degrees.

The music therapy specialization can also support comprehensive undergraduate education through the creation of more programs like the special master's degree tract at the University of Kansas for people who do not have undergraduate preparation in music therapy and do not meet registration and certification requirements as established by national associations. The Kansas master's program appears to be an important step toward greater flexibility in music therapy education. We strongly recommend that national professional associations in music therapy encourage the development of similar graduate level programs for people who did not study music therapy as undergraduates. Temple University acknowledges that its master's degree in music therapy has been designed for music therapists who have already been certified or registered, but the program makes it possible for people with at least sixty credits in music to attend. The Temple program requires the student to complete all undergraduate professional music therapy requirements before the completion of the master's degree. This corresponds to the "music therapy equivalency" programs offered by other schools for college graduates with "expertise in music" but who do not have professional training in music therapy.

The catalog materials that we reviewed indicated that equivalency programs are offered at Florida State University and the Cleveland Consortium Schools (i.e. Baldwin-Wallace College, Case Western Reserve University, Cleveland State University, College of Wooster, and Oberlin College). The Florida State University equivalency program may be combined with graduate degree studies in music therapy. We recommend that every effort be made to integrate post-baccalaureate studies of this kind with master's degree programs. The Temple University, Florida State University, the Cleveland Consortium Schools and the University of Kansas programs are important advances in music therapy education indicating greater flexibility and new directions in professional education. More opportunities of this kind will indirectly support liberal study and greater choice at the undergraduate level. In terms of its long-term planning, the music therapy profession will find that it will benefit from providing educational opportuniteis for both college graduates who did not major in music therapy and vocationally minded undergraduates who have decided to educate themselves for a career in music therapy.

Art therapy undergraduate programs, perhaps because they do not represent themselves as providing comprehensive education in the profession, tend to concentrate on basic introductory courses in art therapy, methods/techniques of art therapy and practicum training. This coursework is typically integrated into the more general program of studies of a liberal arts college or a school of fine arts. The same tends to be true of those schools that offer undergraduate training in dance therapy and drama therapy. The graduate entry level requirements of these creative arts therapy concentrations allow for considerable educational diversity in undergraduate programs. We did observe that individual schools offer programs of study with few humanities offerings. However, the decision to construct a program in this manner is made by the college or university. We also noted how independent schools of visual arts tend to parallel the undergraduate curriculum structures of music therapy education, placing a strong emphasis on professional training in the specific art modality. For example, the School of Visual Arts undergraduate concentration in art therapy lists the following requirements:

Studio art courses . . . . .84/81 credits*
Art history . . . . .12/15 credits
Humanities (including 12 credits in psychology) . . . . . . .32 credits
*15 credits of art therapy are included in the studio total (SVA, 1984)

It therefore appears that music therapy education and registration requirements are built upon a music school model and not on a liberal arts college or general education model. As a whole, art therapy undergraduate programs were focused on comprehensive education in cooperation with professional training. The College of Saint Teresa lists not only art therapy, psychology and art requirements together with "Basic Requirements" and "Breadth Requirements" which include humanities, fine and performing arts, "physical well-being," natural sciences and mathematics, liberal studies, religious studies and a senior seminar (CST, 1984). We noted that specialty schools in the visual arts tend to be committed to comprehensive education and the humanities. For example, in addition to the School of Visual Arts requiring 32 credits in the humanities, the undergraduate art therapy program at the Philadelphia College of Art lists required coursework in philosophy, cultural anthropology, "social and group process," "human origins" and other courses (PCA, 1984).

Undergraduate art therapy catalogs consistently emphasize that the purpose of the program is preparation for graduate study. In addition to the general undergraduate requirements of the school, the programs typically offer coursework in the following areas: introductory art therapy, methods and materials of art therapy, and practical training in art therapy. Some schools also offer an art therapy seminar together with other elective offerings in art therapy. Trenton State College, which lists itself as the first undergraduate art therapy program in the United States, did not exclusively emphasize preparation for graduate studies but states that graduates of the bachelor's program are eligible for both advanced study in art therapy and other fields as well as "employment" in "adjunctive" therapy. Although closer to the bachelor's degree emphasis of music therapy specialization than other art therapy undergraduate programs, the Trenton State College program clearly differentiates between graduate and undergraduate levels of training in art therapy and different levels of professional responsibility (TSC, 1984).

We found that the catalog materials from Albertus Magnus College expressed the major themes in undergraduate art therapy education. Preparatory studies in art therapy are available to both art therapy and psychology majors. Throughout art therapy undergraduate education, there appears to be a cooperation between art and psychology departments with the goal of presenting art therapy as an integration of the two disciplines. Requirements at Albertus Magnus College in art and art therapy are not so extensive that they limit opportunities for comprehensive educational opportunities. Flexibility and choice are encouraged in the college curriculum (AMC, 1984).

The small amount of catalog materials that we received on undergraduate education in dance therapy and drama therapy indicated that these specializations tend to be similar to general characteristics of bachelor's level education in art therapy.

The creative arts therapies profession, much of which has modeled itself after educational traditions in medicine, might carefully review recent criticisms within the medical community of its educational standards. The foremost criticism of medical education concerns its lack of attention to the humanities. At the 1984 annual meeting of the Association of American Medical Colleges, Steven Muller, President of Johns Hopkins University and chairman of a panel proposing major revisions in the country's medical education standards, told the association that changes are "unavoidable." Muller stressed the importance of a comprehensive education in the humanities for medical doctors. He criticized the emphasis on memorization of extensive scientific data in contemporary medical education. Muller stated that reforms are "long overdue." Muller was joined in his criticism by Ernest Boyer, president of the Carnegie Foundation for the Advancement of Education and former United States education commissioner, who stated how medical education standards must not continue to emphasize scientific disciplines and pay little attention to the humanities.

Muller described how medical school education does not necessarily involve students in doctoral level studies and how medical students "have been treated as undergraduates for eight long years" (HPR, 1984). Unless the humanities and other opportunities for more comprehensive education are included in the training of prospective medical doctors, then Muller recommended that the country's medical schools begin to award a "B.S. in medicine" and require six years of study. This approach would eliminate much of the repetition that presently exists in medical education and make better use of educational resources. Medicine would thus begin to align itself with present standards for music therapy education. Medical education critics feel that the ideal situation would involve expanded opportunities for studies in the humanities and we feel that this also applies to the related field of the creative arts therapies.

PRACTICAL TRAINING

Varied forms of practical training are considered to be essential by both graduate and undergraduate programs in the creative arts therapies. Schools for the most part follow the recommendations of national professional associations with regard to the number of hours needed for practical training and the types of placements required. National Association for Music Therapy undergraduate guidelines involve students in a six-month clinical training experience that is required in addition to the credits needed to complete the bachelor's degree. The six-month period of music therapy clinical training is typically initiated after all academic requirements have been completed. Most music therapy undergraduate programs also involve students in practical training experiences during their academic years of study. The Temple University music therapy program believes that practical training should be closely supervised by university faculty, whereas in other music therapy programs the internship carried out six months after the completion of undergraduate coursework does not always require faculty supervision.

Graduate training programs in art therapy, dance therapy and drama therapy tend to integrate practical training with academic and experiential coursework throughout the degree program. In most schools, practical training is required for two years of graduate study. Typically, the clinical hours increase in the second year of the program. Students are often encouraged to work in two different sites or with two or more different client populations during their program of studies. There appear to be few standard principles and a healthy diversity of opinions on the following issues: the length of practical training experiences; whether or not the student should work with one population or different client groups; and whether practical training should be initiated at the beginning of the graduate program or after the completion of certain coursework requirements.

We found that differences in the length and scheduling of degree programs inevitably affect practical training requirements. Some master's degrees can be earned in one year or in fifteen months, while others may be extended beyond two years. In two-year programs, the second year tends to involve more time in practical clinical experiences than academic coursework. All graduate programs appear to agree on a minimum of 600 hours and one academic year of intensive involvement in practical training, during which the student becomes an integral member of the clinical team at the placement site. Programs are in agreement on the primacy of practical training in the educational experience of creative arts therapists.

GRADUATE COURSEWORK

Dance therapy graduate coursework tends to be less varied than the specializations of art therapy and music therapy. This is perhaps due to the prescriptive standards of the American Dance Therapy Association for master's level training. Programs uniformly include movement observation, group process in dance therapy, dance therapy theory and practice, psychopathology, diagnostic techniques, theories of psychotherapy, research methods and a thesis project. Kinesiology and anatomy are taken as part of the graduate program or are presented as prerequisites for admission. Programs with few electives provide a sequential series of dance therapy courses. Other programs vary in relation to opportunities for elective coursework which may include child, adolescent or adult dance therapy; different theoretical approaches to dance and body oriented therapy (e.g. Jungian, Reichian, etc.); and studies in the other creative arts therapies.

Music therapy master's degrees, in contrast to undergraduate studies in the specialization, tend to offer considerable variety and choice to students. All programs appear to have a consistent and strong thesis component. We noted that there tend to be two distinct types of music therapy graduate programs: those that are closely associated with undergraduate education in music therapy (usually in the same school where undergraduate studies are offered) and those offered by schools with no relationship to undergraduate training in music therapy. In some schools where there were also National Association for Music Therapy approved undergraduate training programs, we observed that research coursework was often oriented to behavioral and experimental psychological methods. These programs often offered coursework in the psychology of music, measurement of music behavior, music in society, a music therapy seminar, advanced acoustics and advanced composition, music theory and studies in various aspects of music performance. One school offered a course in music therapy administration and supervision which appears to be in keeping with much of music therapy graduate education's orientation to training faculty members and leaders in the profession as opposed to entry level practitioners. Music therapy master's programs also tended to allow for considerable elective study in psychology. In keeping with the pattern of undergraduate studies in music therapy, there appeared to be little emphasis on "psychotherapeutic" training in many music therapy master's programs. The relatively small number of schools associated with the American Association for Music Therapy are concerned with psychotherapeutic training at the master's level. These programs also appeared to have educational standards that were consistent with master's degree training in the other creative arts therapies. Master's degree studies in music therapy at institutions of higher education that are not involved in the traditions of music therapy undergraduate education, such as Hahnemann University, demonstrated significant commitments to psychodynamic and psychotherapeutic training in a manner that corresponded to the general clinical training trends in art therapy and dance therapy.

There appear to be considerable variety and scope in art therapy master's degree coursework. Art therapy programs had a significantly stronger emphasis on family therapy than dance and music therapy programs. As with the other specializations, virtually all art therapy master's degree programs offer basic and advanced art therapy practice and theory, diagnostic techniques, theories of psychotherapy, psychopathology and research methods. The majority of, but not all, art therapy master's degree programs have a thesis or master's project requirement. In addition to family art therapy courses, art therapy master's degree studies tended to offer many more courses focused on children, adolescents, adults and special populations than either music therapy or dance therapy. A significant number of art therapy master's programs are offering coursework in the other creative arts therapies.

THE THESIS

It is strongly recommended that all creative arts therapy master's degree programs give serious attention to strengthening thesis and master's project components. The thesis is a challenging task for both students and faculty. A successful thesis program demands extensive effort, individual consultation and many other characteristics that are required of both quality education and professional practice. The thesis provides students with an opportunity to integrate all of their studies and clinical experiences while also making a contribution to the profession. My involvement with thesis advisement indicates that the process of producing a thesis is a rite of passage into the profession and an essential quality control for the academic program. It is recommended that approaches to thesis writing and the production of master's projects offer different choices of methodology. My experience indicates that many students benefit from a thesis process which allows them to describe and synthesize training experiences. This is an appropriate approach for clinically oriented training programs. Other students have a need to produce more scholarly or scientific theses.

The profession must try to avoid bias with regard to methods of scholarship. Methods are most effective and creative when they emerge from the person, the context and the purpose of the study. Inevitably, the methods of a thesis program will be largely determined by faculty resources and the mission of the academic institution. Methods of investigation may be descriptive, quantitative, literary/expository/artistic, historical, etc. and should relate to the complexities and essential character of the creative arts therapy profession.

It is important to support artistic methods of scholarly investigation as well as the artistically oriented master's project. Students should be encouraged to express themselves in their areas of artistic strength in addition to mastering skills in written expression. We have required students, who present a series of artworks, a performance or other artistic production as their master's project, to submit an accompanying written text which describes and reflects upon their artistic expression in considerable detail.

Since the creative arts therapies are an interdisciplinary profession drawing together the resources and scholarly methods of the arts, the humanities, psychology, psychiatry and other health disciplines, it is essential to avoid definitions of research methodology which are limited to a single mode of inquiry.

INNOVATIVE GRADUATE PROGRAM STRUCTURES

The majority of graduate programs in the creative arts therapies function on the basis of conventional residency requirements and coursework. There have been notable exceptions developed to meet the needs of working professionals and people with family and other responsibilities that make it difficult to become engaged in a conventional program. As mentioned previously, the Goddard College Master's Program, the Goddard Adult Degree (B.A.) Program, and the Union Graduate School Ph.D. program have pioneered in offering opportunities for graduate study in the creative arts therapies which combine short-term periods of residence with independent study.

Vermont College of Norwich University has developed an innovative art therapy master's degree program involving summer full-time residencies with supervised practical work experience in a geographic region selected by the student. The 42-credit master's degree program in art therapy can be completed in fifteen months and involves two three-month summer residencies during that time period. Students are expected to begin to make arrangements for the practicum prior to the first summer session. A five-credit independent study project resulting in the writing of a "major paper" is pursued during the 35-week practicum. Nine credits are awarded for the practicum. Field work is also required during the summer sessions in Vermont. The graduate program allows students to utilize a variety of training options in different parts of the country. Summer residencies in Vermont can be combined with practical training in mental health centers in San Francisco, Houston, Miami, New York and other regions. The summer period of concentrated studies also provides the college with considerable flexibility in hiring faculty for short periods of time. The school therefore maintains a small resident faculty and draws on other experts in the field on a short-term basis.

The Pratt Institute has developed a similar summer institute program to complement its regular master's degree programs in creative arts therapy. Summer sessions in the Pratt program run for five weeks, beginning with one week of work on the Pratt campus in Brooklyn and followed by a four-week period of study in Jefferson, New Hampshire. A selection of weekend courses and week-long courses are offered to both degree students and continuing education students. Three summer periods of study are required to complete the program, together with three five-day "Spring Institutes" on the Pratt campus. As with the Vermont College model, students are involved in supervised field work over the course of the year in the region where they reside. The 52-credit program can be completed in a three-year period.

In addition to its regular on-campus graduate degree programs in creative arts therapy, Lesley College has initiated special master's and certificate of advanced study degree programs for working professionals from foreign countries. Lesley has developed affiliated training centers in Israel, Switzerland and Sweden. The center in Switzerland presently involves students from that country, West Germany and Austria. The Swedish center engages students from Sweden, Norway and Finland. Ongoing coursework and supervision of practical work is provided in the international training centers throughout the year. In addition to a core faculty from the local countries, Lesley faculty travel to these centers on a regular basis to teach. Students working toward a graduate degree can either travel to the Lesley campus in Cambridge,

Massachusetts for two five-week summer programs or they can come to Cambridge for a longer period of study. The program requires a thesis, which can be done at home or in Cambridge. The international summer school program model has recently been expanded to include working professionals from throughout the United States as students. Degree studies can be completed through summer residencies on the Cambridge campus and by attending a series of courses offered at Lesley College National Outreach sites in other parts of the United States. A supervised practicum and a thesis is also required to complete the 48-credit program.

A number of schools offering graduate level training in the creative arts therapies have developed innovative ways to increase the depth and variety of their course offerings. The University of New Mexico art therapy master's degree program and the Mount Mary College graduate level certificate program in art therapy augment resident faculty resources by bringing visiting professors to their campus for short-term residencies.

Non-academic art therapy training centers have affiliated with colleges in order to award the master's degree. The Toronto Art Therapy Institute which bases its training program on personal growth, seminar integration of theory and practice, and clinical experience has affiliated with Beacon College and International College for the purpose of awarding the master's degree.

SUMMARY

From our review of characteristics of academic training programs in creative arts therapy, we can attest to the vitality and the commitment to excellence that presently exist in both graduate and undergraduate training programs. There have been certain themes and patterns that we have criticized in the interest of strengthening educational standards. We have observed that many training programs do not take a strong stand on the importance of the student's personal growth as part of the educational experience. There are also few school catalogs that address the integration of personal inquiry with clinical and academic development. There is a similar absence of attention given to the student's artistic development in some of the creative arts therapy specializations. We recommend that artistic and personal growth be given a primary place primary place within the creative arts therapy training program. In the creative arts therapies we cannot distance ourselves from the fact that our chief purpose is the education of the whole person as an instrumentality of the healing and creative process. A number of the older and larger creative arts therapy training programs include the student's personal development as part of the core of the training experience. My dialogues with prominent educators reveal that the *person* of the student must be the major objective of training. It is essential to make this position clear in national association educational guidelines and school catalogs.

We also feel that the creative arts therapy profession can be doing far more to support study in more than one art modality during both undergraduate and graduate studies. There have been consistent increases in the number of schools becoming involved in interdisciplinary creative arts therapy education, but more needs to be done to begin to achieve the full potential of the profession.

REFERENCES

Albertus Magnus College: Undergraduate catalog, 1984.
College of Saint Teresa: Undergraduate art therapy brochure, 1984.
Eastern Montana College: Music therapy program brochure, 1984.
Health Professions Report: Vol. 13, 1984.
Philadelphia College of Art: Undergraduate art therapy brochure, 1984.
School of Visual Arts: Undergraduate art therapy brochure, 1984.
Temple University College of Music: Program guide, 1984.
Trenton State College: Undergraduate art therapy brochure, 1984.

Appendix

LIST OF SCHOOLS

Undergraduate..U
Graduate...G
Undergraduate & Graduate ....U/G
Doctoral Studies..D
Certificate...C
Art Therapy...AT
Dance Therapy...DT
Drama Therapy...DRT
Music Therapy...MT
Psychodrama..P

Schools	U	G	U/G	D	C	AT	DT	DRT	MT	P
Adelphi Univ.	X	X	X				X			
Albertus Magnus College	X					X				
Alverno College	X					X				
Anna Maria College	X					X			X	
Antioch New England		X					X			
Antioch Univ./Venice CA	X					X				
Antioch San Francisco		X						X		
Antioch Seattle		X				X				
Arizona State Univ.	X								X	
Augsburg College	X								X	
Avila College	X					X		X		
Baldwin Wallace College	X								X	
Baptist College at Charleston	X								X	
Beacon College		X				X				
Bowling Green State Univ.	X					X				
Calif. Coll. of Arts & Crafts	X	X	X			X				
Calif. Inst. of Integral Studies		X					X			
Calif. State Univ. — Longbeach	X								X	
Calif. State Univ. — Hayward		X					X			
Calif. State Univ. — Los Angeles		X				X				
Calif. State Univ. — Sacramento		X				X				
Capital Univ.	X					X				
Case Western Reserve	X								X	
Catholic Univ. of America	X	X	X						X	
Cheyney State College	X					X				
Cleveland State Univ.	X								X	
College of Misericordia	X					X			X	
College of Mt. St. Joseph on the Ohio	X								X	
College of New Rochelle	X	X	X			X				
College of Notre Dame		X				X				
College of Saint Teresa	X					X	X		X	
College of Wooster	X								X	
Colorado State Univ.	X								X	

Schools	U	G	U/G	D	C	AT	DT	DRT	MT	P
Columbia Coll. of Chicago	X	X	X				X			
Columbia Union College	X								X	
Combs College of Music	X								X	
De Paul Univ.	X								X	
Drake Univ.	X	X	X			X				
Duquesne Univ.	X	X	X						X	
East Carlonia Univ.									X	
Eastern Michigan Univ.	X								X	
Eastern Montana College	X							X	X	
Eastern New Mexico Univ.	X								X	
Eastern Virginia Medical School		X				X				
Elizabethtown College	X								X	
Emmanuel College	X					X				
Emporia State Univ.	X	X	X			X				
Florida State Univ.	X	X	X	X					X	
George Washington Univ.	X	X	X			X				
Georgia College	X								X	
Glassboro State College	X						X			
Goucher College	X	X	X			X	X			
Hahnemann Univ.		X				X	X		X	
Henderson State Univ.	X								X	
Hofstra Univ.		X				X			X	
Howard Univ.	X								X	
Hunter College		X					X			
Illinois State Univ.	X								X	
Immaculata College	X								X	
Indiana Univ. – Ft. Wayne	X								X	
Indiana Univ. of Penn.		X				X				
International College		X				X				
Jersey City State College	X					X				
John F. Kennedy Univ.		X					X			
Lesley College	X	X	X			X	X	X	X	X
Lindenwood Coll. for Indiv. Ed.		X				X				
Loyola Marymount Univ.		X				X				
Loyola Univ., New Orleans	X	X	X					X	X	
Mansfield State College	X								X	
Marian College	X					X				
Maryville College	X					X			X	
Marywood College		X				X				
Mercyhurst College	X					X				
Michigan State Univ.	X	X	X						X	
Montclair State College	X					X			X	
Mount Aloysius Jr. Coll.	X					X				
Mount Mary College	X	X	X		X	X				
Naropa Institute	X						X			
Nazareth College of Rochester	X								X	
New York Univ.	X	X	X	X		X	X	X	X	
Oberlin College	X								X	
Ohio Univ.	X					X			X	
Philadelphia Coll. of Art	X					X				
Phillips Univ.	X								X	
Pittsburg State Univ.	X					X				

Schools	U	G	U/G	D	C	AT	DT	DRT	MT	P
Point Park College	X						X			
Pratt Institute		X				X	X			
Queens College, Charlotte NC	X								X	
Radford Univ.	X	X	X						X	
Saint Mary of the Woods	X	X	X						X	
Salem College	X					X				
School of the Art Inst. of Chicago		X			X	X				
School of Visual Arts	X					X				
Shenandoah Coll. & Consv. of Music	X								X	
Slippery Rock State College	X								X	
Southern Methodist Univ.	X	X	X						X	
Southwestern Okla. St. Univ.	X								X	
Springfield College	X					X				
State Univ. Coll. at Buffalo	X	X	X			X				
State Univ. Coll. at Fredonia	X								X	
St. Univ. Coll. at New Paltz	X								X	
Temple Univ.	X	X	X						X	
Tennessee Technological Univ.	X								X	
Texas Woman's Univ.	X	X	X	X					X	
Trenton State College	X					X				
Univ. of Bridgeport	X	X			X	X				
Univ. of Calif. — Los Angeles	X	X	X				X			
Univ. of Colorado — Colorado Springs		X					X			
Univ. of Dayton	X								X	
Univ. of Evansville	X								X	
Univ. of Georgia — Athens	X	X	X						X	
Univ. of Houston — Clear Lake City	X						X			
Univ. of Illinois — Chicago		X				X				
Univ. of Iowa	X								X	
Univ. of Kansas	X	X	X	X					X	
Univ. of Louisville		X				X				
Univ. of Miami	X	X	X			X			X	
Univ. of Minnesota	X	X	X	X					X	
Univ. of Mo. — Kansas City	X	X	X						X	
Univ. of New Mexico		X				X				
Univ. of the Pacific	X	X	X						X	
Univ. of Wisc. — Eau Claire	X								X	
Univ. of Wisc. — Milwaukee	X	X	X						X	
Univ. of Wisc. — Oshkosh	X								X	
Univ. of Wisc. — Superior	X	X	X			X			X	
Ursuline College	X					X				
Utah State Univ.	X								X	
Vt. Coll. of Norwich Univ.		X				X				
Wartburg College	X								X	
Wayne State Univ.	X								X	
Western Illinois Univ.	X								X	
Western Michigan Univ.	X	X	X						X	
West Texas State Univ.	X								X	

Schools	U	G	U/G	D	C	AT	DT	DRT	MT	P
William Carey College	X								X	
Willamette Univ.	X								X	
William Patterson College	X							X		
Wright State Univ.	X	X	X			X				

5. COMMON EDUCATIONAL ELEMENTS IN THE CREATIVE ARTS THERAPIES

RESEARCH on cross-cultural psychotherapy reveals that in addition to differences between cultural groups there are universal elements which are present in all people. The cross-cultural perspective can be useful in approaching the various mental health professions. Each professional group is in many ways a culture unto itself, with different traditions, concepts and languages. Contemporary approaches to interdisciplinary cooperation and teamwork have, however, emphasized the qualities of clinical work which all professions share. The various creative arts therapies have also developed as separate cultural groups in spite of the fact that they have many commonalities. Among themselves, the creative arts therapies typically emphasize the differences between the specializations. Outsiders are more apt to see similarities. This chapter will investigate elements that are common to training programs in all of the creative arts therapies.

As stated previously, the creative arts therapies can benefit from the definition of how the various specializations are similar and how they are different, where they can share educational and professional resources and where they cannot, and how research efforts in different creative arts therapy modalities can be mutually supportive. It is especially important for the creative arts therapies to strive to eliminate confusing and contradictory aspects of professional presentation. In addition to planning for growth in the field, preparations should also be made for the maximum utilization of scarce resources. Cooperaton of this kind will offer the public and the mental health field a more coherent and clear image of the profession.

Lessons can be gained from the study of older professions. *The Chronicle of Higher Education* has described serious problems in the education of teachers and psychiatrists which can be instructive. Thomas Bittker, a psychiatrist and faculty member at the Arizona School of Medicine, stated at the annual meeting of The American Psychiatric Association that "Psychiatry is in great jeopardy of extinction" (Fields, 1984). Fewer medical doctors are choosing psychiatry in the 1980s. The percentage is significantly less than the 1960s and is resulting in a situation where there do not appear to be a sufficient number of psychiatrists to fill existing positions. While psychiatry is losing ground, other mental health professions have grown significantly during the same period. Greater freedom is being given to them in terms of clinical practice and thus psychiatry's area of influence is not always clearly defined. According to *The Chronicle of Higher Education*, this makes recruitment for the profession difficult.

Psychology, social work and nursing have made the greatest statistical gains in recent years. The creative arts therapies have the potential to substantially increase their influence, but first the image of the profession must be consolidated with all of the separate elements joining together to support their mutual interests.

The Chronicle of Higher Education, in reporting on teacher education, described how critics feel that the multiplicity of training standards and the lack of consistent national guidelines make it difficult to bring coherence and quality to the profession. The American Association of Colleges for Teacher Education maintains that it "does not endorse any monolithic model for teacher training" (Evangelauf, 1984). The association also feels that national examinations will not necessarily improve the quality of teaching and the upgrading of the profession. The creative arts therapy specializations are characterized by even more radically different standards ranging from bachelor's entry level requirements to master's degree qualifications. Because state licensing and certification procedures have yet to be established throughout the country, it is timely for the various specializations to begin to plan for coherence in the future. It is not in our interest to have the present inconsistencies written into law. Colleges and universities also need guidance in planning for the future of professional education for creative arts therapists. As recommended by The American Association of Colleges of Teacher Education, a "monolithic" and standardized formula is not desirable. Clear principles of mutual agreement and interdependence between the creative arts therapies can be established which will contribute to increasing the ability of colleges and universities to design innovative and high quality training programs.

THEORETICAL ORIENTATION

A description of universal elements of creative arts therapy education will not include basic agreement on theoretical orientation. There is, however, relatively consistent agreement between the creative arts therapies on the importance of respecting a variety of theoretical constructs. Psychodrama is the only specialization which has a clearly defined theory of practice and body of knowledge which specifically relates to that discipline. The theory of psychodrama with its accompanying principles of creativity and spontaneity was established by J.L. Moreno with others contributing to further expansion.

The other creative arts therapies are consistent in their willingness to relate to the broad range of theoretical orientations that characterize contemporary mental health. A particular theoretical perspective will commonly be applied to all creative arts therapy specializations. As a result, a situation is established where creative arts therapists with backgrounds in different media specializations may find themselves in a closer operational agreement with each other than with a group of peers from the same specialization who share different theoretical beliefs. Creative arts therapy professional associations have historically been established in relation to commonalities of a particular medium, rather than theory. It can be argued that differences in ideas can separate people far more than differences in materials. Psychodrama is again unique in that fundamental theoretical and media coherence appear to characterize all practitioners.

It is possible to construct a new and cooperative theory of the creative arts therapies which delineates elements that are common to all specializations while still respecting the multiplicity of psychological systems that guide professional practice. The fact that theory has not been able to provide coherence to many of the individual creative arts therapy specializations does not have to reflect negatively on future possibilities. Theoretical coherence can begin with an understanding of the core elements shared by all of the creative arts therapies.

MEDIA AND ACTION

All of the creative arts therapies can be distinguished from other mental health disciplines in terms of the primary role given to artistic action. It will be advantageous to the profession to emphasize how all specializations integrate media-related action with therapeutic treatment. The "sacred" domains of media in the fine arts must not be confused with what is best for the client and the profession as a whole. Comparisons can be made to the professions of recreation and occupational therapy. It might be asked how recreation therapy would appear if the discipline was divided into different forms of recreation, each of which claimed a distinct professional identity. The same situation can be envisioned with occupational therapy being divided according to different media specializations. Since these two professional are so well established today, it would appear absurd to divide them in this way. The gains that both occupational therapy and recreational therapy have made are largely the result of an integrated professional identity which includes various component parts and specializations. Even though creative arts therapists generally tend to have earned higher degrees involving more psychotherapeutic training than occupational and recreational therapists, they are often hired in departments or programs controlled by these disciplines. Professional power in the creative arts therapies demands consolidation of the still separate arts specializations.

All of the creative arts therapy media introduce the healing properties of aesthetic experience into mental health programs. The primary use of fine arts media as a therapeutic process distinguishes the creative arts therapies from occupational therapy and recreational therapy. In addition to the association of the arts with different psychotherapeutic systems, all of the arts have healing qualities that are inherent to the engagement of the medium in itself. The writings of creative arts therapists from many different theoretical orientations consistently state how the art experience as therapy must be considered as a fundamental element of the profession.

In describing attributes that characterize all fine arts media, Israel Zwerling, M.D., Ph.D., in his address to the 1979 Conference on the Creative Arts Therapies sponsored by the American Psychiatric Association, said:

> Two operational concepts are widely acknowledged as having paramount importance in the clinical application of the creative arts therapies. First, and almost universally accepted, is the concept that the nonverbal media employed by creative arts therapists more directly tap emotional rather than cognitive processes in patients . . . . The point, however conceptualized, is that the creative arts therapies evoke responses, precisely at the level at which psychotherapists seek to engage their patients, more directly and more

immediately than do any of the traditional verbal therapies . . . . The second widely acknowledged concept related to the clinical application of the
creative arts therapies is their intrinsic social or reality based character
. . . . There is a visible or audible or tangible link to society in a session involving a creative arts therapist and a patient, and it has a qualitatively more
immediate, more real presence than does the person or the thing a patient
may talk about (Zwerling, 1979, pp. 843-844).

It is an interesting commentary on the creative arts therapy profession to have a distinguished psychiatrist like Doctor Zwerling, from his
vantage point outside the field, conceptualizing and stating the obvious
universal characteristics of all arts specializations and how they cohere
as a single psychotherapeutic discipline. The profession itself must become similarly involved in describing common philosophical and operational elements. A vital starting point is the universal use of media in all
specializations. Differences in media qualities not only exist between
specializations but within specializations as well. Therefore, the separation of specializations according to media could go on indefinitely.

MEDIA COMPETENCE

There is universal agreement among the creative arts therapy specializations that the therapist is to be educated in a way which guaran-
tees competence in the particular artistic media being applied to
therapy. Music therapy has included media-related training in professional educational programs at the bachelor's level, while art therapy
and dance therapy have made media skills a prerequisite for admission
into graduate programs. Since media differences have been the primary
reason for the separation of the creative arts therapies, it would seem
that the evaluation of media competence would be emphasized more in
assessments for professional practice. Within an integrated creative arts
therapy profession, media competence must continue to be valued and
assessed. The precedents established by the music therapy specialization
can contribute to this process. However, competence in artistic media
cannot, and should not, be exclusively determined by taking a standardized set of course requirements. History has clearly shown that competence in artistic media can be achieved through many different forms of
training, self-development and experimentation.

In creating standards for media competence, the history of psychodrama education should be considered. As stated previously, psycho-

drama programs do not require previous training in theater and yet psychodramatists tend to be talented facilitators of the dramatic process. Media competency is developed through psychodrama training. The tendency of the other creative arts therapy specializations to require previous training in particular art media for admission into education programs may exclude potentially competent people. Existing policies related to media competence make it difficult and sometimes impossible for psychotherapists with doctorates in other mental health disciplines to become involved in the creative arts therapies. This could be a great loss to the profession in the future. Every effort should be made to involve talented and committed people. The creative arts therapy field should therefore study a variety of ways in which media competence can be developed and not adopt rigid and exclusionary standards that will excessively restrict participation in the profession.

EXPRESSION

All of the creative arts therapies stress the value of expression in therapy, and their most significant contribution to twentieth century mental health has been the introduction of alternatives to verbal communication to psychotherapy. Sensory expression is encouraged together with communication through imagery. Clinical opportunities have been expanded through the creative arts therapies, and the ability of therapists to respond to the different expressive and communication styles of clients has been substantially developed. Body, mind and spirit integrations have been similarly enhanced by the expressive liberations of the creative arts therapies.

The potential of creative expression in therapy is only beginning to be realized. The future of the creative therapies is secure because of the need that mental health programs have for varied forms of non-verbal therapy. This need is most acutely felt in treatment programs for children, adolescents and chronic adults, because conventional therapies have not been effective in treating them. The creative arts therapies can be equally relevant to all clinical populations. The creative use of imagery and expression can dramatically affect the more spiritual and depth oriented approaches to psychotherapy. A major area for development in the creative arts therapies is the use of multi-sensory and artistic expression with the elderly. Private practice opportunities are also expanding, as well as the application of creative expression to the treatment of life-threatening illnesses and stress. All of the creative arts therapies can work together to promote expression as a core element of health. It is the profession's responsibility to educate the public and transform health policies and attitudes. It is time for the creative arts therapies to present themselves as primary health care providers skilled in the therapeutic use of expression.

CREATIVITY

A distinguishing feature of all of the creative arts therapies is their consistent commitment to the creative process as a primary element of healing. This orientation to creativity is an essential characteristic of the profession's identity. Creativity is approached from multiple theoretical vantage points ranging from psychological constructs attempting to define its nature to therapeutic beliefs which perceive the energy of creativity as being the same as the energy of healing, in that both transform conflict and pain into positive manifestations of life. Commitment to the process and psychology of creativity unifies all of the diverse elements of the creative arts therapy profession, from the most standardized forms of single media practice to the more all-inclusive forms which see all therapeutic practices based on creativity as art.

As the creative arts therapies mature, they will inevitably contribute to deepening our undersanding of the creative process and its application to healing. With the advancement of research and doctoral study, there will be a corresponding progression in the application of the creative process to all aspects of human service professions. The professional application of the process of creativity to health is the single most important contribution of the creative arts therapies. Although the different specializatons have developed with little formal coordination between one another, they have all contributed to the single effort to increase the influence of the creative process in therapy.

The future potential for the use of creativity in therapy is unlimited. Society is hungry for positive and life-affirming approaches to the transformation of stress. The fulfillment of the profession's potential is dependent upon the ability of all specializations to articulate a common identity based on the therapeutic use of the creative process. Without this single focus, and integration of energies, the power of creativity will be dispersed and continue as a relatively diffuse presence within educational, health and human service settings.

The study of the psychology and process of creativity is a primary component of education in all of the creative arts therapy specializations. Perhaps even more important to the profession is the practice of creativity and the personal artistic skills of the therapist. Creative arts therapy education helps students to learn how to inspire creative expression in others, to understand how they either strengthen or obstruct creativity with their personal behavior, and to be skilled in the process of cooperative creativity with others. These skills and their inclusion as primary elements of training are common to all of the creative arts therapies and are combined with knowledge of, and personal comfort with, particular media. As with the different forms of art, every creative arts therapist strives to develop a style and personal form of work which furthers the maximum use of personal creativity.

CROSS-CULTURAL QUALITIES

In the contemporary era, communications between cultures and all parts of the world are becoming increasingly common. In addition to international cooperation, there is a new respect within the United States for the importance of recognizing cultural differences. There is a complementary need in psychotherapeutic practice to define universal elements of life that all cultures share. The arts serve as unique tools for both cultural differentiation and unification. Ethnic art forms maintain the dignity and autonomy of cultures, while the arts also serve as a universal language which transcends cultural differences. The ability to both express the particular qualities of a culture and of a person, while simultaneously serving as a universal human language, is a trait that is unique to all of the non-verbal art forms. These qualities of the arts in therapy are especially vital within today's pluralistic society, striving for better cross-cultural communication and understanding. The arts therefore have special powers within clinical programs directed toward varied client populations. Cross-cultural studies of artistic expression, together with the study of both universal and culturally specific forms of imagery, can in the future become an essential part of the education of creative arts therapists.

All of the creative arts therapies are expressing ancient continuities of healing. Many of the actual behaviors observed in the contemporary practice of art, dance, drama, music and psychodramatic therapies can be observed within indigenous healing practices throughout the world. Historical, anthropological and depth psychology studies of the origins of the various art modalities in healing will reveal that indigenous practices make few distinctions between art media. All forms of expression are naturally integrated with medical, spiritual, social and ritual practices.

CLINICAL INTERDEPENDENCE

A characteristic of all of the creative arts therapies is their present "minority" status in relation to larger and more dominant mental health professions. Consequently, interdependence with other clinical traditions is a necessity. The creative arts therapies can be likened to a small but enterprising cultural group with a language unto themselves but who instinctively learn the more dominant languages of the world within which they must trade. The creative arts therapist is therefore typically "multi-lingual" in terms of being able to understand the conceptual systems and values of other mental health traditions. The need to be knowledgeable about major psychotherapeutic and psychological systems, and to justify our work within a society that is not always familiar with what we do, has helped to create the strong growth momentum and professional alertness that has been present within the creative arts therapies. These traits are universal to all of the specializations, with the rationale for one modality being interchangeable with all the others.

As a result of this need for interdependence, there is much to be learned within creative arts therapy training programs. In addition to the expanding body of knowledge related to the particular specializations, there are also the many conceptual systems and clinical practices of the other mental health disciplines. The need for interdependence is one of the greatest strengths of the creative arts therapies. Because of their recent arrival in the health fields and because mental health, in particular, is at the present time encouraging multi-disciplinary teamwork, creative arts therapists must be knowledgeable in general clinical practice. This interdependence has not characterized the arts in education which accounts for the more peripheral role that arts educators unfortunately often have in schools. Full interdependence would involve the arts educator in all aspects of the school curriculum as opposed to "special subject" teaching. The arts educator is typically perceived in relation to the subject matter as opposed to a complete teaching relationship with the individual child.

Many creative arts therapists have worked to develop the skills that will enable them to serve as primary therapists within the clinics where they work. The clinics themselves have in recent years discouraged extreme specialization and have committed themselves to interdisciplinary cooperation. The creative arts therapist typically shares responsibility for the administration of a caseload of clients together with other professional staff. In addition to receiving referrals for creative arts therapy and running groups in their areas of specialization, creative arts therapists often serve as the primary therapist for individual clients, coordinating their clinical program from intake procedures to aftercare. Complete clinical interdependence and the ability to take on primary clinical responsibilities must be given serious attention in the education of creative arts therapists. Narrowly specialized studies cannot comprise the major portions of a professional's education in the contemporary mental health field.

From my experience in observing the education and career development of thousands of creative arts therapists throughout the United States and foreign countries over the past fifteen years, I can say that those who have most distinguished themselves in mental health careers have been the people who developed the most sophisticated interdependence with other mental health professionals in terms of theoretical understanding, communication and operational methods. Comparable success has not characterized the work of others who have been less attentive to the development of these skills. It can be said that if the profession does not encourage and produce the highest level of clinical competence, it will languish. Until this achievement is a universal feature of the creative arts therapies, salaries and employment responsibilities will remain at the lower levels that unfortunately characterize much of the profession today. Interdependence must become a primary goal of all training programs, rather than specialization. All creative arts therapists, irrespective of specialization and media-related skills, need to develop the following competencies expected of all mental health professionals who aspire to positions of responsibility:

1. The ability to make diagnostic assessments within the context of the area of the therapist's expertise as well as the general life structure of the client.

2. Group skills together with the ability to establish one to one relationships in therapy.
3. The ability to clearly articulate feelings, observations and clinical recommendations.
4. A sophisticated understanding of the varied therapeutic factors working within the milieu of the clinic.
5. The capability to work cooperatively within a team and to adapt to different points of view and the complex psychodynamics of organizations.
6. Crisis intervention skills.
7. The ability to establish and follow through on both short-term and long-term therapeutic plans.
8. The ability to make transitions from one client to another, and from situation to situation, while maintaining personal attentiveness and composure.
9. The ability to engage the context creatively.
10. Understanding of the self and the way in which the person of the therapist effects the therapeutic process; the ability to take criticism and change behavior.

This list can be expanded to include many more interpersonal and clinical skills. There is in this respect a number of specific skills and clinical competencies that are required not only of all creative arts therapists but of all mental health professionals. Every mental health discipline has historically placed much more emphasis on training students in a body of knowledge and clinical procedure considered to be unique to the field. Perhaps these practices have been motivated by a need to justify and validate the existence of the profession as distinguished from other disciplines. A more sensible approach to education would begin with the premise that students must develop basic skills required of all mental health professionals and then complement this training with the development of specialized competencies. In the education of creative arts therapists, the fundamental curriculum would proceed from the development of competencies that are shared by all mental health professions, to skills required by all of the creative arts therapy specializations, to competencies that are unique to a particular art medium, and to skills that are unique to a particular person. All psychotherapeutic professions will benefit by acknowledging that they share the primary educational objective of training the "person" of the student as an instrumentality of the therapeutic process.

CLIENTS AND SETTINGS

The creative arts in therapy have been used with all client populations and within a comprehensive group of clinical and educational settings. History has shown that non-verbal, activity oriented forms of communication are consistently more useful in psychotherapy with children than the exclusive use of spoken language. As creative arts therapists become more involved with the elderly, they are showing that there is a primary place for creative action in treatment programs. The arts have been widely used in residential programs for adults and within the recently developed community day treatment center programs. Art and action methods are used in short-term therapy, crisis intervention and private practice. In the past, all of the creative arts therapies have been primarily used within institutional settings. The pattern is changing as the profession matures and becomes increasingly autonomous and better recognized within the mental health community. The newest and potentially far-reaching applications of the creative arts therapies are in the treatment of life-threatening illness, stress and other forms of physical discomfort. The professional use of creative expression is becoming increasingly wholistic through clinical integrations of the mental, spiritual and physical qualities of art.

PRACTICAL TRAINING

The education of all creative arts therapists places primary emphasis on practical training. Through the practicum or internship, and the accompanying supervision process, media specific and generic skills are developed. In virtually all education programs within institutions of higher education, supervision is provided by both the training program and the clinical site. Non-academic clinical training programs are attractive to some students because of the way in which they immerse participants in practice. Generally speaking, students find that their primary professional identity formation takes place through practical training. Supervision is most effective when it provides both media specific training as well as more general clinical learning experiences. Issues of clinical supervision and practical training will be explored in more detail in Chapter 7.

RELATIONSHIP TO THE ARTS IN EDUCATION

A comparison between the arts in education and the creative arts therapies indicates that there are profound similarities between all applications of the arts to human service professions. There are many arts in therapy programs presently offered in cooperation with arts in education training programs in colleges and universities. Because of their present minority status within both education and mental health, the arts in both fields might consider closer cooperation on the national association level and within colleges and university training programs. In addition to creative arts therapists sharing many interests with arts educators, it is perhaps universally accepted that every arts teacher can benefit from some form of training in the creative arts therapies, in that therapeutic skills will help them to relate more effectively to students. The creative arts therapies can, in this respect, help arts educators, struggling from the need to work with hundreds of children each week, to individualize and transform their work within schools. Many continuing education courses in the arts in therapy are taken by arts educators eager for training. Arts educators also involve themselves in master's level study in the creative arts therapies and attempt to use their training to change the way the arts are used in the shcools. There are also numerous educators of children with special needs who have pursued professional studies in the creative arts therapies.

Differences between the creative arts therapies and special education are often minimal and restricted only by licensing and certification standards which can be formidable barriers to cooperation. In both areas, the relationship with the individual child is approached clinically and within an interdisciplinary context. Arts educators are, however, clearly differentiated from creative arts therapists through the nature of the systems that they work in, by case load and numbers of people that they are responsible for, and by the way in which they are generally perceived by society and the agencies within which they work. Creative arts therapists have historically had to struggle in many situations to distinguish themselves from what were perceived as the negative implications of "art teaching."

Within therapeutic settings creative arts therapists are still actively engaged across the country in demonstrating their clinical competencies, and because we have not yet emerged from this formative stage of professional development, many creative arts therapists maintain a distance from the arts in education. It is unfortunate that there is a need felt for this separation. The situation does, however, reveal problems within the arts in education. In spite of the early philosophical foundations of the arts in education which stressed the vital role of creativity in life and learning (principles that are also part of the genesis of the arts in therapy), the arts in education, because of the need to teach "en masse," have tended to adopt highly structured, methods oriented systems of instruction. Much of music education lends itself naturally to group expression, significantly more so than art education. However, as in the visual arts, individualized relationships are extremely difficult within music education. Dance and drama have not, because of the patterns of educational history, been integrated into the school experience on a universal basis.

The statements of arts educators describing the fundamental competencies of their profession can be compared to what has been presented here as the universal qualities of creative arts therapy education. W. Reid Hastie described how the common elements characterizing the work of excellent art teachers include: self-confidence; a sense of teaching as an important profession; a sophisticated knowledge of the subject matter; a personal commitment to continuing education; expressiveness and clarity in communication; sound aesthetic judgment; motivation to create original forms; the ability to inspire students and organize educational experiences; the ability to "create" curriculum without standard guides; the selection and management of varied materials; the ability to create an environment supportive of expression; personal involvement in the creative process and ideally being perceived as an "artist-teacher"; an orientation to others rather than the self within the context of professional service; an understanding of the history of art in different cultures; an understanding of human behavior and social relationships; the ability to prescribe appropriate art experiences for the learner; an understanding of the psychological dynamics of visual perception; counseling skills; the ability to speak enthusiastically and "even dramatically" in order to motivate artistic expression; evaluation and administration skills; the application of educational theories to art; an understanding of child psychology; a liberal education; the ability to understand and direct "all of the variables, especially their own behaviors, that determine learning" (Hastie, 1964, p. 257).

Ultimately, according to Hastie, the quality of art teacher education programs is determined by "the imagination and vision of the persons responsible" (Ibid, p. 255). Elliot Eisner feels that it is important for art educators to take an interest in scholarship; develop clinical competencies; be capable of self-confrontation in order to understand how personal behavior affects others and to make conscious use of the self; have the ability to understand the psychodynamics of children's artistic expression; and be able to apply varied personal life experiences and liberal academic interests to art (Eisner, 1964).

All of the competencies necessary for excellent art teaching as described by Hastie and Eisner are interchangeable with the primary competencies of the creative arts therapist. The major differences between the arts in education and therapy appear to be related to contrasts between school systems and clinical environments. Although the primary artistic and interpersonal competencies may be quite similar, creative arts therapists and arts educators work within different "cultures" and theoretical systems. Success and competence are related to the ability of the person to function within the cultural environment of the workplace. Although basic art and human relations competencies may be interchangeable, the cultures of education and mental health are not.

SUMMARY

The creative arts in therapy, as well as the arts in education, share fundamental operational elements. The arts in education and the arts in therapy are distinguished from one another in terms of the "cultures" that they operate in, each demanding an understanding of different approaches to methodology and theoretical purpose. It is the ability to function effectively within systems, and to adapt to the manner in which they approach clients, that determines the success of professionals. All creative arts therapists not only share the common elements of practice described in this chapter but work within the same clinical systems. Therefore, it appears that there are profound commonalities between the various creative arts therapies, extending from universal qualities of media and artistic expression to the structure of the workplace. These universal elements, and the relatively small size of each of the specializations, encourage the perception of all of the creative arts therapies as a single field which, like other mature professions, can also support specialization and differentiation within itself. The following chapter will present features that distinguish the creative arts therapies from one another and which are to be addressed within training programs encouraging interdisciplinary study.

REFERENCES

Eisner, Elliot: Graduate study and the preparation of scholars in art education. In Hastie, W.R. (Ed.): *Art Education*. Chicago, The National Society for the Study of Education, 1965.

Evangelauf, Jean: Up to half of teacher-education programs should be closed, critic says. *The Chronicle of Higher Education, 29*, September 5, 1984.

Fields, Cheryl: "Extinction" of psychiatry seen as possible with fewer doctors choosing to specialize. *The Chronicle of Higher Education, 28*, May 16, 1984.

Hastie, W. Reid: The education of an art teacher. In Hastie, W.R. (Ed.): *Art Education*. Chicago, The National Society for the Study of Education, 1965.

Zwerling, Israel: The creative arts therapies as "real therapies." *Hospital and Community Psychiatry, 30*: 12, 841-844, 1979.

6. SPECIFIC MEDIA COMPETENCIES

DURING TWO TERMS as Chairman of Professional Standards for the American Art Therapy Association, I worked with my committee to define the competencies required for the practice of art therapy. Our goals were to give definition to the profession, to provide guidelines for the evaluation of qualifications for professional registration, and to articulate specific objectives for professional training. The list of competencies can be divided between skills that are shared by all creative arts therapists and skills that are unique to the particular medium. Not only does each art form require the development of media-related skills, but I have consistently observed how different practitioners within a particular media specialization tend to have very different skills. What one experienced and competent person is capable of achieving with a particular art form might not be realized by a person equally experienced within the same medium, and vice versa.

Clients will also respond to media in different ways. Every art material stimulates a response or lack of response in relation to its unique formal qualities. Certain materials are apt to be more effective in relation to the intellectual and expressive styles of individual clients than others, and therapists must be skillful in assessing these clinical aspects of media. The tendency to justify specialization within a particular area of competence can therefore go on into infinity. It is possible to be an advocate of media competence by creative arts therapists without supporting the division of the profession according to media specializations and the containment of professional activities within the boundaries of a particular art form.

Professional training is also a lifelong process. As skills are developed in one area, it is natural to continue to grow in new ways. A person who establishes mastery in one art form can naturally expand into others.

This chapter will define specific media competencies within the creative arts therapies and discuss how educational programs can help to develop them. As we discovered when compiling the core competencies for the American Art Therapy Association, the definition of specific skills resulted in a definition of art therapy. In spite of the many commonalities to all psychotherapeutic practices, the art therapist does have unique qualities not present in the professional identities of other mental health disciplines. When approaching training, it is beneficial to learning and practical, in both clinical applications and the proper distribution of resources, to determine how all mental health professions are alike and how they are different. As stated in the previous chapter, this evaluation of similarities and differences will bring the creative arts therapies into a logical and unified grouping, distinct from other disciplines.

Within the larger perspective of all human service professions, the different creative arts therapies have many more similarities than differences. However, both commonalities and different qualities must be investigated within training programs. It would be harmful to the professional practice of the arts in therapy to suggest that the different specializations should not be separated for the purpose of training. The particular qualities of every medium must be seriously studied in the pursuit of competence. Most contemporary training programs on both the undergraduate and graduate level in the United States take this orientation to the extreme of maintaining not only that the particular qualities of a medium are to be studied in isolation in order to develop competence, but also that the total program of study is to be focused exclusively on a single medium. This position is then taken further by national associations which attempt to control the practice of the creative arts therapies through single medium specializations.

It is not only possible but also highly productive, both within the context of clinical efficacy, academic excellence and artistic vitality, to include different media focused educational experiences within a single training program. Experience with this approach to educating creative arts therapists reveals that students integrate the various concentrations in varied and personal ways in relation to their learning styles and professional objectives. Our experience with integrated training indicates that most people approach the different creative arts through a single art form in which they feel most competent and comfortable. This concentration becomes the trunk of their professional tree. For example, a dancer may concentrate in dance therapy while actively pursuing studies in music therapy, drama therapy, psychodrama, art therapy and poetry therapy with the goals of enriching and expanding the dance therapy experience and developing the ability to be more responsive to the different expressive styles of clients.

Others may wish to study only the performing arts of dance, drama and music as they are related to therapy. All three may be approached with equal emphasis or in a fashion where one is more dominant and the others are studied in relation to what they can contribute to the "primary" media. These concentration patterns may be established during a student's university training and may change during later professional practice, either by becoming more expansive or more focused. We have observed how long-term professional cycles of development in the work of a creative arts therapist may result in alternating periods, where at one time there is intense concentration on a single medium and during other periods the emphasis is on the integration of other media.

Students with a strong professional background in a particular art form have sometimes found it more useful to concentrate on another media during graduate study. For example, a professional visual artist may become deeply engaged in psychodrama and movement training as major concentrations while simultaneously studying art therapy. Moving into areas other than the one where a person is most comfortable, established and habit-bound may stimulate profound learning for mature students, and the same applies to mature professions. Obstacles that are encountered can become a source of instruction if properly engaged. Less experienced students find it better to focus on their areas of strength and comfort as they begin to take on new and challenging responsibilities in clinical work. Media from other art modalities are incorporated carefully, under supervision and in response to client needs.

Often students will utilize their training in different creative arts therapy modalities to become more comfortable with, and knowledgeable of, expressive behaviors that clients manifest in every relationship. Movement, sound, visual imagery, dramatic action and the personal use of language tend to be present in every human encounter and do not have to be introduced by therapists. In working with one art modality, the others are generally involved. For example, language, movement, sound and dramatic enactment have a strong presence in art therapy which cannot be conceived as exclusively "visual." Movement and the enactment of feeling are as vital to this art form as visual imagery. It does not harm a musician to be competent in movement. The Zurich and Winterthur conservatories require creative movement of all students in order to improve their sense of rhythm. It benefits the dance therapist to be able to produce music rather than depending on records and tapes. Music skills expand the dance therapist's ability to reach clients; they can talk to people through drums and other sound sources. Drama therapy must train in all art modalities in order to correspond to the fullness and multiplicities of life which are the medium of theater. Sensory interdependence characterizes all of the creative arts therapies. Comprehensive training in the different specializations expands the range of the therapist's clinical competence.

In summary, there are many different ways to combine the creative arts therapies within the context of training programs. The particular structure of the integration should respond to individual needs, interests and learning styles. This type of integrated training is difficult to achieve within programs with limited resources, and for this reason cooperation between the different creative arts therapies is encouraged. However, it is true that specific traits connected to each art form are best understood through focused study. Without this concentration, the varieties would lose definition and power. It is also important to maintain the different identities of the creative arts therapies in relation to training, research and practice. What is not realistic is the belief that the different specializations are unable to form relationships with one another. This segregation of media and basic elements of expression blocks the expansion and free functioning of the creative process which is forever establishing different combinations and separations in response to the needs of a given situation. Our experience reveals that integration skills and the ability to adapt creatively to new situations and problems are fundamental to successful professional practice. Every specialization is best achieved through a sensitive relationship to the need for integration with other disciplines.

THE DEFINITION OF COMPETENCIES

The work that we did in defining the professional competencies of the art therapist for the American Art Therapy Association offers specific examples of the qualities that are unique to a given specialization in the creative arts therapies. Of the twenty-eight competencies of the art therapist used as a guideline for evaluation for registration by the Association, sixteen competencies were specifically related to the visual art medium (i.e. 57%). Twelve of the core competencies attributed to the practice of art therapy can be described as interdisciplinary skills (i.e. 43%). An understanding of commonalities and differences between all of the creative art therapies was not listed as a basic skill of the art therapist.

This list of art therapy competencies was developed through the involvement of many art therapists and art therapy educators from throughout the United States. The final list was produced after extensive editing of an original list of fifty-six competencies, of which thirty-three were specifically related to art therapy (i.e. 59%).

The American Association for Music Therapy lists competencies to be used as the basis for educational programs. Ninety-seven competencies are listed, the majority of which deal with music therapy principles. One of the competencies addresses the importance of interdisciplinary cooperation with the other creative arts therapies (AAMT, 1984). This lengthy list of competencies has been consolidated by the association for the purpose of reviewing applicants for professional certification. Twenty-five general categories of competence are established which include the ninety-seven skills listed as guides to educational programs. They are as follows:

> Music Theory
> Aural Skills
> Music History and Literature
> Composition and Arrangement
> Major Performance Medium
> Keyboard
> Guitar
> Voice
> Non-Symphonic Instruments
> Improvisation
> Conducting
> Movement
> Exceptionality
> Dynamics of Therapy
> The Therapeutic Relationship
> Foundations and Principles
> Client Assessment
> Treatment Planning—Individual and Group

Therapy Implementation
Therapy Evaluation
Therapy Closure
Communication about Therapy
Interdisciplinary Collaboration
Supervision and Administration
Ethics

Each of the music therapy competency categories is accompanied by a statement describing specific skills within that area. For example:

KEYBOARD (Plays basic chord progressions in all keys, intermediate piano compositions, and traditional songs by memory: harmonizes and transposes at sight and by ear; sight-reads, and accompanies self and others while singing) . . . . THERAPY IMPLEMENTATION (Creates environment conducive to therapy; selects, designs, or adapts appropriate musical materials; provides music that motivates client; provides appropriate directions and cues; improvises music reflecting client; engages client in musical interactions; sequences and paces therapy session; responds appropriately to significant events) (AAMT, Application for Music Therapy Certification, 1984).

The twenty-eight competencies listed by the American Art Therapy Association are divided into four categories: theory, method, artistic expression and professional development. Four of the six theory competencies were focused exclusively on art therapy (i.e. 67%). Eight of the sixteen method competencies involved specific art therapy skills (i.e. 50%). Both of the two artistic competencies concerned art therapy (i.e. 100%). And two of the four professional development skills were specifically associated with art therapy (i.e. 50%). In order to present a complete example of professional competency definition, the art therapy list is presented in its entirety. Each category is divided into media specific and generic clincial skills. This division is not made in the art therapy association listing.

1. THEORY

(Specific Art Therapy Skills)

- Understanding of the art therapy literature, history and research.
- Understanding of different applications of art therapy (individual, group, family, special populations).
- The developmental stages of visual art expression.
- Understanding application of theories of motivation, perception and development to the practice of art therapy.

(Generic Clinical Skills)

- Understanding of different psychological theories of human behavior.
- Theories of psychopathology, behavioral disorders and developmental disabilities.

2. METHOD

(Specific Art Therapy Skills)

- Ability to adapt art therapy methods for special populations.
- Ability to use art therapy with different populations including groups, individuals, families.
- Ability to relate art to treatment methods.
- Ability to utilize different art materials to facilitate art therapy.
- Ability to initiate, structure and maintain a therapeutic relationship through the medium of art with individuals and with groups.
- Ability to translate the art therapy experience into psychological concepts.
- Ability to carry out art therapy treatment plans.
- Ability to present the goals and methods of art therapy to other professionals.

(Generic Clinical Skills)

- Ability to approach treatment with the goal of assessing client's strengths and weaknesses.
- Ability to assess interactional patterns of individuals and groups.
- Ability to alter one's therapeutic approach in response to the requirements of the session.
- Ability to establish and constantly evaluate treatment goals.
- Ability to create an environment in which a client can communicate through both verbal and non-verbal expressions.
- Ability to stimulate creative potential in clients.
- Ability to relate to and interact with other professionals in a team approach to treatment.
- Ability to present case materials orally and in written form.

3. ARTISTIC EXPRESSION

(Specific Art Therapy Skills)

- Personal expression through art.
- Level of involvement in personal artistic expression and commitment to ongoing artistic exploration.

4. PROFESSIONAL DEVELOPMENT
(Specific Art Therapy Skills)
• Personal Contributions to the theoretical and/or clinical development of art therapy.
• Commitment to continuing education as an art therapist.

(Generic Clinical Skills)
• Understanding of the way therapist's personality and behavior affect clients and therapeutic process.
• Ability to receive and respond to criticism and supervision (McNiff, 1981, pp. 7-8).

The competency lists created by the American Association for Music Therapy and the American Art Therapy Association can be used as models for defining specific media skills needed in the practice of other creative arts therapies. Generic competencies are interchangeable with all specializations, while specific media skills can be substituted with comparable competencies in other specializations. In evaluating a person's comprehensive ability to work professionally with all of the creative arts therapies, competence in each of the different media specializations can be assessed as well as additional skills in understanding similarities and differences between the creative arts therapies in terms of theory and method, together with the ability to determine when the use of a particular medium is appropriate.

The listing of specific competencies in all of the creative arts therapies clearly reveals the many commonalities between specializations as well as differences. The value of lists of this kind lies in their ability to define the profession and educational objectives. Competency lists should be perceived as an attempt at a particular time by a particular group of people to define a profession. Lists can become dated and therefore need ongoing review and revision from all segments of the profession. The art therapy association list was developed over a period of years by a committee of educators from different schools who shared varied theoretical orientations. All other educators in the field, as well as all professional members of the association, were given the opportunity to participate in the process. Competence listings must be tested over long periods of time to determine which elements are relatively unchanging and permanent as opposed to those which fluctuate according to the demands of a particular era. Experience with the evaluation of competence may also reveal overlap and repetition in the list as well as omissions. And finally, all evaluations and educational programs must deal with the assessment of the whole person and individual abilities to integrate the many different elements of professional practice addressed in these competency lists. Detailed lists of professional attributes are to be perceived as guides to comprehensive and wholistic learning rather than as vehicles for the fragmentation of professional identity and training. Every individual skill is interdependent with all others and the synthesis that the person achieves tends to be unique and expressive of an individual style.

UNDERGRADUATE PREPARATION

In keeping with the policies of the American Art Therapy Association, the American Dance Therapy Association, the American Society for Group Psychotherapy and Psychodrama and the National Association for Drama Therapy, it is recommended that professional entry level training in the creative arts therapies is to take place on the graduate level. Undergraduate training is to be considered preparatory to graduate study. It is recommended that diversity and liberal studies be encouraged in undergraduate education. Major concentrations in the creative arts therapies at the undergraduate level are to be considered as one of many preparation options. If a student is to major in the creative arts therapies at the undergraduate level, every effort should be made to complement this early specialization with liberal studies. A variety of choices can be presented to students interested in undergraduate preparation for graduate studies in the creative arts therapies. The long-term interests of the profession will be served by graduate programs encouraging liberal study at the undergraduate level and diversity in their admissions requirements as well as competency in the arts and psychology.

Early and complete specialization at the undergraduate level goes contrary to the major clinical service patterns of contemporary mental health systems which emphasize interdisciplinary cooperation and general skills together with specialized competencies. Total specialization at the undergraduate level tends to promote subsequent professional fragmentation and a narrow vision of clinical responsibility and resources. Contemporary educators are critical of these patterns in the education of medical doctors. Because of the driving need not only to specialize but also to achieve high grades and test scores during college studies, some medical schools are experimenting with accepting students into combined college and medical school programs of study directly from high school. The goal is to eliminate excessive stress and competition and to encourage more liberal and creative studies.

Undergraduate education in preparation for the creative arts therapies can potentially address the many different scholarly and practical areas that are integrated into the profession: the humanities, behavioral sciences, fine arts and preliminary clinical training. In addition to psychology, studies in philosophy, religion, cultural anthropology, history, literature, education and the physical sciences can be most useful in preparing for graduate study. Individually guided studies are encouraged, and if students interested in the creative arts therapies do not have access to courses, then preparatory study may be pursued on an independent basis.

With regard to uniformity, virtually every graduate program in the creative arts therapies, regardless of theoretical orientation, requires previous study in psychology or the demonstration of psychological competencies and similar preparation in the fine arts. Graduate programs also emphasize the importance of previous clinical experience, either in relation to academic studies or through previous professional or volunteer experience. Undergraduate programs offering students the opportunity to major in the creative arts therapies guarantee these core areas of preparation. The seriousness and focus achieved through undergraduate training has merit and does appeal to those who are ready to begin concentrated study in the creative arts therapies. Others will prefer broader liberal studies during the college years. Many will not choose a career focus until after college. The growing number of people who find themselves in this category within contemporary society is the strongest argument for encouraging varied undergraduate forms of preparation.

At the present time, graduate programs in the creative arts therapies attract many students from the country's finest liberal arts college who have had comprehensive training in the arts and humanities. It is in the long-term interests of the profession to engage the best possible students. Graduate entrance requirements must not become so overly specialized, as in other professions, that the potential field of applicants is unnecessarily limited. Professional programs run the danger of placing more emphasis on narrowly defined admissions criteria than on admitting the most talented students. Liberal admissions standards must also be maintained if the profession is to continue to attract a large percentage of adult learners who are fully qualified for graduate study. The adult learner can be severely limited by professional programs which limit admission to those who have completed a prescribed series of undergraduate studies. The narrow definition of undergraduate preparation will result in the situation, commonly seen in medical education, where the professional schools are predominately filled with recent college graduates. The creative arts therapies should also continue to be flexible and open in providing training to mid-career professionals in related fields who wish to expand their skills.

It is recommended that graduate admissions standards be based upon the assessment of the applicant's ability to succeed within the training program and the profession, rather than upon a prescribed series of undergraduate courses. The successful completion of specific undergraduate courses is one of many measures for assessment, which tends to be oriented toward the experience of those people who have recently graduated from college and who have planned their undergraduate studies in preparation for graduate school in the creative arts therapies.

As a result of fifteen years of involvement in the higher education of creative arts therapists and direct experience with the training of over one thousand professionals from throughout the United States and thirty-five other countries, I can confidently report that the completion of a prescribed course of undergraduate studies has little to do with either excellence in graduate study or excellence in professional work. My experience as an educator and my observations of the performance of successful and innovative professionals with whom I have not worked as a trainer indicate that a broad variety of educational and life experiences is the best preparation for psychotherapeutic work. Motivation, talent, creativity, native intelligence, the ability to integrate specific and broad areas of knowledge, adaptability, interpersonal skills, good work habits, responsibility, commitment and other primary personal attributes are the fundamental ingredients for success. Clinical skills and a sophisticated understanding of the varied approaches to psychology within contemporary culture, as well as artistic competence, ar essential to successful performance as a creative arts therapist. However, it has not been proven that the only way, or even the best way, to achieve these specific competencies is through a prescribed series of undergraduate courses. Our experience in graduate education does indicate that excellence in the total training experience is furthered by the presence of people with varied life experiences.

INTERPERSONAL SKILLS

The primary emphasis of psychotherapeutic training must be on the person as the basic instrumentality of clinical work. In the case of the creative arts therapies, the core competencies of the profession involve interpersonal and artistic skills. Theory and clinical knowledge are also essential, in that they serve as guides to action and reflection. Certain elements of psychological and psychotherapeutic training may be likened to language and cultural education, in that creative arts therapists will be ineffective within human service institutions in applying interpersonal competencies if they do not speak and comprehend the particular clinical language and feel comfortable and competent within the professional culture.

Educational programs in the creative arts therapies for the most part reflect the importance of interpersonal training. These core competencies cannot be developed through standardized learning structures and testing systems directed at "objective" assessments of competence. Interpersonal learning and assessment demand inner reflection and self-evaluation; the direct supervision of performance, experiential engagement, and ongoing communication between the learner, peers and supervisors. Personal involvement and action, together with feedback and sharing, provide the foundation for the learning process. Within interpersonal learning, individual differences and common areas of concern are recognized together with the definition of personal strengths and weaknesses. Rigid formulas are discouraged, since the laboratory of life, with its many uncertainties and its emphasis on the ability to act decisively, is the ultimate vehicle for the development of interpersonal skills.

ARTISTIC SKILLS

The creative arts therapies demand knowledge and skill in the artistic process. Graduate level training programs typically do not place significant emphasis on the development of artistic competence, largely because of the demand to acquire clinical skills. However, personal artistic expression is typically encouraged within creative arts therapy training groups. Perhaps the only resolution to the growing split between personal artistic expression and clinical practice is the perception of the work of creative arts therapy as an art unto itself. Psychodrama has followed this course. Psychodramatists do not tend to feel the separations between art and work that are more characteristic of other creative arts therapists.

During my tenure as Chairman of Professional Standards for the American Art Therapy Association, we had applicants for registration submit portfolios of personal artwork as part of the application process. We did not evaluate the portfolio materials because there is no clear mandate within the art therapy profession requiring personal artistic competence for clinical practice. Many would argue that there are people who can inspire creativity in others without having personal skills in the particular medium. It is, however, generally accepted that media-related knowledge does increase competence, sensitivity to artistic expression and the therapist's ability to relate to technical problems with an artistic medium.

Our goal in requiring portfolios in the art therapy registration process was for the applicant to demonstrate personal commitment to the artistic process. There were no serious objections to submitting portfolios, and applicants on the whole seemed to appreciate the consideration given to their creativity. Attention to personal art affirmed the basic image making nature of art therapy. It is recommended that education programs in the creative arts therapies consistently make efforts to design systems for the affirmation of creative expression in relation to training. The profession must support personal artistic expression and give it value as a core element of clinical work.

The assessment of artistic quality is a controversial subject, as is the suggestion that personal artistic skills are a prerequisite for the practice of the creative arts therapies. Notable exceptions to every general principle exist and rigid standards of professional practice are not always in the interest of quality. However, it can generally be said that personal artistic competence is necessary for successful professional practice. It is not practical or realistic for a person without these skills to become involved with a career in the creative arts therapies. In most cases potential students make these decisions for themselves. But there are talented and experienced therapists, with little or no personal background in the arts, who wish to become involved in creative arts therapy training.

These people have a fervent desire to increase their clinical skills through the use of the arts. It would be unfortunate to block aspirations of this kind.

Artistic competencies can be evaluated without bias and educators will best serve applicants and students by providing direct assessments of competence. Our experience with portfolios in the registration applications in the American Art Therapy Association provided interesting data on artistic assessment possibilities. The portfolios of applicants who qualified for registration varied significantly in artistic competence. Many were of high professional and creative quality, while others were stereotypic, unimaginative and without exceptional skill. It remains to be determined to what extent success in the clinical practice of art therapy relates to personal artistic competence. Prominent creative art therapists do not always demonstrate excellence in artistic expression. The same applies to the other creative arts therapies. The profession should focus on the "art" of creative arts therapy. Personal artistic competence is to be encouraged but cannot be separated from therapeutic practice when making determinations of what is best for the profession.

Our research on portfolio evaluation within the standards committee of the American Art Therapy Association documented how a group of art therapy educators involved in the review of artworks will generally agree on the assessment of competence (McNiff, 1981). Evaluation criteria included spontaneity, originality and technical competence. We asked ourselves whether the evaluation of the artistic skills of creative arts therapists contradicted the basic values of the profession which values the artistic expression of all people, in all art forms. It was decided that the assessment of competence does not contradict these values and the profession benefits by demonstrating to its members, as well as the society as a whole, that media competence is valued in professional practitioners. It is therefore recommended that graduate and undergraudate training programs address themselves seriously to the evaluation of media competence, as well as to the assessment of clinical and interpersonal skills. Opportunities should also be made available within creative arts therapy training for the development of media skills. Mental health professionals from related disciplines, such as psychology, social work and psychiatry, who wish to become seriously involved in the creative arts therapies are to be urged to engage themselves in the process of investigating and developing their personal artistic skills as an integral part of training.

At the present time the more dominant emphasis placed on clinical skills may be undermining the essential and formative place of art within the creative arts therapy profession. The lack of external pressure calling for the development of artistic competence can result in a damaging lack of attention to the unique elements which give the profession its definition. Students are in need of encouragement and support in developing themselves as artists. The methods of instruction in many creative arts therapy training programs tend to place primary emphasis on traditional verbal learning processes. To a certain extent, this orientation contradicts the media being studied. Verbal methods and modes of communication can be integrated with non-verbal and artistic learning structures which place the arts and creativity at the core of the educational process.

REFERENCES

American Association for Music Therapy: Manual on AAMT Approval of Educational Programs in Music Therapy. Springfield, N.J., 1984.

American Association for Music Therapy: Application for Music Therapy Certification. Springfield, N.J., 1984.

McNiff, Shaun: Competency evaluation in the American Art Therapy Association. *AATA Newsletter, 11*:4, 1981.

7. SUPERVISION AND EVALUATION

THE FORMAT OF SUPERVISION

ALL OF THE creative art therapies are dedicated to training which integrates theory and practice. In addition to developing clinical skills through work with clients, creative arts therapists are encouraged in training programs to integrate theory with their personal lives. The context of practical training inevitably includes the behavior, attitudes and personal histories of students. Supervision is the primary vehicle for learning in practical training. Students typically crave supervision, and training programs find that it must be given a primary position within the total educational experience. Within supervision there is a discussion of the details of clinical experience and a sharing of personal difficulties, doubts and achievements. Supervision tends to be a time where the teacher listens to the student who is responsible for preparing the agenda of what will be discussed and reviewed. This opportunity to present questions and needs within a relationship, where attention is focused on the individual student, is what makes supervision a core element of education in the creative arts therapies.

Most clinical training programs within institutions of higher education offer multiple forms of supervision. A practicum is universally required and the student receives supervision from both the academic institution and the clinical site. In some situations, practicum training sites are affiliated with the college or university and a clinical site supervisor may also be a faculty member in the training program. Certain schools have followed the medical tradition of giving clinical site supervisors faculty appointments. This is a clever and cost-effective way of dealing with supervision. Clinical supervisors often desire academic recognition and titles and are paid for their work by the clinic rather than the institution of higher education.

Clinics also find benefits attached to becoming training centers. Student interns typically expand services while working as non-salaried staff. Regular staff generally discover that serving as a supervisor and mentor to students expands the scope of their professional roles. Clinical training centers tend to have an image of prestige within the health professions, since training heightens the intellectual and research dimensions of the clinic.

It is generally true that the more the clinical and academic functions are integrated, the better the educational experience will be. Perhaps the same can be said of clinical practice. Eduational quality is enhanced by ongoing communication between site supervisors and faculty. Although there are advantages to combining the two roles into one person, the student can also benefit from having a distinct separation between supervision at the clinical site and the academic program. This separation is particularly valuable in the case of interpersonal conflict between the site supervisor and the student. The academic supervisor can thus serve as a mediator and help to improve communication and cooperation.

In many educational programs students receive supervision from more than one person at the clinical site. They may have a principle supervisor and attend other supervision sessions which may focus on the development of skills in group therapy, family therapy, crisis intervention, diagnostic assessments, etc. It is generally accepted that a student benefits from both individual and group supervision. The one-to-one session provides the private time and week-to-week continuity necessary to go deeply into personal concerns and problems. Group supervision encourages peer learning, sharing, criticism and validation. The experiences of other students are a vital part of training. Supervision groups serve as both support systems and forums for confrontation. They can be composed of students from different disciplines or a single discipline, both of which have their advantages.

Faculty members from the training program typically visit the clinical training site and maintain regular channels of communication with site supervisors. Many programs offer supervision groups at the school which are composed of students working in different practicum sites. These groups allow the student to expand clinical experience by working with peers who are engaged with different populations and different types of clinical settings. The supervision group also keeps the academic institution closely engaged with the realities of clinical practice. It serves as a bridge between the academic training program and the clinic, guaranteeing that faculty do not become estranged from clinical practice. This form of ongoing group supervision within the academic institution is not present within external degree programs which are focused more on the training resources offered by the clinical site. The external degree program may, however, involve residency periods when students come together to share experiences and receive supervision. These residential supervision sessions have advantages, such as the intensive period of time spent together with few distractions, which can offset what is lost by not having an ongoing group within the academic training program.

In a Southern Illinois University study of college supervision of student teaching experiences involving university supervisors, student teachers, public school administrators and cooperating teachers, all of these groups agreed that *liaison* was the most important function of the university supervisor who "serves as the link between the university and the public school in which the student teacher serves. The visits of the supervisor help to maintain unity of action in the overall task of teacher preparation. Relationships would be too impersonal if the attempt were made to supervise the program only through correspondence, telephone conversation, or some other method of indirect communication" (Neal, Kraft and Kracht, 1974, pp. 164-165). Other functions of the university supervisor included helping student teachers, fulfilling university responsibilities to student teachers, establishing a cooperative effort in all aspects of the training program, introducing and interpreting the student-teaching program to the cooperating public school teacher, and providing continuity to the program over a period of years (Ibid., 1974).

The Southern Illinois study documented how university supervisors tend to identify "many more roles" for themselves than the cooperating school personnel or student teachers expect of them. Liaison and the other roles listed here were given far more importance than what was described as the traditional role of directing and critically evaluating the student teacher. Direct supervision was therefore not what was desired of the unversity supervisor. The liaison function is equally important in clinical practicum training. Visits and regular communications initiated by the university supervisor express a commitment to the student and recognition of the important training functions being undertaken by the clinical staff. The university supervisor in this respect supports the field supervisor, who is responsible for directing and evaluating the student's day-to-day clinical work.

University supervisors can easily find themselves in a situation where they are attempting to do everything and not utilizing their resources to their best ability. It is essential to realize that fundamental responsibility for the student's clinical work lies with the site supervisor, who is the "primary clinical supervisor." The responsibility of the university supervisor is to develop the best possible clinical training sites for students and maintain close communication with the site supervisor. The university supervisor can be perceived as having primary responsibility for the student, whereas the site supervisor has primary responsibility for the clients that the student is working with. University supervisors must understand these distinctions in role responsibilities and focus their work appropriately. For example, problems will inevitably present themselves if university supervisors feel it is their responsibility to take over the clinical supervision of the student and suggest how a particular case is to be handled within a clinic. The university supervisor may in a situation of this kind be advising the student in a manner that is contrary to the suggestions of the site supervisor. University supervisors may certainly provide additional consultation to students on how to work with clients, especially in areas of their expertise, but it must be clearly understood that all recommendations are to be considered in relation to the procedures and systems of the clinic. It is strongly recommended that university supervisors be actively involved with their students in a didactic manner concerning clinical work. However, university supervisors will strengthen the overall clinical training experience by focusing on their liaison role with the clinic and becoming actively involved in the development of sites, ongoing communication and cooperation with supervisors and clinic administrators with reference to the individual student and the goals of the university training program, regular assessment of the performance of clinical training sites, and general program improvement.

QUALITY SUPERVISION

The maintenance of consistent standards of quality clinical supervision is a challenge to a relatively new profession like the creative arts therapies. New training programs, in new professions, typically do not have access to a wide range of experienced supervisors in the field. It takes years to build a comprehensive supervisory network, and in many cases graduates of the program must be groomed to take over the responsibility of clinical supervision shortly after they begin jobs as creative arts therapists. The recent graduate, though short on experience, is typically a highly dedicated supervisor who understands the student's role.

The excellent clinical supervisor is self-confident and possesses diversified theoretical and practical knowledge of the creative arts therapies as well as the principles of various psychotherapeutic systems, has the respect of colleagues within the clinical setting and the ability to clearly articulate the clinic's orientation to professional practice, is flexible and adaptive to the differing needs of students, is empathetic and able to transcend personal perspectives, encourages students to allow their unique qualities and therapeutic styles to emerge, has a sophisticated self-understanding and is aware of how personal behavior affects others, does not insist upon a single theoretical model for therapy, is able to clearly articulate what is happening within the supervisory relationship and when necessary confronts problems, inspires the student with standards of quality, provides both professional and personal support and affirmation, assists in the resolution of ambiguity while maintaining respect for the complexities of clinical practice, and helps the student to integrate theory and personal values with therapeutic practice.

DETAILS OF STUDENT PLACEMENTS

In the early years of creative arts therapy education, students in their practicums would often act as pioneer therapists, developing the first arts programs in the clinics. The absence of creative arts therapy clinical sites, and a senior creative arts therapist to serve as a role model, were sometimes compensated for with opportunities to create programs and develop leadership skills. As the profession continues to grow, practicum training tends to take place within established creative arts therapy programs and under the supervision of an experienced therapist.

Graduate programs vary as to when they involve students in practical training. Some programs believe that students should take introductory coursework before beginning a practicum. The rationale of this approach is that the student should first be prepared and oriented before entering the clinic. Careful preparation of this kind tends to involve students in clinical observations before becoming involved in practical work. The majority of graduate training programs involve students in practical training during all stages of their study. The rationale for this approach is that clinical experience is vital to all aspects of the educational process. It is felt that students who are well prepared within the clinic, and who receive good supervision, can begin to make professional contributions early in their training programs. Many creative arts therapy graduate students are experienced professionals or they have had previous practical training experiences. External degree students often use their jobs as practicum sites.

Most practical training experiences involve the student in the clinic for at least fifteen hours per week. This time is necessary to provide an exposure to the total treatment program. In addition to individual and group therapy experiences, students typically attend staff meetings and other programmatic events. Practical training is concerned with learning how institutions operate and how one is to function effectively in them.

There are two distinct traditions in mental health practical training. One approach involves multiple clinical exposures, or rotations, introducing students to a variety of clinical sites within a relatively brief period of time. Advocates of this approach feel that students benefit from working with different populations and different institutions and that *more* will be learned in this way. The other approach to practical training is based on the belief that longer training residencies in a clinic are necessary in order to receive adequate exposure to clients, systems and changes that occur. It is felt that time is an important ingredient in the training experience. Time is needed for the student to feel comfortable, to understand how the clinic functions, to receive the respect of staff and clients, and to become involved with treatment programs. Time is also necessary to understand changes and cycles in client behavior. Short residencies interrupt and cut off some of the most important learning experiences available to students. It is generally recognized that short-term residencies are not as helpful to clients and the general functioning of the clinic, since both the individual client and the total treatment program benefit from continuity and stability in staffing. The negative effects of students leaving can be minimized by careful efforts to integrate them into the activities of the clinic in a manner which encourages continuity rather than abrupt change.

Decisions as to whether or not short-term or long-term practical training experiences are to be encouraged will depend upon the nature of the clinical site. Certain clinics lend themselves to short-term practical training residencies, whereas most are suited to longer training experiences over the course of an entire school year.

METHODS AND PROCESS OF SUPERVISION

Supervision of practical training is based on two primary elements: direct observation and the presentation of case materials. Through direct observation, the principles of apprenticeship training are carried into contemporary professional education. Video and audiotape recording equipment have provided new opportunities for the expansion of direct observation. Videotape has been particularly revolutionary within the context of supervision. Dance and movement therapy, together with all of the creative arts therapies, have been major beneficiaries of videotape technology. A major feature of videotape in supervision is that it allows students to critique their work and become their own supervisors. This form of self-evaluation is effective in serving as a stimulus for change. Video playback also enables students to work together in peer supervision.

Special features of videotape in supervision include possibilities for viewing work over sustained periods of time and giving focused attention to specific behaviors. With videotape, supervision groups within the academic training program can directly observe what is taking place within the clinic. Videotape also enables supervisors in external degree programs to observe students.

Psychotherapeutic supervision has not traditionally placed primary emphasis on direct observation. The classical technique involves students meeting with supervisors in private sessions in which they discuss experiences with clients. The student presents case materials while the supervisor listens, questions and sometimes comments. Art therapy supervision makes extensive use of drawings and other objects created during therapeutic sessions. By focusing on these materials, supervision engages in a form of observation not present in other mental health supervisory processes. However, the object is best understood in relation to the process of its creation within the session and this again reinforces the importance of direct observation of performance. In spite of its value, videotape playback is not a standard process in most supervisory relationships. This can be attributed to the unavailability of videotape materials in most clinics, the difficulties involved in having a session taped, and the fact that supervisors do not typically have their offices equipped with playback equipment.

Supervisors and students may also feel that the videotape *hardware* can be dominant in their supervisory sessions and interfere with interpersonal relationships. It is possible for both students and supervisors to avoid personal encounter by focusing on technological materials. These potential problems are to be carefully considered when introducing videotape to supervision.

Paolo Knill has experimented with creative uses of videotape in both the United States and Europe (Knill, 1983). During site visits to practicum students, he avoids many of the practical problems of videotape technology by doing the recording himself or by having another person with video skills assist him with the equipment. He enters the group as a participant engaged with the videotape process as opposed to an observer. If it is appropriate, the videotape playback is shared with clients and is integrated into the therapeutic experience. The supervisor becomes involved in the artistic process and contributes something to the group. Media competence is essential in maximizing the therapeutic potential of video. Skillfull in-camera editing, selection of subject matter and visual appeal have a direct effect on the emotional reaction of the person viewing the tape. There is a correspondence between what is perceived and what is felt. It is also difficult for a student who does not have professional video skills to go into a practicum situation and maintain composure and accessibility to clients while trying to operate the recording equipment. Because the camera focuses so completely on one vantage point at a time, it is also difficult to be aware of everything that is happening within the therapeutic environment while using the equipment (McNiff, 1975, and 1980).

Videotape may be used as a tool for *micro-teaching* in which five minutes or less of a videotaped session are played back to the supervision group and evaluated. Playback may also take place within the therapeutic session with clients and staff responding to what was videotaped

(Knill, 1983). Videotape can thus introduce information which stimulates self-evaluation and communication.

The use of videotape provides the opportunity for the evaluation of brief time intervals which can be isolated through playback. Attentiveness to "particulars" and specific qualities of the student's performance can encourage a more focused and thorough analysis of interpersonal behavior. Supervision can potentially involve so many aspects of what occurs during a session that material has to be selected for the purpose of presentation, concentration and careful review. A thorough evaluation of a brief interval of a therapeutic session will demonstrate how much there is to be aware of within human relationships. This approach to details contrasts to attempts to cover everything that occurred in a session. Clinical and emotional depth require focus and concentraton.

Supervision in the creative arts therapies offers many opportunities for the use of the artistic process as a primary mode of communication between the supervisor and trainee. Because conventional verbal modes of supervision have been such a large part of twentieth century psychotherapeutic history, many creative arts therapists simply adopt them for the purpose of supervision within the profession. Creative arts therapists have been, and still are, often supervised by psychologists, social workers and psychiatrists and tend to internalize the supervisory styles of their mentors. Exclusively verbal supervision, especially when offered by other mental health disciplines, can be useful to the creative arts therapist who not only learns the skills of the other professions through the process but develops the ability to articulate the psychotherapeutic dynamics of the creative arts therapies. One of the advantages of supervision with other psychotherapeutic disciplines, not thoroughly familiar with the creative arts therapies, is that nothing is taken for granted. Everything must be justified and explained within the context of another approach to therapy. All supervisory relationships might similarly benefit from assuming little and questioning every belief and action.

However, the creative arts therapies must initiate art-based modes of communication within supervision. In art therapy supervision, students and supervisors can create artworks expressing their perceptions of what is happening within relationships with clients. This process can also be applied to the supervisory relationship. All of the other media of the creative arts therapies may be similarly engaged. In body oriented therapy, supervisors can work directly with the student's personal movement style and explore its effects on others. Psychodramatic enactment, role playing, dramatic simulation, sound improvisaton and other art experiences have extraordinary potential for recreating specific incidents and expressing feelings and perceptions about key issues. It is recommended that creative arts therapists engage the arts as primary modes of communication in supervision. The use of the media of the profession helps the student to develop a deeper understanding of how to work with the arts in varied situations. When supervision parallels the process of the profession, it is more complete and integrated. We must demonstrate to ourselves and our students how the arts can be primary forms of clinical analysis and expression. Without this integration, we de-value our media.

The use of the arts as vehicles for communicating a student's perceptions of what is taking place within the therapeutic relationship may be considered by certain supervisors as less accurate than written process notes. Expert observers of conventional psychotherapeutic supervision maintain that, "It is commonplace that no recording can be a faithful rendering of the total therapeutic experience . . . . There is, in fact, no absolute concept as to what ideal process recording is . . . . What is ideal in each instance depends on the student's present capacity, on the specific use of certain recording methods in specific learning situations, and perhaps also on some of the capacities of the supervisor . . . (Ekstein and Wallerstein, 1972, pp. 274-275).

The arts, rather than being less precise than written process notes, allow for the presentation of more comprehensive information. Just as the arts expand the scope of communication in therapy, they do the same in supervision. They allow students to give more of themselves to the learning situation. Only biased attitudes toward the arts would insist that written notes offer the only "verbatim" record. Ideally, all modes of representation can be used in creative arts therapy supervision. Written notes and oral accounts certainly have value. Artistic, poetic and dramatic expressions are especially useful in conveying the student's emotional response and present feelings toward the client and the relationship with the supervisor. Flexibility is recommended with regard to the recording and presentation of case materials during supervision. Both conventional process notes and artworks will express the student's selection and formulation of issues, understanding of patterns in behavior, sensitivity to needs and change, openness to different forms of expression, organization, awareness of personal feelings, tolerance, self-confidence, and ability to share feelings with the supervisor. Ekstein and Wallerstein note that the recording process may change dramatically as skills develop and students may become engaged in "an entirely spontaneous" supervision process. They describe how it takes a sophisticated and experienced supervisor to approach supervision and teaching with flexibility and spontaneity (Ibid, 1972).

THE SUPERVISION AS THERAPY CONTROVERSY

Supervision is conducted by therapists with students wishing to become therapists. The primary purpose is training, but the therapeutic process being studied inevitably manifests itself in the supervisory relationship. Those of us who are involved with the psychotherapeutic *culture* cannot always make neat distinctions as to where therapy begins and ends. Supervision itself is oriented toward helping students to *live* the process of therapy with professional competence. Descriptions of psychotherapeutic supervision that we have encountered emphasize the importance of studying the psychological and emotional details of relationships between therapists and clients. Analytically oriented professionals refer to this process in terms of *transference* and *countertransference*. Supervision thus focuses on how the client perceives the therapist and acts within the relationship. Similar issues are addressed with regard to the therapist's feelings about the client and the details of performance. Supervisors help students to understand the effects of their behavior on others, to question their motives, and to improve their ability to relate to people.

Problems with self-confidence, intellectual and practical knowledge of psychodynamics, the negative effects of anxiety, overly enthusiastic interventions and confrontations, pushing for results and communication, and a general inability to accept clients for who they are at the moment, and what they are capable of doing, are typical of beginning therapists. Personal habits are brought to the attention of the student as well as projections onto clients, supervisors, other staff and the organization. A major problem of beginning and experienced therapists is the tendency to overlook how people perceive situations differently and function within different roles. There is a common assumption that others share a similar frame of reference. The emotional complications of the supervisory relationship are further intensified by problems that supervisors sometimes have with students. Inexperienced supervisors are apt to manifest many of the same problems that are typical of the beginning therapist. Both new and experienced supervisors may express rigidity or intolerance in what they perceive as relevant to training. Supervisors can be overly controlling and defended, vulnerable and unable to receive criticism. Supervisors who are themselves unable to receive feedback on their behavior place themselves at a disadvantage when attempting to help beginning therapists open to criticism and assistance.

It can be gathered from this list of potential problems that supervision is not always conducted under ideal circumstances. When group dynamics are introduced, the problems become magnified. Frustration and a lack of trust can be intensified when an overly controlling, dogmatic, or insecure person is leading a supervision group. The student's interpersonal problems are thus often multiplied and further complicated in relation to clinical work. Insecure students and supervisors who protect themselves with feelings of superiority can add to the complexities and ambiguity of the learning environment. Within the context of psychotherapeutic supervision and training, every aspect of interpersonal relationships, both good and bad, has its place. Ambiguity and confusion often result when the supervision process does not deal clearly with underlying psychodynamics and when supervisors present mixed messages to students.

Although psychotherapeutic education, as a result of the long history of personal analysis as an essential part of psychoanalytic training, respects the student's personal involvement in therapy, many educators maintain that supervision should be distinguished from therapy. A recent study of art therapy supervision takes this position.

> The supervisor's role is one of teaching students how to ask questions. "Why did the patient paint that then? Why did I say what I said?" . . . This essential self-examination on the part of the student in supervision needs to be clearly separate from the self-examination of personal therapy. It is the supervisor's role to identify personal difficulties which interfere with a student's clinical work, but I believe it is not appropriate to work therapeutically with those difficulties in the educational setting of supervision. Instead, the students should come to realize that the supervisor is there to help them with the specifics of their clinical work and not with their personal problems no matter how much these two areas may become intertwined (Wilson, 1984, pp. 100-101).

Another perspective on supervision is presented by those who find it more difficult to determine a specific and consistent place "to draw the line" between therapeutic and didactic issues in supervision. Supervision has in this respect everything to do with the student's or therapist's personal problems and patterns and how these are projected onto clients and psychotherapeutic relationships. The way students are within a supervisor's office cannot be separated from the way they are with clients. Problems in one area will manifest themselves in others. The skillful and sensitive supervisor will guide students and make them more aware of how personal style affects psychotherapeutic performance. This type of guidance is not necessarily called psychotherapy but, rather, it is supervision. Supervisors may, of course, approach the situation with different boundaries and needs for limits. This is a projection of the supervisor's style and personality. Some are more comfortable than others with both intimacy and conflict. "Although supervision often in practice takes the form of sideline coaching, this is hardly its essence. And the misconception leads not only to the coaching-versus-therapy dilemma but also to crippling restrictions on the fullest, creative utilization of the supervisory process . . . . Supervision is a therapy of therapy; in other words, it is metatherapy" (Abroms, 1977, p. 82). The rationale for this approach is that the structure of the supervisory relationship will inevitably correspond to the structure of the therapeutic relationship within teaching situations that wish to work with the essence of the psychotherapeutic process. The role of the supervisor is to demonstrate, clarify and serve as a model for becoming aware of the complex, and sometimes obvious, elements of human relations. Some supervisors are either not capable of functioning or simply do not choose to work in this way, and this is a fact within the mental health field which I do not wish to dispute. However, personal values which advocate clear boundaries between the personal and professional must not be projected onto every form of supervision.

The debate as to whether psychotherapeutic supervision and training should, or should not, be perceived as therapy is to me unnecessary. Students typically pursue supervision for the purpose of training and not personal therapy, although there may be exceptions to this general principle. We are also speaking of an educational process, fully grounded in traditions of professional training. The therapy versus training dichotomy presents a thesis and anti-thesis which are united through a synthesis of the two. Psychotherapeutic education is neither pure personal therapy, nor pure didactic presentation, but rather a synthesis of the two, a new combination that has evolved as the most effective way of educating therapists. Training, in order to be fully effective and practical, must embrace the subject matter of the profession as it is experienced within the educational context.

This form of education demands skill and sophistication on the part of teachers. The educator or supervisor needs to be more than just a talented therapist. The transition must also be made to the synthesizing role of teacher-therapist. Experienced and gifted teachers will find it difficult to function expertly in clinical training without psychotherapeutic experience. They may be able to instruct students in related studies, but they will not be capable of engaging the pure process of the work and what it evokes in students.

In West Germany and Switzerland, psychotherapeutic training programs have a clear conceptualization of the interface between therapy and teaching. Students become involved in training experiences referred to as *studientherapie* (study therapy) which are personal therapeutic relationships pursued for the purpose of gaining insight into clinical work. The focus of the therapeutic relationship is on the technique and process of doing therapy. Teachers and supervisors are fully engaged in the process through a concept called *intertherap* which also makes the supervisor a subject of the supervision process. Within the context of *intertherap* the total dynamic of the supervisory process is engaged. The style and performance of the supervisor is evaluated and discussed together with the assessment of the student. The *intertherap* model recognizes that the two cannot be separated (Knill, 1984).

Ekstein and Wallerstein (1972) maintain that both supervision and psychotherapy involve the use of interpersonal relationships with the object of helping others. They feel that even though the two deal with the same emotional materials, there is a fundamental "difference in purpose," with therapy being directed toward the resolution of emotional difficulties and training oriented toward the development of psychotherapeutic skills. Again, as Abroms indicates, it is difficult to draw the line between therapy and training. The clearest and most unambiguous resolution is to perceive psychotherapeutic training as a third process, distinct from personal therapy and traditional education, but yet integrating the two polarities into a new combination. The "either/or" duality inevitably negates vital elements which yearn for integration. Problems will emerge when supervisors "try to convert the teaching relationship into a therapeutic one" or "defend . . . against this temptation by rigorously avoiding any aspects of a 'therapeutic' relationship and by becoming a teacher who remains simply 'didactic' " (Ekstein and Wallerstein, 1972, p. 255).

The relationship between supervisor and student, as with psychotherapy, cannot avoid the intricacies and simple facts of how people relate to one another. Rigid boundaries avoid the total context of the therapeutic process and deny opportunities for learning and creativity. Master teachers project a clarity and security to students, giving them the feeling and confidence that there is an overriding element of control and protection within the learning environment. Expert leadership conveys trust and increases student participation by demonstrating how the educational experience will not become involved in unnecessarily destructive and chaotic emotional confrontations. Psychotherapeutic training, like therapy itself, is an art that demands well-developed skills and emotional sensitivities. It is clearly a process that is more than doing therapy, and more than the teaching of a particular subject matter. This can be validated by examples of people who have been gifted in the professional practice of one or both of these areas but who have found it difficult to integrate the two in psychotherapeutic education. The creative arts in therapy further complicate the skills needed for the successful educator with demands for media competence. It is a challenging and difficult role that takes special gifts and the ability to accept criticism, learn from it and continue to perfect the work.

PERSONAL THERAPY AND INTRAPERSONAL LEARNING

Psychotherapy has become identified with diverse practices. The many varieties, ranging from strategic life planning to catharsis, are all based on the common desire to understand, accept and transform life situations and feelings through relationships with others. The effects of psychotherapy are universally based on the motivation of the client and the artistry of the therapist. Regardless of theoretical orientation, what really matters in terms of the therapist's competence is human understanding and the ability to work competently with the subject matter of human feelings and interpersonal relationships. The competence and "image" of the therapist will inevitably influence the client's motivation to seriously engage the therapeutic process. There are few psychotherapeutic educators who will say that understanding of the self has little to do with successful clinical practice. Differences begin to emerge with regard to where and how this psychological inquiry into the self is to take place.

Mental health training programs take different and sometimes opposing positions on the place of personal therapy in training. In the early days of psychoanalysis, personal analysis was a major element of training. As psychotherapy began to expand, training became increasingly controlled by professional association standards and teaching traditions in colleges and universities which did not originate for the purpose of training psychotherapists. Today psychotherapeutic education takes place primarily through affiliations between institutions of higher education and clinical sites, both of which are not typically prepared to do training through personal analysis. Institutions of higher education offer systematic studies through academic and professional curricula, while clinics are busy providing services to clients. Because of the intensive orientations of universities to academic content and the clinic's commitment to service, it is unusual to find institutions which can easily accommodate the student's personal self-analysis into the training program. Institutions of higher education, clinics, hospitals and other human service settings involved with mental health training do not perceive private therapy for staff and trainees as a priority or something that they should be concerned with at all. Even programs which totally integrate personal and interpersonal experiential learning into the curriculum find that for certain people, the program of study is not sufficient and that an outside therapeutic relationship is recommended. There are people whose needs for personal attention and self-understanding cannot be accommodated within the structure of the training program.

There is an unfortunate confusion with regard to the proper context of psychotherapeutic training, resulting from the history of the mental health profession.

> Because modern psychology was born in the consulting rooms of two Viennese physicians and in the locked wards of a Zurich psychiatric asylum, it has been assumed to be an offspring of medicine. Those who work in psychology are considered to belong to the family of the healing arts . . . and our work as psychotherapists is considered to be limited to the care and service of the ill psyche. That the psyche at the turn of the century was so ill that it appeared mainly in medical surroundings is no reason for it to remain there. The psyche in the medical consulting room was a necessary fantasy of the nineteenth century . . . (Hillman, 1978, pp. 11-12).

The origins of modern mental health practices spread to empirical and clinical psychology, which together with medicine helped to formulate the present partnership between the university and the clinic. The creative process, the arts and the ancient traditions of spiritual disciplines had little to do with the establishment of the major patterns of contemporary health systems and training practices. Psychology, in response to pressures encouraging the field to be "more scientific," separated itself from its historic alliance with philosophy. As a result of these trends there is not a complete integration within contemporary mental health training environments of the historic components of therapy. Academic and clinical issues are too often separated from personal self-discovery, spirituality, creativity, interpersonal relationships and the total context of knowledge.

The historic missions of institutions of higher education in the United States has not included the personal therapeutic experiences of students and faculty. The same applies to clinical centers. Therefore, we typically have to go elsewhere for these educational experiences. This fact is a consequence of history and the evolution of institutions and does not necessarily reflect ideal conditions for training. Private, non-academic training centers can easily, and successfully, base the complete educational experience upon an integration of personal growth and clinical training. The same integration could be achieved if spiritually oriented centers were to become involved with psychotherapeutic training. These environments are established upon an inseparable integration between the *responsibility and necessity* of intrapersonal learning and service to others. It is therefore essential to look carefully at the influence of historical patterns on what some consider to be the fundamentals of clinical education.

Most psychotherapeutic and creative arts therapy training programs are in agreement in finding that it is useful for the student to have a personal therapeutic experience that is related to training. Programs and individual faculty members differ on whether or not they require, strongly recommend, recommend, or occasionally suggest personal therapy for students. There are also differences within the creative arts therapy profession as to whether or not students in training should go into therapy with another creative arts therapist or a more conventional clinician. Both have their advantages, and certain students have explored learning through involvement in varied forms of therapy. Students involved in personal therapy, with few exceptions, affirm the vital role that the therapeutic process plays in relation to training. There is little evidence to suggest that personal therapy should be a required part of the training of the psychotherapist, and especially in educational situations where personal and interpersonal dynamics are thoroughly integrated with teaching and supervision. However, there must be a place within the total experience of training, where the primary focus is on the student as a person. Private fears, conflicts, fantasies and aspirations, aroused by clinical training, need to be fully engaged.

Both academic programs and clinical training sites will improve the quality and depth of professional education by focusing on the student's needs in this way. It is recommended that both theoretical training and clinical supervision actively involve the *personal* pscyhe as a core element of professional identity.

Private training centers that are not associated with large institutions often place much more emphasis on the systematic inclusion of personal growth as a core, and integral, element of training. This integration of the personal and the professional, as suggested by traditional psychoanalytic training, is essential to the education of psychotherapists. The institutions of higher education and clinics that have become the primary centers of training in the health professions have shown little interest in changing their historic functional patterns in order to provide this integration. Psychodrama training programs typically involve students as protagonists in psychodramatic enactments and as active participants in the group psychotherapy process. The essence of psychodrama education is the experience of the psychodramatic process under the supervision of an experienced trainer. This tradition has resulted in a high degree of demonstrated excellence in training. The success of psychodrama education, largely conducted without the involvement of universities and colleges, can provide important data for higher education and help professional schools to return to a more direct and pure process of training and practice. Perhaps the power and efficacy of the psychodramatic process, and its training methods, can be attributed to the fact that institutions of higher education have not been significantly involved. The same can be said about centers for psychoanalytic training.

The academic industry has, in the interest of what it perceives as important, taken education on a different course than that which has historically been followed by the non-academic psychotherapeutic training centers which have done so much to create and define contemporary psychotherapy. Early twentieth century psychotherapy as developed by Freud, Jung, Rank, Moreno and others was keenly sensitive to the integration of personal and professional experience, together with the synthesis of medicine, psychology, philosophy, history, mythology, the arts and all other sources of knowledge. Because medical doctors were so instrumental in developing the process of psychotherapy, medical schools and psychiatry have for many years dominated psychotherapeutic practice and have established precedents for specialized education within a single discipline. Other professions, in order to become involved in the psychotherapy, followed suit and have similarly established special fields of study, which attempt to provide a different angle on the psychotherapeutic process.

The result of this progressive fragmentation, supported by the academic industry, has been an increasing alienation from the intellectual, clinical and spiritual sources of the psychotherapy. Mastery of a circumscribed body of knowledge and the completion of a prescribed series of courses, research activities, clinical experiences and various other forms of initiation into professional practice have been required. Many of these directions are in fact vital to competent professional practice within an increasingly complex world. The constant differentiation of skills and the expansion of knowledge is recommended and respected. However, it is important to question the extent to which training has been fragmented in order to accommodate new interests. Technical sophistication and clinical competence need not be pursued at the expense of intellectual, personal and professional integration. The separation of intrapersonal learning from the mainstream of professional mental health education is an unfortunate result of this missing synthesis. It is strongly recommended that education programs for creative arts therapists seriously study how intrapersonal learning can be furthered in the future, even though institutions of higher education do not presently consider this to be part of their mission. In the pursuit of excellence, institutions and professions must consider change and transformation.

GROUP WORK AND CREATIVE ARTS THERAPY SUPERVISION

Creative arts therapy supervision addresses itself to elements of clinical practice that are relatively unique to the profession. One important feature is the way in which creative arts therapists tend to work with groups as a common mode of treatment. Similarly, training sessions often take place within groups. Psychodrama developed as a form of group therapy and all of the other creative arts therapies have special features which allow them to be effective in large and small group settings. This ability to engage groups does not negate the importance of introducing the artistic process to one-to-one relationships and family therapy. However, the fact is that the creative arts therapies have made far-reaching and influential contributions to clinical settings throughout the world through various forms of group work. This has probably occurred because the tools of the profession are uniquely adapted to group participation and action. Other mental health professions have not had comparable means for fulfilling such a wide variety of clinical needs for group activity. In addition to being able to parallel the services of conventional, verbal group therapy, the creative arts therapies introduce action, enactment, imagery, the construction of tangible objects, musical improvisation, chant, rhythm, videotape, poetry and various other art media.

The average creative arts therapist, working within a clinical or educational setting today, sees both individuals and families, and engages a larger number of people through different forms of group therapy. There are many exceptions to this general principle and therapists who do not choose to work in groups for various reasons. The frequency with which the creative arts are engaged in group therapy needs to be addressed by training programs. In addition to making it necessary to train students in areas related to this mode of treatment, group work presents numerous practical opportunities for supervision.

Group creative arts therapy experiences allow students to work along with the supervisor as an assistant or co-leader. The presence of a more experienced therapist gives the student more of an opportunity to observe and take on responsibilities gradually. Having the supervisor present will generally allow the student to relax and feel more comfortable. However, this situation can be reversed if the supervisor is overly critical of the student's performance. Beginning students will become inhibited and unspontaneous if they feel that every move they make is being scrutinized by a judgmental supervisor. Other positive features of working togther with the supervisor in a group situation include learning how to cooperate with a co-therapist and share clinical responsibility, the opportunity to study the style and performance of an experienced therapist without interfering with the privacy of the therapeutic relationship, immediate feedback and consultation for the student, and the intimate alliance that can be created between the supervisor and student as a result of working together as a team.

VULNERABILITY, AFFIRMATION AND ABILITY

Informality and a sense of respect for what the beginning student has to offer a therapeutic situation are encouraged. I have repeatedly observed how students and experienced therapists cannot be themselves and work to their full ability when they are anxious and uncomfortable. People must feel "at home" within a work setting if they are to act creatively to their full potential. It is equally important to acknowledge the student's inexperience and occasional incompetence, recognizing mistakes, oversights and conflicts as opportunities for learning. Tension, conflict, crisis, vulnerability, feelings of inadequacy, depression and anxiety are the subject matter of psychotherapeutic work. Without problems, there would be little need for therapy and the training of psychotherapists. The wise supervisor approaches conflicts and errors of judgment as opportunities for constructing learning experiences. This approach gives the student a feeling for and cognitive grasp of how psychotherapeutic transformation takes place. There is a natural rhythm to engaging a conflict, opening to it, discovering what it has to communicate and internalizing the experience into a better understanding of the self and the psychotherapeutic process. The overly guarded student cannot interact naturally and with maximum sensitivity to the client. Too much energy is placed on self-protection and fears of losing control and appearing inadequate. The opposite situation of over-identification with the client can be equally ineffective.

Continual respect and compassion for the limitations of the beginning therapist are highly recommended. Affirmation and the recognition of the various contributions that students make to the therapeutic process are essential. Affirmation of the student must be ongoing and at the forefront of the educational experience. I try to acknowledge the significance of the student's simply being present with the desire to learn and be of use to others. The presence of the student as an active participant in the therapeutic process is in itself a major contribution. We try to take little for granted. By affirming the importance of an open and attentive *presence* (and even through silence and inactivity), students can begin to feel that they have something to offer and that they have value within the therapeutic process. This attitude helps to minimize the tendencies of beginning therapists to *over-act* and push too much for immediate results. A primary objective for the beginning therapist is the acquisition of a therapeutic consciousness which respects the need for timing, inaction, waiting and sensitive intervention. The most profound therapeutic transformations take place within an environment of trust and inspiration, established by the accepting and calm presence of the mature therapist. Pushing for change and results tends to create resistance and emotional rigidity.

Cooperative work with an experienced therapist can offer guidance on how to take risks and act decisively when necessary. This is particularly true with groups of children and aggressive adolescents where a primary element of the therapeutic process is limit setting and group cooperation. There is probably no greater challenge to the beginning therapist than a group of aggressive children. Therapy cannot begin until order and cooperation are established. Working toward these objectives, and the struggles along the way, are often the basic therapeutic processes with children's groups. The presence of an experienced therapist is extremely useful within emotionally volatile groups. Beginning therapists realize that what is necessary is the ability to project an image of control and an understanding of what is going on to the children. If the therapist is confused, frightened, inconsistent and unsure of how to proceed, chaos will most likely occur.

At some point during training, the student needs to be given complete responsibility for the therapeutic process. Supervisors vary on when this autonomy is to be encouraged. Some programs will start students off immediately with primary clinical positions, while others will proceed more gradually. These determinations may also be made in response to the ability of individual students, who can be given different degrees of responsibility in relation to their capabilities. University supervisors typically take the level of student skill into consideration when selecting appropriate field placements. I do not wish to suggest that there are different levels of clinical populations or training sites. Every population has its depths, challenges and learning opportunities. Distinctions can, however, be made between settings in terms of the specific demands that they will place on students. Aggressive and volatile clients require quick and decisive emotional reflexes and judgments. Less responsive clients will require different skills, such as patience and the ability to work seriously with the most rudimentary behaviors.

THE ORGANIZATION

In helping students to become engaged with appropriate clinical sites and individual clients, supervisors take on dual responsibilities to students and the clinical program and serve as advocates for quality standards in both training and clinical service. Supervisors are often essential in helping students understand the administrative functions and staff relationships in clinics which are sometimes perceived by new students as obstacles to the therapeutic process. Supervision and clinical training frequently give considerable attention to the complex psychodynamics of institutions.

Students often have strong personal reactions to the organization and staff relationships and find it to be a challenge to work through their feelings toward how things are done within the clinic. The beginning student is typically idealistic in contrast to the more weathered attitudes of certain staff. As with the supervision of the student's clinical work, supervision of the ability to work within an organizational context focuses on problem areas, attempting to define the nature of the student's conflict and use the situation as an opportunity for learning. Conflicts between students and staff are often more pronounced because they are easily articulated by both parties, because the bonds of intimacy and personal responsibility are not as strong as they are between students and clients, and perhaps because there are a number of competitive and territorial emotions involved. Negative attitudes are more easily projected onto staff and onto the organization than onto the client, who is the focal point for the student's therapeutic energy. There is often a resentment and anger aroused by the fact that the organization consumes so much energy that could otherwise be directed toward clients.

However, students are typically not as empathetic with the problems of staff and administration as they are with clients. Consideration of the total dynamic of the clinical organization will benefit the supervision process. The student is not working in isolation with clients but is part of a cooperative community effort. Students sometimes find themselves in crisis in response to the general values of the clinic. For example, the heavy use of medications, electro-shock therapy, strict behavior management systems, rigid staff hierarchies, and other features of certain clinical environments can provoke strong feelings in students. Others may find the liberal and permissive values of a particular clinic difficult to accept. As with crises in relationships with clients, the supervisor can be useful in helping students to objectify the situation and plan a strategy with regard to the problems. If a student is to work within the organization, it can be said that there has to be some degree of acceptance of the way in which things are done. The organization must make an effort to give serious consideration to student criticisms. If the student chooses to work within an organization whose values are not totally accepted, then care is to be given not to mix these issues with client relationships. It is highly recommended that clinical training sites undergo constant self-evaluation and provide student interns with the opportunity to assess the quality of their training within a formal system of feedback. University supervisors should also maintain detailed files of student evaluations of clinical trianing sites so that future students will have comprehensive data to use in making their decisions about clinical placements.

It is recommended that institutions of higher education give students the opportunity to choose clinical placements and that the same choice be given to the clinic. This mutual-choice principle corresponds to the realities of the professional world and gives the student the opportunity to go through the various stages that will be encountered in seeking employment after completing the training program. In the event that there are serious conflicts between the student and the training site, it helps in the resolution of the situation if both parties have freely selected one another. The arbitrary assignment of students to placements can be an administrative convenience to the student, the clinic and the academic institution, in that the uncertainties and time spent in the selection of sites are largely avoided. However, vital professional learning opportunities are also missed and the basis of free choice does not exist. It can be argued that university supervisors know better than students as to which site they are best suited and that students will often *choose* certain sites out of insecurity and a variety of other misconceptions. Close and careful supervision can minimize the possible negative effects of the free-choice process. Supervisors and students can also use the various issues related to the choice of a placement as subject matter for learning.

The ideal training site engages the entire organization as a resource in the educational process. All aspects of the environment contribute to deepening the student's understanding of the therapeutic process. The best training sites encourage autonomy rather than dependency in students, assisting them in creating a personal style of doing therapy as opposed to operating within dogmatic methods adopted by the organization. Experimentation is valued together with self-evaluation and the ongoing transformation of programs in order to most effectively meet client needs. Students are highly regarded and given the impression that they have something important to offer to the clinical program and that their recommendations will be carefully considered. Creativity is encouraged and the organization perceives itself as establishing a cooperative interdependence between its parts. Multi-disciplinary sharing is stressed rather than separation. Staff from different disciplines make themselves available to students with the goal of providing a comprehensive educational experience.

The excellent clinical organization, even though it may employ many experienced staff and have a distinguished history of training, approaches every new problem with attitudes of openness, flexibility, an eagerness to learn and a conviction that members of the staff are most effective when there is a pervasive atmosphere of mutual support. Administrators and leaders are particularly open to the contributions of students and staff and convey the feeling that they are there to help and provide support. The outstanding training site inspires students with high standards and its collective clinical performance. The actions of the organization correspond to the core elements of training presented as goals to the student. The organization as a whole demonstrates how to engage conflict and transform it into affirmations of life; problems are perceived as opportunities for learning; openness and compassion are consistently maintained; the purpose of the organization is to give and be of use to others; innovation and change are encouraged when necessary to meet new needs; intelligent reflection on the efficacy of services and the utilization of resources and constant self-evaluation are encouraged; organizational structures are not rigidly established but rather formed in relation to the individual and cooperative styles of staff; criticism is accepted and considered; variety and differences are recognized and encouraged within the staff and this respect for the individual gives the organization its collective identity; training is valued and perceived as an opportunity for continuing education within the organization as a whole; and all staff members are considered to be learners who transmit the value of continuous self-improvement to students.

It is recommended that training programs in the creative arts therapies be sensitive to the way in which environmental and organizational
dynamics affect the work of individual therapists. The future success of
the creative arts therapy profession will be largely dependent upon the
skills that the graduates of our training programs develop in this area.
The organization and its functional patterns are to be engaged as a clinical and artistic challenge. Rather than scorn, avoid or simply tolerate ineffective organizational structures, the creative arts therapist can take
the institutions on and transform them with the creative spirit that has
until now been focused more on the therapeutic treatment of individual
clients.

EVALUATION

Interpersonal, artistic and experiential learning experiences are primary components of the education of creative arts therapists. Informational learning is essential to training, but action and live process are the
principle elements of education. It is recommended that evaluation procedures be designed in a manner which provides the opportunity for the
assessment of interpersonal skills and interpersonal learning. Clinical
placements, university courses and relationships with faculty and peers
are laboratories for experiential learning. Cognitive reflection is
directed toward understanding actual experiences. Practical problems,
feelings of inadequacy and clinical challenges motivate students to
further their conceptual learning and extend informational resources.

Performance skills are best evaluated through expert observation.
Since personalities and individual values inevitably enter into the assessment of clinical skills, reliability is strengthened by cooperative faculty
evaluation of students.

Self-evaluation is an essential part of the assessment of interpersonal
skills. The student is ultimately the instrumentality for the implementation of change and improvement. Evaluation procedures validate the
learning process and provide the opportunity for becoming more conscious of performance. The experience of assessment is in itself an important learning activity. Evaluation is most effective when it combines
ongoing and informal assessment with periodic and more formal assessment procedures. The periodic ritual of evaluation encourages the student to prepare through extensive self-appraisal and reflection.

Objectives for the improvement of performance are established and both short-term and long-term assessments are made in relation to the student's complete educational history. The more varied and flexible the approach to evaluation is, the more capable it will be of assessing the complex interplay of skills needed for psychotherapeutic work.

The assessment process should be thorough and complete and avoid determinations based on limited data. Progress is more likely when agreement can be established between students and faculty, and when students can articulate evaluation objectives and outcomes while taking full responsibility for the learning process, with the faculty member serving as a guide and consultant. This approach to assessment gives power, control and accountability to the student. Evaluation sessions strive for clarity and precision in assessment. Specificity is desirable when describing what is observed and how we are affected by these observations. It is common, especially with groups inexperienced with this type of communication, for people to be unable to clearly articulate their feelings and perceptions. It is therefore necessary to create a patient atmosphere encouraging students to restate their observations and feelings in order to eliminate misconceptions. When communication becomes misunderstood and is expressed inaccurately, emotional confusion results and it is difficult to go further in the relationship. Teachers and supervisors can set an example for clinical thoroughness in striving to reach the point where communication is clear. The process of evaluation ideally serves as a model clinical learning experience for the student which is applied to work with clients. Assessment should be comprehensive and involve the review of clinical performance, theoretical understanding, self-awareness and feelings of competence.

Educational programs which do not offer personalized evaluation opportunities for students are overlooking a core element of the clinical learning process. The primary skills of the psychotherapist, and particularly the creative arts therapist, have to do with performance and interpersonal competency. Both practicum supervision and university-based learning experiences are most effective when they are direct, personal and in correspondence with the spirit of the psychotherapeutic experience. It is recommended that clear distinctions be made between the assessment of different competencies. Areas of strength can be contrasted to weaknesses. It is important for students and faculty to realize that problems in a particular area will not necessarily impact negatively on a total performance evaluation.

Evaluation sessions are most effective when they are conducted with pervasive attitudes of support. Successful assessment procedures help to clarify problems with performance while increasing self-confidence and the ability to correct weaknesses. Affirmation and the documentation of strengths are vital to educational achievement. Although educational programs operate with the goal of achieving generally recognized standards of excellence, the uniqueness of the individual student is important to emphasize within the assessment process. Students need to internalize goals and standards of proficiency, rather than perceive them as separate from their personal behavior.

It is recommended that peer evaluation play a primary role in the education of the creative arts therapist. Within the context of clinical practice, students who are working together become involved in what can be described as a cooperative educational experience. The extent to which they can communicate openly with one another, offering support and criticism, will provide a model for team cooperation, vitally necessary in the mental health field. Peer evaluation tends to be ongoing and an integral part of group process in all aspects of the training experience, from supervision to experiential learning situations. The faculty member is often an experienced guide who assists the students in their communications with one another. Developing the ability to give clear and useful feedback to peers is one of the core elements of the training experience. Equally important (and often more difficult) is the development of the ability to receive feedback from others.

Cooperative Assessment of Experiential Learning (CAEL) is an educational association which has produced extensive publications and research activities on the subject of assessing experiential and interpersonal learning. CAEL emphasizes the need for developing competence in "basic interpersonal literacy" which involves "knowing when (a) and how (b) to communicate what (c) to whom (d) in order to achieve specified goals (e)" (Breen, Donlon and Whitaker, 1977, p. 8).

CAEL research projects have developed comprehensive strategies for evaluating both verbal and non-verbal communication. The timing, content, focus and medium of expression are considered as part of the evaluation process. These approaches to interpersonal learning can be of assistance to creative arts therapy programs desiring to become more conscious and deliberate in articulating assessment practices.

CAEL guidelines place emphasis on the improvement of performance. Attention is given to the intent of communication and to becoming aware of objectives in relation to personal feelings. "The person who is interpersonally literate will be able to use communications skills to maximize the attainment of goals that are congruent with his own and other's feelings, actions, and interpretations and be able to recognize when they are not congruent" (Ibid., p. 8).

Guidelines for interpersonal assessment developed by CAEL stress the importance of direct observation of performance; flexibility; self-evaluation; the use of as many raters as possible to avoid bias; expert evaluation; student-centered approaches; minimizing undue stress and anxiety; multiple-assessment procedures designed for consistency and the elimination of chance evaluation; a dynamic, open and supportive atmosphere that allows evaluation to be a major component of learning and self-improvement; intelligent and comprehensive evaluation systems which engage the total range of interpersonal skills, both verbal and non-verbal, and the complexities of their interdependence within professional practice. The development of student and program assessment practices, if carried out in an open way, provide the creative arts therapy profession with the opportunity to give definition to the field. Interpersonal assessments including faculty evaluations of students, student peer evaluations, student evaluations of faculty and programs, faculty peer evaluations, administrative and faculty evaluations of educational programs and clinical training sites, etc., can be perceived as vital research and professional development activities within the creative arts therapies. The scope of evaluation in this respect extends beyond the individual student to the profession as a whole.

Within the context of evaluation, documentation and careful record keeping are essential. Programs should be involved in ongoing self-study and planning. Short-term and long-term evaluations are necessary to ensure excellence in performance. University evaluation procedures and reviews by professional associations should be directed toward assisting programs in careful self-evaluation and documentation. As with the evaluation of individual students, assessment procedures should relate to the unique identities of programs rather than force them to fit into arbitrary external standards which lack flexibility and the encouragement of differences in style. Standardization must be minimized if excellence, innovation and creativity are to prosper. Agreed upon *standards of excellence* are not necessarily served by standard procedures and content. The emergence of the particular personality of the training program is to be supported as a primary objective within professional education. These values are in turn projected to students and the profession as a whole. Standardized education produces standardized professional practice. All of the objectives listed for the evaluation of individual students can be applied to programs — flexibility, the avoidance of bias, ongoing self-evaluaton, program-centered approaches, the minimization of undue stress, support and affirmation, openness, comprehensive review, and varied forms of assessment. The same principles are to be applied to faculty evaluation.

Academic excellence demands constant and rigorous evaluation of all aspects of the educational experience. Problems begin to develop when there is an imbalance in assessment procedures and when certain aspects of the learning community are not subject to evaluation as, for example, when programs place heavy emphasis on the assessment of students but do not involve faculty, supervisors, the academic program, and clinical sites in comparable evaluation processes. It is also important for professional associations interested in evaluating academic programs to undergo ongoing self-evaluation and evaluation by the programs they are charged with assessing. The learning community in the creative arts therapy profession is all-inclusive, involving students, faculty, university administration, university support services, clinical sites and professional associations. If a successful interdependence is to be established, all sectors need to be involved incontinuing evaluation and mutual support.

MUTUALITY

Evaluation of clinical work and the assessment of interpersonal competencies demands that programs construct a general atmoshpere in which criticism is valued and acted upon. As I have stated, evaluation must be mutual if this environment is to be created. My years of experience in higher education have revealed that the effective giving and taking of criticism is a formidable challenge for faculty, supervisors and students. People are often afraid to give criticism because they fear the consequences. They fear hurting others, and in many cases faculty and students fear that their personal weaknesses will be revealed when they confront others. Inexperienced faculty are not always secure in their critical abilities and sometimes doubt their mastery of the interpersonal skills that they are assessing in students. For example, the faculty member who is not a skillful listener might be confronted by a student who is being evaluated in this area, and the same applies to other aspects of clinical and interpersonal sensitivity.

Psychotherapeutic education is without standardized and objective criteria for evaluation when it comes to the most challenging areas of interpersonal competence. Evaluators inevitably project their values and personal perspectives into the assessment process and must be prepared to deal openly with ambiguity and conflict that may result within the assessment relationship. This aspect of the educational experience, perhaps more than any other, calls for experience and sophisticated interpersonal skills on the part of the faculty member or clinical supervisor.

Those who give excessive effort to their self-protection and the justification of their personal point of view will encounter many problems in evaluating students. To be successful in evaluating others, the person making the assessment or offering criticism needs to genuinely show more concern for the well-being of the other than for defending, empowering or expressing the self. This emotional attitude is essential if an atmosphere of trust and cooperation is to be established, which is difficult for inexperienced and insecure evaluators to achieve.

When people involved in evaluation sense insecurity and a lack of complete concern for the well being of others, together with bias and a lack of mutuality, destructive emotions and communications enter the environment. These problems inevitably arise when the assessment process serves the needs of the evaluator more than the person being criticized.

A primary objective of the educational program must be the creation of a cooperative and positive attitude toward evaluation. Rigid standards will consistently work against this process because emphasis is placed more on the standard than the person. Flexibility and the assessment of the unique learning objectives of the individual are essential to a spirit of collective cooperation. Differences of opinion, interpersonal irritations and conflict are vital elements within every learning community. It is recommended that they be openly acknowledged and engaged as part of the learning experience. The evaluation process takes place spontaneously and on a continuous basis in every student and faculty member as a primary emotional need, serving the purose of self-assessment. If open communication is not encouraged, evaluation will take place nevertheless. It is recommended that the evaluation process be respected, recognized and formally integrated into the educational program.

I will now go into more detail on what I see as core elements of the training process. The elements that I will describe have emerged through my experience as fundamental and ongoing challenges. I have had struggles and failures as a teacher in not being adequately aware of the primary needs of students and the unique qualities of psychotherapeutic training in the creative arts therapies. The section that follows is personal, in that it has developed from my most significant learning experiences as a teacher and my attempts to become conscious of the core elements of the therapeutic process. This book would not be complete for me unless I attempt to reflect on the deeper psychodynamic elements of education in the creative arts therapies. In the following section, I will try to complement information about systems, programs and general professional practices presented in the previous chapters, with a description of the therapeutic learning process as it relates to art.

REFERENCES

Abroms, Gene: Supervision as metatherapy. In Kaslow, F.W. (Ed.): *Supervision, Consultation, and Staff Training in the Helping Professions*. San Francisco, Jossey-Bass, 1977.

Breen, Paul; Donlon, Thomas; and Whitaker, Urban: *Teaching and Assessing Interpersonal Competence—A CAEL Handbook*. Washington, D.C., Cooperative Assessment of Experiential Learning, 1977.

Ekstein, Rudolf and Wallerstein, Robert: *The Teaching and Learning of Psychotherapy*. New York, International Universities Press, 1972.

Kaslow, F.W. (Ed.): *Supervision, Consultation, and Staff Training in the Helping Professions*. San Francisco, Jossey-Bass, 1972.

Knill, Paolo: *Medien in Therapie und Ausbildung*. Suderburg, BRD, Ohlsen-Verlag, 1983.

Knill, Paolo: Private conversation. Cambridge, Massachusetts, 1984.

Lucio, William (Ed.): *Supervision: Perspectives and Propositions*. Washington, D.C., Association for Supervision and Curriculum Development, 1967.

McNiff, Shaun: Video art therapy. *Arts Psychotherapy, 2*:1, 55-63, 1975.

McNiff, Shaun: Video Enactment in the Expressive Therapies. In Fryrear, Jerry and Fleshman, Bob (Eds.): *Videotherapy in Mental Health*. Springfield, Illinois, Thomas, 1980.

Neal, C., Kraft, L., and Kracht, C.: Reasons for college supervision of the student-teaching program. In Johnson, J., and Perry, F. (Eds.): *The Supervision of Clinical Experiences in Teacher Education*. Dubuque, Iowa, Kendall-Hunt, 1974.

Oneida Community: *Mutual Criticism*. (Introduction by Levine, Murray and Bunker, Barbara) Syracuse, N.Y., Syracuse U Pr, 1975.

Wilson, L., Riley, S., and Wadeson, H.: Art therapy supervision. *Art Therapy, 1*:3, 100-105, 1984.

Wilson, Laurie: The beginning phase of supervision in art therapy. *Art Therapy, 1*:3, 100-102, 1984.

8. AN ARTISTIC THEORY OF MENTAL HEALTH AND THERAPY

THERAPY AS ART

EDUCATION in the creative arts therapies can make an important contribution to more general psychotherapeutic education by applying principles of artistic training to clinical practice. Therapy can be considered as a performing art, the efficacy of which is determined by the skill of individual and team performance. It is assumed that competent artists have an empathy with others and an understanding of the emotions which are reflected in their expressions. Without this sensitivity and artistic intelligence, the artwork would have little appeal. The history of the arts demonstrates how artists go deeply into themselves in order to reach others. The process of therapy, which deals with the intricacies and problems of the human spirit, is one of the most challenging forms of art. In ancient times, and within indigenous cultures, there were few distinctions between sacred, artistic and healing actions. Education in the creative arts therapies, because of its use of ritual, imagery and all forms of dramatic enactment and sensory expression, has a unique potential to restore this lost unity.

The art of the therapist is characterized by the ability to respond personally, and with depth, to each person and situation. All of the therapist's resources, and those that can be engaged within the environment, are channeled to the person in need of help. One of the primary skills of the therapist involves adjusting focus from person to person and from situation to situation. Whatever is before the therapist becomes the focal point of complete concentration. These clinical skills closely parallel the dynamics of art.

Artists tend to be acutely aware of the contributions of science which they incorporate into their work. Art by definition can be perceived as an integrating activity which makes use of the range of materials offered by a particular context. The artistic consciousness is concerned with the style of expression, sensitivity, timing and the general heightening of experience. The power of art to heighten and focus consciousness through varied forms of communication suggests many possibilities for a cooperative relationship between *artistic* and *clinical* skills.

Both the artist and the clinician are concerned with understanding of the self and others, observing environments, emotional transformation and the creation of new relationships. Artists are trained to express emotion with quality and to cultivate their sensory awareness. The same skills are demanded of the therapist but are not adequately addressed in most training programs. The artistic consciousness and artistic methods of training, when applied to therapy, can help students to develop the core competencies needed in clinical work. Major advances in psychology and psychiatry have been made by people with highly developed creative sensibilities who have extended the boundaries of conventional thought and practice. However, the primary relationship of the artistic process to psychological thinking and psychotherapy has not been adequately investigated. Even the creative arts therapies tend to base training methods on conventional psychological concepts. Ultimately, the value of both psychological thought and clinical practice is determined by the artistry of the people involved. The psychotherapist can be perceived as an artist, working creatively with the varieties of the human spirit.

There is no evidence to indicate that one particular professional orientation to therapy or approach to training will be more effective than others in the education of psychotherapists. Most teachers recognize that the gifted therapist works with innate abilities and perfects skills though experience and supervision. The same applies to the training of artists. Psychotherapy is not an exact science, yet training programs are typically identified with these approaches to human understanding rather than with the systematic improvement of interpersonal skills and creative performance.

Before the artistic process can be fully integrated with psychotherapy, misconceptions about the basic nature of art and artists must be corrected. Art will be forever kept off to the side, together with creative arts therapists, unless the artistic process is conceptualized as a fundamental element of life for all people in all cultures. The creation of the self, relationships, families, communities, environments and organizations, together with the perfection of skills, style, expressive abilities, emotional sensitivities, and critical judgment, can be perceived as part of the artistic process. The expansion of the artistic consciousness is particularly relevant to contemporary culture because of the need for integration within all aspects of society. Through art objects, people and situations are placed into new relationships with one another. Human beings long for art in their daily environments and instinctively act according to the principles of the artistic process in the most commonplace activities. Art is elevated and the concentration of its power is heightened through discipline and commitment. Those to whom we refer as *artists* are people who have consciously dedicated their lives to this discipline. Their careers can be likened to a religious vocation. The life of art evokes the image of the blue flame, the most intense heat of transformations. Art, like religion and spiritual sensitivity, can consciously direct and permeate all action in the daily life of every person. The close relationship between religion and art throughout history attests to this mutuality. Art, like religion, creates value, serves as a means of transformation, intensifies commitment, heightens sensitivity and appreciation, encourages communication and catharsis, and generally sanctifies life. These are also primary objectives of psychotherapeutic change.

ART AS PSYCHOLOGICAL INQUIRY

In both the psychology of art and aesthetics, the process, concepts and conventions of the dominant discipline (psychology and philosophy) are applied to art. The creation of art is perceived as behavior to be studied, rather than as a philosophical or psychological process of inquiry. The language and established systems of psychology are in this way used to reflect upon, analyze and describe the artistic process. Within the creative arts therapies, influential constructs have been created which follow conventional psychological theories: Freudian, Jungian, developmental, behavioral, etc. Psychopathological approaches to the analysis of art have had a major impact on the creative arts therapies, and especially art therapy, because of the way in which Freudian theory and pathologically oriented psychiatry have influenced the mental health field during the early and mid twentieth century. The psychiatric and medical dominance of the mental health profession is coming to an end and this is creating opportunities for re-thinking the basic elements of health, psychological inquiry and therapeutic transformation.

The creative arts therapies have for the most part adopted the language and conventions of psychology as vehicles for conceptualizing what the profession is. There have been notable exceptions, such as Nietzsche and Thoreau, who integrated artistic process with philosophy and psychological understanding. Their philosophies are expressed passionately and with poetic language, achieving an integration of artistic process with philosophical process. James Hillman has made similar contributions to psychology and speaks of "the poetic basis of mind." Theology can also be perceived as a poetic discipline. The great books of the world's religions are inspirational and poetic statements, rich with imagery, description, story-telling and the generally creative uses of language which are appropriate for the word of God.

Stephen Levine presents the ideal of the philosopher/artist who integrates imaginative and intellectual inquiry. This synthesis also applies to psychotherapy and psychology.

> Plato's banishment of poetry from the just city resulted in a banishment of art from the domain of philosophy. The philosophical tradition is primarily oriented either toward science or toward religion, and it is not until our own time that the presence of art begins to make itself felt in the domain of thought. I am not speaking here about the development of esthetics as a philosophical discipline; just such a development points out the distance between philosophy and art . . . philosophers have once again become poets. From Nietzsche to Heidegger, philosophical speech has no longer the transparency of mathematical statement nor the movement which takes place in proof. Rather, it is a matter of a speaking which has in it a depth and vibrancy that transcends the pure thought of science, and of a style of demonstration which is based upon imaginative connection rather than formal rules of procedure (Levine, 1969, pp. 438-439).

The integration of art and psychotherapy can be perceived as a pragmatic quality of clinical practice as suggested by the following six points:

1. Therapeutic effectiveness is determined by the manner in which personal actions influence others. Competence in this area can be evaluated in the same way that an actor's expressions engage an audience.

2. Art, theory and professional judgments are constructions. The

extent to which human creations influence others is dependent on quality, skill, style and sensitivity to what is needed within the particular context. The interpersonal, environmental and historical context is in constant flux, requiring imaginative adaptation. The artist acts in relation to context.

3. The archetype, or abiding essence, complements creative construction with continuity, providing the primal matter from which all personal transformations take shape. The creative transformation of stress is itself an archetype, the universality of which transcends contemporary systems of psychology.

4. Art still suffers from the "platonic" split whereby: "The imitator or maker of the image knows nothing of true existence, he knows appearance only" (Plato). A separation has been created which maintains that there is a hidden truth, or meaning, that lies concealed and beyond immediate action and perception. Art suggests the contrary: that appearance is a manifestation of essence and that true competence involves the ability to act within the material world. A philosophical system based purely on intellectual and rational analysis projects its incompletion onto the world. Classical western thought has separated art from the mainstream of academic inquiry. One form of reflection on existence has been promoted over another and philosophical and psychological inquiry have been limited by their modes of operation.

5. All of the primary modes of human expression and understanding are to be integrated into psychology and psychotherapy.

6. Art has not claimed health, psychological inquiry, learning, psychotherapy and other life studies as part of its sphere of influence and has been excluded for this reason. Responsibility for this situation does not lie with conventional psychology but is to be attributed to art for its lack of initiative and vision.

CREATING AN ARTISTIC PSYCHOLOGY

A rationale for the arts in psychotherapy can be established on the basis of artistic principles rather than by searching for justification solely within conventional psychological systems. However, it is of practical use to creative arts therapists to provide explanations of what they do that are intelligible to the more dominant clinical modes of thought within contemporary mental health systems. All points of view have their place within the creative process. Yet, in the interest of developing the full powers of the creative arts therapy profession, it is necessary to relate clinical practice to theories which correspond completely to the depth of the artistic process. A full integration with the historic continuities of artistic thought will enable the arts in psychotherapy to realize their potential as primary modes of healing which can transform the mental health field. If the arts in therapy are exclusively perceived in relation to conventional clinical thought and procedures, they will remain on the periphery of health systems as adjunctive therapeutic modalities. Within training programs for creative arts therapists, much more attention needs to be given to theoretical principles which emerge directly from the artistic process.

Art has historically opened itself to the varieties of human experience with all methods and personal points of view being considered by the artist who tends to be keenly aware of the concerns and discoveries of psychologists. The creation of a major psychological system corresponds to the inner working of the artistic process. Influential psychologists then inspire the creative work of others.

> Each psychology is a confession and the worth of a psychology for another person lies not in the places where he can identify with it because it satisfies his psychic needs, but where it provokes him to work out his own psychology in response. Freud and Jung are psychological masters, not that we may follow them in becoming Freudian and Jungian, but that we may follow them in becoming psychological. Here psychology is conceived as a necessary activity of the psyche, which constructs vessels and breaks them in order to deepen and intensify experience (Hillman, 1977, p. xii).

If psychology is defined as the search for the truths and continuities of human nature, in their many forms, then it is artistic inquiry which has consistently undertaken this task throughout the centuries, never abandoning the desire to grasp the source of motivations, perceptions, dreams, expressions, contradictions, illusions, injustices and achievements. Psychological thought has become over-identified with fitting experience into established systems and formulations, rather than with the creative process of being psychological in observing experience, and expressing what is perceived in forms that are best suited to the intent of the message. The artistic consciousness respects variety and differences and strives to "save the diversity and autonomy of the psyche from domination by any single power" (Ibid., p. 32).

Formal psychology and art deal with the same principles of human behavior but often from different vantage points. Eugene O'Neill, irritated by the suggestion that his plays were adaptations from Freudian themes, spoke of how authors were psychlogists, and profound ones, before psychology existed. Literary ambition is manifested by the great psychologists — Freud, Jung, Rank, James. Hillman cites how Freud said of himself, "A man of letters by instinct, though a doctor by necessity, I conceived the idea of changing over a branch of medicine — psychiatry — into literature. Though I have the appearance of a scientist I was and am a poet and novelist. Psychoanalysis is no more than an interpretation of a literary vocation in terms of psychology and pathology" (Papini, 1934). Freud acknowledges the way in which his work corresponds to the process and forms of art, but these essential elements of his creativity are overlooked by the conventions of medicine and psychiatry. The work of the most influential psychologists of the twentieth century is based on methods of literary research within the context of psychology and psychotherapy. Artistic and imaginative inquiry are always at the forefront of major advances in human understanding.

Artists are not only psychological in relation to understanding the people and situations that provide the subject matter of their work but also in terms of their expressive styles. The psychological sophistication of expressive style is what distinguishes great artists and psychologists. Master artists are capable of expressing themselves in forms which correspond to the deepest and most complex emotions. Because of these sensitivities and powers of communication, the artist as psychologist has offered many of the most important insights into the human condition which include what Melville said about human motivations and evil; O'Neill on guilt and family conflict; D.H. Lawrence and Anais Nin on passion and sexuality; Lawrence Durrell on the complexities of love; Edna O'Brien on relationships and loneliness; W.B. Yeats on symbols and myths; Puccini, Verdi and Franck on the sacred; the imagination of Dante; the prophecy and vision of Blake; the sensitivity of Dickinson; the perception of Joyce; the social consciousness of O'Casey; the dedication and love of the gospels; the transformation of Nietzsche; the ambition and desire of Faust; the scope of Shakespeare and Leonardo; the intensity of Strindberg; the humor of the storyteller in the street . . .

Psychological education, and especially the training of creative arts therapists, can benefit from more comprehensive studies of the varied forms of psychological thought. The arts in therapy profession is in a unique historical position to bring about the integration of art and psychology. In order to achieve this objective, equal attention is to be given to both traditions. What exists today is an imbalance in creative arts therapy psychological thought and research methodology. Students characteristically feel a split between their artistic and psychological identities. The same tends to be true of practicing creative arts therapists. Because of the dominance of conventional psychological thought within their training and places of work, they have not been introduced to theoretical constructs supporting the integration of artistic and clinical identities. A sense of cohesion can be achieved by perceiving all of psychotherapy as an artistic process utilizing varied conceptual and sensory materials. Classical art forms which include drama, storytelling and image making are involved with all forms of psychotherapy and can be amplified in relation to the needs and interests of both therapists and clients. Creative arts therapists will approach a more complete professional integration when they no longer feel that their art is something that they do outside of their clinical practice. We choose the work of the arts and psychotherapy because we desire a broader application of our creative and artistic process. If this integration is to take place, creative arts therapy training programs will have to take a leading role in helping students to discover deep personal affinities between their artistic and clinical activities. Courses of instruction that continuously separate art from psychology, and the student's creative expression from psychological reflection, will reinforce the separation which is established in conventional academic and clinical institutions.

James Hillman's psychology is based on the principle that the basic structures of life are revealed through imagery, religion, myth, ritual and the arts. This contrasts to the biochemical, behavioristic and psychopathological approaches to psychology that dominate much of contemporary mental health. Hillman believes that the image refers to nothing beyond itself and that it is a primary psychic structure. He speaks of "the driving necessity in the arts, for they provide complicated disciplines that can actualize the complex virtuality of the image" (Hillman, 1983, p. 10). In keeping with the belief that the creative functions of mind are poetic, he maintains that "the method of therapy is the cultivation of imagination" (Ibid, p. 4).

IMAGINATION AND PSYCHOSIS

Psychotherapy is an imaginative art. Clinical work with imagination and imagery demands an understanding of culture, history, aesthetics, mythology and symbolism, together with an awareness of cross-cultural and universal patterns. This is necessary because myth patterns pervade daily life. Contemporary psychology with its quantitative bias is without an artistic or poetic base.

Art is not a specific product but rather a process that includes all of the senses and imagination. The specific product may be referred to as an "artwork." Art and creative transformation involve the emergence of imagery and expression with the guidance of consciousness. This definition of art can be similarly applied to the psychotherapeutic process. Imagination can take both life-threatening and life-affirming forms. Within psychosis and severe conditions of inner stress, the imagination turns against itself. The psychotherapeutic process can be perceived as a redirecting of the transformative powers of imagination and image making. Rather than creating illness and anxiety, imagination is directed toward life-affirming actions.

In *The Genealogy of Morals*, Nietzsche describes the instinct for expression and creativity that can be considered as the most basic motive for art.

> Every animal, including *la bête philosophe*, strives instinctively after an *optimum* of favorable conditions, under which he can let his whole strength have play, and achieves his maximum consciousness of power; with equal instinctiveness, and with a fine perceptive flair which is superior to any reason, every animal shudders mortally at every kind of disturbance and hindrance which obstructs or could obstruct his way to that *optimum* (it is not his way to happiness of which I am talking, but his way to power, to action, the most powerful action, and in point of fact in many cases his way to unhappiness) (Nietzsche).

Illness is often an expression of choice and personal creation. I have explored this issue with colleagues in different parts of the world. Eckhard Krause, a West German psychiatrist with special skills in psychosomatic medicine, told me that when he first meets a person at his clinic he asks, "What is the advantage of this illness to you" (Krause, 1983)? He then engages the person in trying to determine what can be done so that life without illness is more attractive. Therapy is an exploration of possibilities for helping imagination to grow stronger. Doctor Krause believes that every physical illness has a psychological background and can be treated most effectively in terms of what he calls "the body-soul union" (*leib seele einheit*) which to him is the basis of health.

Doctor Krause and I worked on the problem of talented people who are preoccupied with fears. We explored how to help people who express a desire to escape from the control of fears and negative thoughts, but who nevertheless persist in having life structured by them. Fears and obstructions to creativity become habitual over time and direct the course of a person's life. Power is projected onto obstructive elements and a source of control outside the self. The person does not want to accept inner choice and control. Fears become a form of protection from responsibility and the acceptance of the consequences of action.

All too often, according to Nietzsche, we have an "evil eye" for "natural inclinations" so they have become transformed into fears. People oppress themselves with guilt because their natural inclinations to freely express anger, rage, sensuality and intimacy are blocked and they turn these feelings inward against themselves. Psychosis and sickness result from the destructive internalization of the passions and desires of the soul. Unable to find fulfillment, the will to power and freedom is reversed and the energy is turned against the self. Sartre would insist that this self-torment is always a matter of choice. If we cannot fully express our power in the external world, we express it within ourselves. Sickness, self-destruction and self-torment are manifestations of personal power turned against the self.

Sartre believed that there are no controlling forces outside the self. He called those who hide from their complete freedom *cowards*. "There are no accidents in a life . . . . For lack of getting out of it I have *chosen* it" (Sartre, 1977, p. 64). Each of us creates life. We are not simply shaped by events. Every form of life is a core element of the creative process. Self-torment and sickness are just as much our creations as the successes and affirmations of life that are commonly associated with art. The psychology of creativity can engage every element of life, perceiving everything as opportunity. The tradition of creativity emphasizes action and imagination; it is the opposite of psychological and biological determinism. Health can be best realized through association with creativity and assertive actions of the imagination, striving for optimum personal power. This perspective also places responsibility on the individual for opportunities missed and for the creation of the unpleasant dimensions of personal life. Imagination is a powerful psychological process that can either radically improve the quality of life with bursts of insight, humor and new possibilities for action or it can turn the human instinct for creation against the self. Psychosis is a condition in which imagination expresses its creative power through self-torment, provoked by guilt, fear and alienation.

After years of working with people referred to as "severely emotionally disturbed" and "psychotic," I grew increasingly convinced from my relationships with them that their mental conditions and ways of interacting with others were largely volitional. I would repeatedly observe how they moved from emotional confusion to clarity through acts of choice. When I asked people with whom I had a close relationship to speak in a manner that I could understand, they would often stop their flow of random associations and communicate with focus. They had learned how to use their withdrawal and bizarre behaviors as ways of empowering themselves over others, as protection, as an avoidance, and as a means to either attract people or frighten them away. Our "health" institutions generally approach the person in ways which place little emphasis on the creative faculties of the human spirit. We expect little from the sick and place them within environments which leave few opportunities for engaging the maximum powers of the imagination. We also do not perceive the sick person as the creator of the illness. Causality is attributed to chemical or environmental elements and difficulties, perceived by the sick person as determinants which are not within their control.

The more we make a mystery of the causes of illness and fears and attribute them to sources over which we have no control, the more the imagination loses its healing power. When we are confident and clear thinking in taking responsibility for the creation of what afflicts us, only then can we fully engage powers of imagination in controlling thoughts, emotions and bodily functions.

Deterministic psychology has decreased our sense of responsibility for ourselves and our awareness of life as creation. External causes, the past and a host of other elements have been blamed for our difficulties. Thomas Aquinas in *Summa Theologica* suggests the eternal nature of the debate between free will and determinism when he addressed the question as to "whether there is anything voluntary in human acts." In support of free will he cites scripture, "God made man from the beginning, and left him in the hand of his own counsel . . . That is, in the liberty of choice" (Ecclus. xv, 14). The idea of God as Creator in so many of the religions of the world is in itself an acknowledgment of life as creation.

In describing the divine, humans use the most sacred element and the greatest power that they possess (i.e. creativity) and project it onto the deity.

Aquinas, in keeping with the classical tradition of the West, presented intellectual judgment as the force of the will. He believed that choices based on deliberation are higher than those resulting from natural instinct. Judgments of reason are valued more than the instinctual desires of the "lower appetites." With Aquinas we can see how morality and decisions between "higher and lower" begin to suppress primary passions and, as Nietzsche said, attribute evil qualities to our most human and life-enhancing instincts. Although Aquinas and Nietzsche might agree on the primacy of will, Nietzsche would say that the hierarchical split between reason and instinct is the fundamental illness of humanity. Suppressed and devalued, the animal instincts turn against people. Nietzsche's will is one of spontaneity, action and imagination. It is not less intelligent, but perhaps more so, because mind and passionate instinct are not separated. Desire and knowledge work together through a disciplined, yet liberated consciousness.

CONTAGION

Healthy people are contagious and imagination is stimulated by the actions of others. Qualities perceived in other people can significantly influence a person's life. The word *contagion* is associated with illness in western medicine where sickness is the focus of health care. Power is thus given to sickness and its contagion. Concentration on problems and illnesses strengthens that which a person may wish to let go. Negative obsession is an inner wind to destructive fire in both therapy and training.

Emphasis on a particular emotion results in the creation of corresponding conditions. Such is the power of imagination in creating reality. The therapist provokes contagious reactions which restore the creative power within the self, a contagious person who offers an example of a creative and spontaneous life, realizing personal power with sensitivity to others. The therapist not only prescribes but *inspires*. The artistic impulse is transmitted from person to person through inspiration. "It is the creative, and this alone, that kindles the creative in the other . . . " (Hillman, 1978, p. 77).

A student asked me, "How does this process of contagion work?" I said that it involves an exchange of energy. The healthy person provides an image of health to the other as opposed to an image of illness. The therapeutic relationship is based on empathy and internalizing the energy of the other. The sick receive help from therapists, who accept their sickness and allow it to pass through them. Therapists function in dual roles, taking in the problems of others while simultaneously giving strength through inspiration and support. Successful therapists and artists establish ways of working which allow them to increase their powers through difficult life situations, inspiring others through example. The same applies to educators who inspire contagious reactions in their students. Successful therapists find ways to receive energy and strength from pathology and conflict.

In therapy, efficacy is largely determined by the abililty of the person to inspire action and transformation in others. The *best* teacher is the one who most thoroughly affirms and clarifies beliefs and who inspires the refinement of innate abilities. Education is a process of demonstration, example and inspiration. What is being *taught* is process itself, how to act in life to the full range of ability. Within the more advanced teacher-student relationship, the teacher is valued for critical and observational abilities together with the capacity to serve as a model.

PERSONAL FORM

A fundamental principle of art that can be applied to clinical training is the necessity of establishing a personal style, or form, which allows creative powers to emerge. It is assumed that artists will express themselves naturally and that their styles will be different. Within the arts, a person's style and expressive skills are the primary factors in determining the extent to which others are influenced. Training involves the emergence and refinement of innate powers. The accumulation of techniques, methods and ideas will not result in the creation of art which requires the individual psyche to give shape to materials. Personal discipline and extensive practice is a fundamental quality of artistic training. The convergence of art and mental health, brought about by the development of the creative arts therapies, is presenting the opportunity for a new advance in clinical training involving the synthesis of two closely related, yet previously separate, professions. The creation of a personal therapeutic style demonstrates how this synthesis can be achieved.

The artistic model of training, when applied to psychotherapy, suggests that there are core skills that every therapist must develop. These primary skills are then used to give shape to the unique style of the individual. Training programs often become so focused on the need to develop basic competencies that they overlook the complementary process of supporting the creation of personal form. The training *system* takes precedence over the individual and identity becomes associated with a particular systematic orientation. Efficacy studies similarly tend to give more attention to the effectiveness of systems than to the actual performance of the people who work within them.

CONCEPT

Theory provides a focus and channel for energy within the vastness of possibilities. Students are eager for theoretical explanations as a source of power and as a remedy to the confusion that characterizes the entry into a complex profession. Theory guides action and thought, eliminating confusion and strengthening self-confidence. Tangible answers are presented as alternatives to ambiguity, and within the theoretical framework everything seems to fit. The multiplicity of theories available to therapists and students today sometimes results in an environment of uncertainty and separation. When the teacher does not give students a single theoretical system to dispel confusion but suggests that they study all systems and make their own theory, the emphasis of learning is placed on creation rather than indoctrination.

The source of conceptual confusion is usually a lack of self-confidence, originating in the belief that the opinions of others have more value and truth than one's own. Theoretical certainty demands self-certainty which allows the person to interact with others, listening to different beliefs and opinions without losing or doubting the self.

In my work with training groups, I have discovered that I can never assume to know another person's psyche. The revelation of the thoughts of another is a process of constant discovery. Theoretical inquiry requires an ongoing openness to the nature of the thoughts and feelings of other people, and the self. As a teacher, I try to establish a theoretical *equality* with students, demonstrating the *interdependence* of our thoughts.

Concept formation is a creative process.

On the issue of training, the poet Vincent Ferrini said to me, "The simplest and most difficult thing is to walk in your own shoes" (Ferrini, 1983). My goal in training others, and myself in the process, is to provide us all with the self-confidence, skill and inspiration needed to work with personal resources in the manner which is most natural. The forms of our behavior do not have to be established by convention but can be created by ourselves. Professional style can be an extension of personal style. Training becomes a process of refining personal strengths into abilities that can be of use to others. The power of professional form is determined by the extent to which personal passion is integrated with work.

Walt Whitman urged artists to "Make the works" and stay clear of criticism and the academic analysis of art. He encouraged natural and passionate expression. Creative action in therapy and art loses power when based on derivations or "secondary sources." The training and performance of the therapist, as well as the artist, can be based on the primary sources of the self, interactions with others and the skillful engagement of archetypal principles. Many of the core elements of the therapeutic process are transpersonal or archetypal. They are not created by the individual and have an existence in their own right. The universals include rhythm, imagery, the dynamics of interpersonal relationships and other factors included in the "common elements" chapter of this book. Training itself can be perceived as an archetypal process. Like the artist, the therapists might work for years to develop a particular quality which ultimately becomes part of their repertoire during performance. Training never ends. The therapist, like the artist, is forever sharpening skills and sensitivities through the practice of the work.

Yeats described how the universal object of artistic inquiry is a common search for knowledge and life. He felt that if we understand our thoughts and what longs to be expressed through our consciousness, then we affect others by establishing a relationship with the primary elements of all life and creation which emanate from the same source.

THE ART OF TEACHING

It becomes quickly apparent to the advanced training group how inappropriate it is to respond to the deep feelings or pain of another with an analytic or judgmental statement. A woman in her sixties told me how she was discovering in her training how "to have the spirit rather than formulas." Action and technique flow naturally from empathetic and compassionate feeling. The therapeutic form will always emerge in response to the context and cannot be established in advance.

In the beginning of their training, virtually all students believe that their goal is to accumulate methods. This way of learning is contrary to the nature of art. In my training groups there are often differences between the sensitivities of participants. The more secure, self-confident and skillful person is attuned to *process* and the feelings of other people. Others are more focused on the self. Experience with training groups begins to reveal what works and what does not work in creating an environment that allows people to take risks and open themselves to learning. Advanced students describe how this type of environment is characterized by an *energy*, or collective feeling, that provokes introspection and expression. The teachers who they admire are capable of creating this energy within groups effortlessly, through attitudes of acceptance, empathy, an ability to understand and conceptualize situations and problems, the capacity to teach through example and an actual demonstration of the healing process, personal openness to transformation and learning, active participation in the therapeutic process, and, most importantly, total commitment to the principles and process that are being taught.

The teacher is tested through conflict and struggle. These are usually areas that students fear. If the teacher shows panic and an inability to understand, then the students do not receive the lesson and demonstration that they need. Conflict and disturbance are the subject matter of therapeutic work. The teacher's role is to show the student that problems can be sources of strength. Fear is not always a sign of weakness. It can be an important form of communication and caution. Fear becomes destructive when it immobilizes creativity.

In order to create a therapeutic learning atmosphere in a training group there must be confidence in the leader and the participants then internalize this confidence. An environment of trust and commitment stimulates and supports individual learning. The skillful teacher does not *push* students but rather inspires them to take risks and challenge themselves. Teachers who push are often expressing their personal insecurity, their needs for immediate results and their inability to create a context for learning where students are highly motivated to work. On the other extreme, some teachers find it difficult to confront a situation directly and forcefully, to give specific and strong feedback to students and provide a clear sense of purpose. These difficulties are often an expression of insecurity and a lack of confidence on the teacher's part. There is an art to expressing criticism and providing specific learning objectives with attitudes of compassion and a sincere commitment to the student.

My experience in the professional education of creative arts therapists has revealed that students are constantly in need of both personal affirmation and critical feedback from teachers that they respect. An educational relationship which emphasizes only one of these elements will generally produce conflict. I have also observed that students do not seek out criticism from teachers who they do not respect. Strengths need to be identified and supported, while weaknesses are similarly in need of attention. Experienced educators are aware of the fact that strengths are often closely associated with weaknesses and vice versa. For example, the attentive listener/observer might have difficulties with assertive expression; the self-confident and verbally competent person may find it difficult to listen for sustained periods of time; and the accepting, tolerant and patient student may find critical evaluation to be a formidable task.

A sense of affirmation is transmitted by teachers who convey total commitment to their students. The affirming teacher encourages students to articulate their feelings and observations about the learning process and to participate in dialogue in which the student's perceptions are given serious consideration. A relationship is created in which both student and teacher open themselves to taking risks, expressing uncertainty and requesting help. Relationships of this kind differ from those where excessive energy is given to self-protection. Affirmation is particularly necessary during periods of self-doubt when students lose their confidence and sense of personal value. In these situations the teacher can help students to realize that resistance and depression may be signs that they are drawing close to major discoveries and changes which are upsetting the former balance of their lives. As faculty members, we consistently find ourselves encountering similar situations which can be shared with students and peers rather than concealed.

The *critique* is of primary importance within the classical tradition of educating artists. Teachers are valued for their ability to bring attention to flaws in performance and expression. Critical evaluation is equally essential to the education of creative arts therapists. The skillful teacher knows how to maximize the impact of affirmation and criticism through proper timing and communication. As with the classical training of professional artists, creative arts therapy students learn how to participate in the process of critically evaluating their peers. Education is as much concerned with learning how to give criticism and support as it is with learning how to receive feedback.

Influential teachers often reverse students' perceptions and help them to look at experience from a different perspective. The reversal of conceptual orientation attracts a person's attention. Cognitive reversal is a primary element of the creative process, since it is often the key to problem solving. Resolutions are often contrary to what people take for granted and it can be said that the more accepted an idea is, the more it lends itself to reversal. What we need is not always found in what we think we need. As Heraclitus said, "The opposite is beneficial . . . . what is opposed in helpful."

In psychotherapy training the most profound learning involves the reversal of primary instincts and habitual behaviors. Students who are rigidly contained in a particular position find dialogue with the opposite difficult. They may need a combination of support and confrontation in order to open themselves to creative dialogue.

EMPOWERMENT AND SELF-CONFIDENCE

Effective performance in the creative arts therapies is dependent upon the ability to focus personal resources on a particular purpose. In training psychotherapists and in clinical work, loss of power is commonly due to a lack of self-confidence. Repeatedly, I have seen talented people crippled by self-doubt and the loss of faith in their ability to achieve objectives. Competent people maintain a belief in themselves through times of stress and alienation. They persist through conflict and struggle and become stronger by learning more about their vulnerable areas and how to use the energy of conflict to their advantage. The full realization of personal power demands the taking of risks and an openness to the full range of emotions.

In the pursuit of competence, mistakes and the loss of balance are inevitable. The skilled artist often perceives "errors" as deviations which suggest a better resolution. If a rigid balance is maintained by a person fearful of failure, there will be no growth and an absence of opportunities for the expansion of the limits of consciousness.

Concentration, discipline, persistence, an openness to all feelings and the ability to use all of one's personal resources are key elements of power. Other factors include adaptability; the ability to transform and reverse the energy of pain and conflict and direct it toward objects of desire; the cultivation of the creative consciousness; and the ability to avoid wasting energy on excessive restraints, fears, negative thoughts and self-protective attitudes which limit possibilities. Creative people are always taking themselves beyond conventional boundaries while respecting human limits. Faith in personal power does not have to mean defiance of the principles of nature and blind self-confidence. The powerful person has learned how to live in relation to the rhythms of nature and properly direct energy. Power is ultimately a spiritual and creative discipline involving the cooperative interplay of inner and outer forces in a single course of action.

A student told me that the strongest substances in nature are flexible; they give under pressure and allow for the influence of other forces acting upon them. Rigid forms crack under stress and do not support interaction with other elements. Flexibility and adaptability are primary ingredients of power. The adaptable person is responsive to the influence of external forces but maintains a consistent inner core of being. The combination of sustained clarity of purpose together with adaptability enables people to use whatever is most available and suited to their objectives.

Inner flexibility does not have to result in confusion. The confused person does not have a consistent and positive sense of self and a belief in the powers of creative consciousness. Confusion typically comes from living by contradictory standards. For example, a student once told me that he was confused by the multiplicity of psychological theories that he came into contact with. Each theory presented a different answer to a particular problem. Confusion was replaced by clarity when he began to believe in the value of his personal experience and his ability to create his own theories, concepts and explanations of behavior. In coming to personal resolutions he was able to consult with the various theories to strengthen, expand and confirm his opinions. He did not fear being consumed by each point of view. His value giving power remained constant, allowing him to freely enter into relationships with many other theories without losing himself in the process. Theoretical integration has to come from the core of a person's being and relate directly to experience.

The confused person has lost the power to give value and tends to simply follow the opinions of others, maintaining a dependence on external sources for direction. Nietzsche, the greatly misunderstood philosopher of power, believed that strength lies in the ability to give value to experience. Values are themselves creations which, when distanced from their origins, become rigid convention.

Education is a process of *empowerment*. Rather than simply incorporating the creations of others, learning is itself a creative process. An objective of the student of therapy and art is the discovery of a personal vision which serves as a vehicle of empowerment. The ancient history of the power search of healers engages the initiate in the private vision quest. Each must find the personal way to archetypal elements of power. Action thus proceeds from the personal source of creativity and in a manner which is true to the emotions. When students strive to act according to a way of being that is not their own, action will be less spontaneous and always derivative. Actors who perform according to scripts and therapists who work within prescribed systems must somehow make the established procedures their own if they are to act forcefully and creatively in their roles. Interestingly enough, the archetypal and universal forms of the artistic and therapeutic process are engaged through the particulars of personal experience. Art demonstrates how a sense of well-being is achieved through aesthetic appreciation of the particular forms of everyday life.

Many never realize their potential competence because they do not discover how to focus energy into ways of being which enhance natural abilities. Energy is thus placed into external forms which go contrary to the inner nature of the person. As a result, a split occurs within the self and this condition is projected into professional performance.

GOING TO THE LIMITS

The more experience you have, the more you can think about what you are doing while you are doing it. You arrange things carefully before, but once you are in it you cannot be too careful or too wise, you just act. If you think too much you cannot go to the limits. You have to be free in your mind, in good physical and mental condition. You must have self confidence and the belief that you can make it. You cannot doubt yourself. You just go (Gonen, 1983).

This statement could have been said by any person who deals in high risk situations, survival and creativity—athletes, artists, psychotherapists, teachers, adventurers. It was made by a pilot who believes that success is determined by an ability to "go to the limits." Within any profession that requires the exploration of limits, technical procedures must be mastered, but ultimately it is the openness, the range of responses and spontaneity that are demanded by the engagement that determine success. The situation cannot be controlled by techniques and directions but only by spiritual, physical and mental discipline, creativity and excellent reflexes. The person must know the technical medium and the self, but the true test is experience, to survive in the work and go out again and again, cautious after success and with an abiding trust and humility after failure. Experience allows us to know the context with every element of our beings, to be totally in the situation while simultaneously watching it unfold.

Rigid and tight boundaries, operating "by the book," are rarely of use in any life situation involving change and a complexity of emotions. As Jerzy Grotowski says, "Art doesn't like rule. Masterpieces are always based on the transcendence of rules . . . the test is in the performance" (Grotowski, 1968, p. 56). Training is an opportunity to explore limits, surpass old boundaries and sharpen instincts. Students can often go closer to their emotional limits in training than in therapy. There is usually more raw emotion and conflict between teacher and student, between the students themselves . . . . and perhaps competition, too, though disguised. People are observed closely in training. There is an ongoing process of evaluation taking place, even in the most humanistic environment—assessments of students, teachers, the self, the process. The line between competence and incompetence can be thin, invisible at times. In therapy the emphasis tends to be more exclusively focused on support, even within the context of confrontation. Training can, of course, be characterized by attitudes of support, but there are always the other elements of evaluation, competence, credentialing and personal achievement. Because of the complexities of the training process, and the demands it places on what are assumed to be strong and motivated people, personal limits are typically challenged and expanded. Training, as initiation into sacred and socially valued professions, has since ancient times consistently been a passage rite engaging the exploration of limits and, for the ambitious, the transcendence of limits.

I asked my pilot friend what distinguishes people who can go to the limits from those who cannot. "First I must find the objective. We are always receiving instructions and guidance but I cannot fly according to rules and orders. I must reach a point where I forget about all these things and think about nothing but the objective. Nothing else can enter the mind. I cannot tell you what it is . . . a madness perhaps, which can be disciplined" (Gonen, 1983). Training then appears to be a sharpening of innate abilities and sensitivities. Technique is perfected, but it is ultimately part of something more important.

It might be said that therapy and personal encounter have no standardized forms. A goal of training is the discovery of what our bodies, minds and emotions are capable of doing—alone and within the exchange of relationships. Like the actor, we test ourselves through performance. In addition to the challenges of conflict, we explore the limits of love, intimacy and affection. For many, these areas are more threatening than confrontation, in that some are better at opening to conflict than to sustained intimacy.

OPENING

Existence Opens
Lao Tse

"I work at opening up, at being sincere. I try to go into the deepest places in myself so that other people can go deeply into themselves" (Stahre, 1982). Birgitta Stahre, a Swedish actress, made this statement during a course that I was teaching in Gothenburg on rituals and symbols in psychotherapy. She was a member of a group of artists, psychologists and other therapists who were working in the training group. Since reading Stanislavski's *An Actor Prepares* years before, I have believed that actors have much to teach psychotherapists. In course after course my graduate students in the creative arts therapies told me that the Stanislavski book, which in no way claims to deal with psychotherapy, was one of their most useful and inspirational readings.

Birgitta Stahre described how the actor must "go through many life places to get to simple and direct communication. As Brecht said, 'The simplest is the most difficult' " (Ibid.). Her statement about "opening" allowed me to see that my work has always been fundamentally concerned with the theme. The ability to open the self is at the essence of the artist's and therapist's work, and it can be a formidable challenge to the beginning student. All the confusions of theories melt in opening to the simple communion with another. When we reach the place where personal depths are one with our work, no barriers between, we reach the place of strength, healing and art. Therapists open their souls so that others may enter themselves. We find ourselves through other people. This principle is at the essence of both psychotherapy and art.

Giving can be seen as the guiding attitude of opening the self. When self-revelation is considered as a gift to others, the fears which typically accompany the process of opening can be minimized. The majority of every group that I have worked with have experienced fear when engaging in the open expression of feelings with new people. Judgmental attitudes and fears of what people will see in us, and what we will see in ourselves, have to be let go. In one group a sophisticated man with years of mental health experience shared how he, too, felt intense fear when opening to others. "When I open myself sincerely, I tend to fumble and feel awkward so I allow myself to be elegantly distant."

Opening involves dealing with doubt, pain, grief, loneliness, guilt, demons and inner conflicts. The process is not always pleasant and gratifying. We may find ourselves opening to illness and distasteful parts of our characters. In training groups, I attempt to work toward creating an environment in which leaders and participants are free to open to areas of difficulty and insecurity. When the expression of frightening, unattractive and awkward emotions is perceived as giving to others, we are living in the realm of the therapeutic where the gift takes the form of the open expression of feeling. The guiding skill of the therapist is "compassionate intelligence" (Cobb, 1977) which involves the ability to be empathetic with another and support the healing process. The natural tendency to project personal feelings and values onto another person or environment goes contrary to compassionate intelligence. Students eager to give, and be of use, routinely project their private perceptions onto others, especially in response to stress and uncertainty. In training groups, we engage the problem by encouraging compassion as the first response in determining what may be happening within a given situation. This process of putting the other before the self helps to temper the more instinctual tendency to project the personal position. Compassionate intelligence thus holds projection in check and prepares the person to give.

Opening tends to have negative connotations within the conventional psychotherapeutic context. Fears are constantly expressed about "opening people up" or "opening too much." Terms like "closure" and "clinical distance" arouse more positive feelings amongst psychotherapists. Negative associations to opening result from misunderstanding and a lack of sensitivity to the process. Opening in this sense is feared as a potentially damaging intrusion. These fears have often evolved from real events and traumas where people are forced or confronted into opening themselves against their will and are subsequently abused or abandoned. These intrusions have occurred in most of our lives and have resulted in honest fears. Other forms of resistance to opening are concerned with the person's inability to deal with and control emotions that are provoked. Many forms of contemporary therapy are concerned with the management of behavior and do not always value opening.

The training of psychotherapists is heavily directed toward "intervention skills." In training groups that I have led, the major expectation of many participants unfamiliar with our work is that they will learn how to make interpretations, interventions, decisions and various other clinical judgments which are of course vital parts of therapeutic practice. However, there is sometimes an imbalance in expectations related to training. Beginning therapists often assume that power is related to the ability to intervene rather than the ability to open themselves to the person and the context. Insecurities that therapists and students have about their ability to make clinical judgments and interventions result in a further distancing from the people that they work with.

A common misunderstanding and fear is that openness involves an absence of structure and control. Students fear the loss of power and control and sometimes become overly concerned with methods which structure interactions. There is much to learn from the training of actors. The powers of actors are determined by their ability to go deeply into themselves, to allow expression to unfold naturally and spontaneously, to grasp and understand their motivating passions and to create an authentic personal style. Actors realize that their goal is to reach the realm of pure and simple acts which forcefully communicate emotion. They know that honest feeling is what reaches and transforms others and that form will flow naturally from it. In the training of therapists and teachers, and perhaps even artists, too much emphasis is placed on standard methods as opposed to the inner place from which all external forms originate. The external forms of a therapist's work are most convincing when they correspond to the person's total style of living. The education of therapists is most sophisticated when it avoids training "method actors" who operate within the realm of clinical stereotypes.

Every life situation contains its innate definition and motivating energies. Structure is always present. We must simply have the ability to perceive it. As the gnostic gospel of Thomas suggests, many people can understand the most complicated patterns of nature but cannot see the person before them. The primary powers of artists and therapists involve the ability to engage and understand the moment. The skillful performer knows how to go into a situation prepared, open and without rigid plans. Form and structure emerge through spontaneous action. In this respect the psychodynamics of creativity parallel those of therapy.

SENSITIVITY

In Hösseringen, West Germany, Doctor Eckhard Krause described to me how he became interested in the creative arts therapies because of his desire to open himself to creative expression in professional and personal life. Having established himself as a psychiatrist, he was trying to balance what he described as the rigid formalities of his professional education with artistic sensitivity. I was speaking about opening and Doctor Krause told me how this had become a major theme of his work. "German education teaches us only to analyze and establish clinical distance. Everything is ordered, classified and formal. Psychiatry needs to unite its analytic tendencies with open expression and feeling" (Krause, 1983). He described how he was involved with studying the way in which the face expresses feeling and conflicts.

> I am trying to feel the faces of others. The communication must begin with feeling and then move to rational thought. The process is the opposite of my analytic training. I find that I am good at feeling the souls of others through their faces but not as good at opening my spirit to them . . . . I am trying to *feel into* the other person, through my emotions and sensitivities, while putting my thoughts aside. The face seems to contain everything. Yet it must be engaged together with the whole body. You cannot become obsessed with only one part of the body. After hearing about my studies of the face the staff at the clinic went about looking only at people's faces. We German's in particular have to learn how to open ourselves to, and feel into the whole body (Ibid.).

Doctor Krause described how he sees the development of "sensitivity" as the process of his life. "When this process ends, my life ends. I am always trying to improve my ability to feel into others and open myself to them" (Ibid.). This development of the ability to feel and act is the art of psychotherapy. It is a process that freshly presents itself in each life situation. "I believe that people seeking training in psychotherapy as well as experienced therapists who do not *feel* their clients, do not know and feel themselves. If I am sure of myself, I do not have to worry about boundaries or distance, nor do my clients. If we know and respect ourselves we do not have to fear the personalization of our work" (Ibid.).

In therapy it is necessary also for clients to be able to *feel into* their therapists. Often the major goal of therapy is to help clients to sensitively "feel" the presence of another person. Openness on the part of the therapist is necessary in order to give the clients real emotions and a real person to relate to.

Eckhard Krause, a psychiatrist, and Birgitta Stahre, an actress, express two complementary features of human relationships: feeling others and opening the self. The successful artist is sensitive to the mood and possibilities of the moment and the surrounding environment. It might be asked whether there is any difference in the work of the therapist. Opening and sensitivity to others are skills that can be developed through training. As Doctor Krause said, their perfection is a lifelong process. I believe that most therapists long to live with the creative vitality of the artist, while the artist desires to penetrate the mysteries of human relationships.

THE ULYSSES MYTH AND TRAINING

Advanced training in the creative arts therapies does not follow a blueprint for construction. Both psychotherapy and art engage complexity, ambiguity, spontaneous events and creative transformation. Interpretive ideas guide the therapist's work rather than laws of behavior. The psychotherapist's task is even more complex than that of the artist who is "grounded" in a specific medium and technical mastery. The instrument of therapy is the total person of the therapist. Training in the use of this vehicle of psychotherapy involves serious and extended inquiry into the self. The psychotherapist's competence is thus determined by knowledge of the professional instrument together with its skillful and confident use. If psychotherapy is perceived as a process of self-understanding and personal transformation, then the training of therapists is to be based on the mastery of these core elements so that they may be transmitted to others.

There are universal principles and training experiences that all therapists become involved with: the study of theories of human behavior; practicum education with different clinical populatons; and, in the case of the creative arts therapies, focused study of the properties of varied materials of expression. In the psychotherapy process these core methods, materials, theories and clinical training experiences are part of the therapist's being. Training is a rite of passage through which the self is applied to a new social context and human use.

Inquiry into the self for the purpose of psychotherapeutic training is a journey which corresponds to the Ulysses myth. The initiate, or traveler, is a pilgrim who encounters varied obstacles, challenges and tests, demons, surprises, disappointments and doubts. The process parallels the classic myth structure of the wandering and searching hero. The vision quest of the shaman, the heroic journey and spiritual discovery, are as necessary to psychotherapeutic training as meeting the requirements for professional licensure or registration.

My experiences in training psychotherapists and the experiences of other educators in the profession indicate that the continued reenactment of the Ulysses myth is at the core of the educational process. It is important to concentrate on the myth patterns of Oedipus, Electra, Narcissus and others, but it is the myth of the wandering and searching Ulysses that corresponds to the total process of both psychotherapeutic training and practice. The story of Ulysses is an archetypal manifestation of the journey and search for meaning in the world and within the individual psyche.

The Ulysses myth in its Hellenic and Irish (James Joyce) forms provides coherence to training by giving a sense of purpose and unity to the emotional inconsistencies and struggles that characterize the pursuit of self-understanding. The journey of the student therapist involves trips into the underworld; encounters with fear and pain; excursions into dreams, soul and the world of imagery; and meditation, flights of spirit and uses of imagination. The journey structure allows the student to separate from routine and establish a fresh perspective for looking at the self and the environment. Inevitably, the traveler gets lost and requests assistance from the teacher who becomes a guide. It is important to let students know that confusion is part of the journey.

The mythic aspect of psychotherapeutic training does not proceed according to a fixed schedule or course syllabus. The dynamics of the process correspond more to the structures of dreams, artworks and life. It is impossible to determine in advance what will occur. The student cannot follow a plan, outline or text. As with art, the image will emerge or appear in its own time. Meditation, relaxation and waiting are sometimes more useful than purposeful and directed interventions. The process must be open and inquisitive.

The destruction of barriers and obstacles to personal fulfillment is a core element of the myth structure of the heroic quest. We creative arts therapists are so concerned with the positive transformation of stress and illness that we often find it difficult to accept the place of destruction in creativity. Obstacles to expression need to be destroyed and let go in order for art to progress. The enactment of destruction in therapy and training can be an essential element of creative transformation; the two processes complement one another and can be perceived as interdependent within the life cycle. In *Zarathustra* Nietzsche maintains that the creative person must be able to destroy and "break values."

A key element of health and a primary objective of psychotherapeutic training is the ability to direct destructive energies toward creation. Psychosis and harmful anxiety are expressions of destructive energy used against the self. The psychotherapist in training needs to be deeply exposed to the workings of psychic destruction in the self and others in order to direct these energies toward the enhancement of life. Destruction must be perceived as part of the life rhythm. Expectations, plans, desires, values and needs must sometimes be let go in order to engage new opportunities and a changing context which is not always subject to our control.

G.A. Gaskell interprets the Ulysses myth as "A symbol of courage, arising out of Love and Faith, in learning by experience to rule the lower nature in the interests of the higher" (Gaskell, 1960, p. 547). In keeping with Gaskell's interpretation, the creative arts therapist builds self-confidence and knowledge, hopefully guided by love and faith, through experiential learning. It is important not to make the error of associating the passions, instincts and senses with lower realms of being. Within psychotherapeutic training the "higher" nature involves developing values which emphasize action in the service of others. The "lower" nature is expressed when others are used to serve the self. However, in order to use the self properly in psychotherapy, it is necessary to have comprehensive knowledge of, and sensitivity to, this instrumentality. The weakness of the medical prescription approach to therapy is that it is focused on the application of something external rather than the use of the self. A guiding principle of experiential learning is the fact that a person cannot know something that has not been felt either through direct experience or the imagination. The soul of the therapist must be fully engaged with the work, with the moment, and with the soul of the client. The separation of the soul from the context and the reliance on external mechanisms results in a distancing of the therapist and the loss of power.

James Hillman emphasizes the need for the therapist to maintain the inner search and dialogue through all stages of psychotherapeutic practice.

> The analyst furthers a process which is fundamentally the analysand's own. Primary to all interpersonal relations is the intrapersonal dialectic, the relation to the unconscious psyche . . . . An analyst thus tries to practice the maxim of 'physician, cure thyself'; applying his own medicine upon himself. He tries to maintain his own consciousness in order not to be unconscious with each of his pateients. If he begins to slip, he falls into the roles they put him in . . . Only by maintaining his own pole through his own dialectic with his own dreams, fantasies, emotions, and symptoms can he be of service to the analysand (Hillman, 1983, pp. 144-145).

Since the therapist helps the client to open to the universal forces of healing, it is necessary to be in constant communion with this process. "An analyst appears as Healer only to the distorted vision of the ill, because the ill cannot find the source of healing in themselves . . . . If an analyst identifies with the divine role of Healer he forces the analysand into an identification with the compensatory role of patient" (Ibid., 1983, pp. 124-125).

The journey of self-investigation never ends for the therapist. Otto Rank perceived the therapist as an "artist type" who studies the self in order to be of use to others. Profoundly influenced by Nietzsche, Rank believed that "self-consciousness" is the most important characteristic of the artist. In the German tradition of Goethe, Schopenhauer and Nietzsche, Rank believed in the importance of willful acting and learning from the effects of action. Dream interpretation and all other forms of therapy were perceived by him to be an art. Rank perceived therapy as an art in which life is the artist's subject matter. Within this context the supreme artwork is the artist's creation of life. Rank's work provides an important guide to the definition of art in relation to therapy. The use of a specialized skill and repetitive system of operation is much more of a craft than an art.

Rank believed in the necessity of the psychotherapist's inner search and journey. He said that he "looked too deep into the workings of the world" to be a novelist or poet (Lieberman, 1985, p. 35). Rank's respect for the artist's soul is at the essence of his philosophy of psychotherapy. He referred to Freud as "a medically proven artist." According to Rank, the search for self-understanding is endless: "The masters never come to know themselves completely . . . . Instead of 'Know Thyself,' I would write over the gates of the temples of modern thinkers: 'Seek to Know Thyself.' The search—that's the most important thing" (Ibid., p. 43).

TRANSFORMATION THEORISTS

Generation after generation of artists have understood how emotional difficulty is a primary source of art. As James Joyce suggested, the angels have the power to summon beauty from murky and disturbing places. Thoreau advised that the apparently banal aspects of daily life, sometimes full of conflict and boredom, are sources of beauty which exists "wherever there is a soul to admire. If I seek her elsewhere because I do not find her at home, my search will prove a faithless one" (Thoreau in Volkman, 1960, 6). He realized that the noblest subject matter for creative transformation is the commonplace. "To affect the quality of the day, that is the highest of the arts" (Ibid., p. 22).

The core ideas of psychological transformation can be traced back to Lao-Tse in the East and Heraclitus in the West. In ancient Chinese philosophy, the life force was perceived as involving an interaction of conflicting elements. Lao-Tse (b. 604 B.C.) spoke of establishing an ongoing rhythm of life through a respect for the simple patterns of nature. The ancients believed that the creative interaction of conflicting forces occurs within a world of perpetual change. All opposites were considered as part of the same entity, with everything in nature being related. Within this context the different parts of a person fit into a whole which accepts contradiction and inconsistency. Everything is changing, conflict is unending and the key to health lies in the ability to move rhythmically in relation to these forces. In the *Tao-teh-ching* Lao-Tse describes how "the rhythm of life" involves an understanding of the creative force behind the apparent contradictions of life — "This is the subtle light." The Tao flows in all directions and unites opposing tensions. Lao-Tse advises the person to "flow everywhere" and eliminate all boundaries.

In Greece, Heraclitus (500 B.C.) developed a school of thought parallel to the teachings of Lao-Tse. He was also a believer in eternal flow, perpetual change, the beneficial powers of contradiction, and strife as the life force. Heraclitus felt that life cannot exist without tension. Resolutions lie within the problem which can be helpful and a source of growth if the person has the ability to learn from it and transform its energy. Teaching oneself from direct experience takes skill since "Nature is wont to hide herself."

Heraclitus used the self as a laboratory for learning. Observing and analyzing others invariably lead back to self-examination. He felt that only by understanding the self could a person gain access to more universal understanding.

The ancients perceived tension between the opposites as the source of life. The human response to tension includes the options of stress, collapse and transformation. Through the transformation process the duality of the opposites provokes a third force of creative action which does not deny or eliminate the tension between the opposites. William Blake, who anticipated all of the major transformation psychologies of the West, wrote in his *Marriage of Heaven and Hell*: "Without Contraries is no progression." W.B. Yeats perceived the powers of emotional alchemy as divine. Through this process the lowliest person could in his view join in the universal transmutation of one substance into another. Anything can take on value and become sacred as a result of the person's perceptual powers and creative imagination. However, Yeats wrote of how the greatest ambition of the alchemist, the transformation of "the weary heart into a weariless spirit," was far from his reach. According to Yeats, the poet thrives on this tension, "sings" in response to "uncertainty" and lives within "whirlwinds." Withdrawal and the renouncing of experience are less desirable responses to the poet. Yeats' "vision" is a transformation of the realization that the passions cannot have total and endless gratification. A life of intense feeling provides access to the opposing forces of the emotions which potentially fuel creative transformation. Art heals by willfully focusing on desired transformations.

C.G. Jung perceived the history of alchemy as an external projection of inner feelings of transformation. Theories of transmuting lead into gold were for him a "pseudo chemical language" originating in projections of psychic processes. "As a result of the projection there is an unconscious identity between the psyche of the alchemist and the arcane substance, i.e., the spirit imprisoned in matter" (Jung, 1977, p. 267). The alchemist, in exploring these substances, "projected the unconscious into the darkness of matter in order to illuminate it. In order to explain the mystery of matter, he projected yet another mystery, his own unknown psychic background, into what was to be explained" (Ibid., p. 244). As with shamanic enactment and the healing charms of folk healers, the alchemist followed a carefully prescribed series of ritual procedures in carrying on the transmutation ceremony. What unifies all of these procedures is the universality of faith in the process of emotional transformation. According to Jung, "the method of alchemy, psychologically speaking, is one of boundless amplification" (Ibid., p. 289). All healing traditions are in this respect amplifications of the primary transformation of emotion.

Alchemical transformation is directed toward the release of the imprisoned soul. The nature of the soul's prison changes with the mental set of the particular historical epoch. Within shamanic and folk cultures the soul is abducted and held captive by spirits; in the days of medieval alchemy, when scientific explorations were beginning in Europe, the soul was held within the prison of physical matter; and today the soul tends to be held captive by the self.

Consciousness creates various prisons for the soul. The self has become a prison for the spirit because of the great emphasis placed on the *ego* within our epoch. The same applies to earlier beliefs in the abduction of the soul by spirits and the soul being imprisoned in physical materials. The soul thus has the twofold power of creating its prisons and its means of liberation, both of which are expressions of the ongoing process of emotional opposition and transformation. The soul thus creates its sickness and its cures.

Freud's thinking was based on the tension between contrary forces. His pleasure principle was in conflict with death instincts and the destructive dimensions of life. Freud's theories were but one more presentation of the ancient belief that the life force consisted of conflict. Both Freud and Jung were preceded by Nietzsche, who resurrected passionate origins of western culture. His commitment to the liberation of passion suggests a daring therapeutic approach to the human condition. It is unfortunate that Nietzsche's insights have never been shaped into a psychotherapeutic theory. Although the depth psychologies of Freud and Jung correspond to many of Nietzsche's ideas, they were part of the more general medical/psychiatric approach to mental health which demanded that phenomena be explained in scientific terms. Nietzsche was an artist/philosopher whose prescription for healing was of a passionate, expressive nature.

Nietzsche revived an ancient healing tradition which involves the acceptance of struggle, conflict and passion and the transformation of these forces through the creative ACT. The mental health field has followed a course contrary to Nietzsche's thinking and has encouraged attempts to extinguish passion and conflict through mind-altering drugs, thus realizing his worst fears for the future of humanity. He described how taking away the conflicting force of the emotions is equivalent to taking away life itself. In *The Will to Power*, Nietzsche encouraged "Mastery over the passions, not their weakening and *extinction!*" He described human nature as being motivated by numerous "contrary drives and impulses." The tensions created by the drives stimulate transformations which Nietzsche associated with art, the creative response to conflict. He believed that people are strongest when engaging the most powerful instinctual conflicts. Nietzsche's theories are projections from his experience. His greatness has been determined by the intensity of his pain, and his openness to it, by his humanity and his ability to deal directly with the furies within himself. In an 1882 letter to his friend Franz Overbeck, he wrote, "Unless I can discover the alchemical trick of turning this muck into gold, I am lost."

Nietzsche was an *internal* revolutionary. His message is that the change must begin within the self and spread out to the world. Social manipulations and controls can never produce high levels of spiritual and creative consciousness. These most human attributes can only be produced by inner struggles and the transformation of experience. Nietzsche believed that creative perception and action were the greatest powers that human beings have in dealing with the eternal conflict of life. Art affirms life by transforming tension and giving it value. The artist perceives the underlying necessity of strife and how the forces of conflict bring about the creation of an artwork. Creation is the eternal cure. All healing is a creative process, an artistic transformation of one thing into something else. Through creative transformation the opposites, conflict and all contradictions make sense and affirm life — they are the source and the inspiration for the creative act. Nietzsche's perception of the formative powers of conflict is an antecedent to Freud's theory of sublimation which deals only with the ventilation of conflict and not with the powers of art in giving value to life. Creation is a cognitive and spiritual challenge and not simply an overflow of pathological tension or an excursion into the world of fantasy.

Life for Nietzsche was an artistic manifestation; the creative person an "artist god"; and art a "sorceress expert in healing." He was influenced by Heraclitus, in perceiving the world as eternal flux and strife; and his Dionysian theory of art which presents existence, in spite of its pain and setbacks, as "eternal delight," is reminiscent of William Blake. There is a continuity of action in the works of major transformation theorists which suggests that the creative transformation of conflict is a primary human instinct. The creative arts therapies can be perceived as part of this tradition:

> This world—an immensity of force, without beginning, without end, a firm, brazen magnitude of force, which does not increase, does not decrease, does not consume itself, but only transforms itself, unchangeable as a whole in its magnitude . . . a sea of forces raging and flowing into each other, eternally running back, with immense years of recurrence with an ebb and flow of its forms, moving from the simplest to the most complex, from the uttermost calm, rigor, cold into the uttermost heat, wildness, self-contradiction, and then returning home from plentitude to simplicity, from the play of contradictions to the delight of concord, affirming itself even in this similarity of its courses and years, blessing itself as that which must eternally return, as a becoming which knows no satiety, no surfeit, no fatigue—this my Dionysian world of eternal self-creation, eternal self-destruction . . . " (Nietzsche in Middleton, 1969, p. 245).

Within the context of the arts the passions are given a vehicle for release which can be characterized by order and emotional discipline. According to Euripedes, the passions are the fire that does not die. If they are blocked, their energy will be turned against the person. Nietzsche anticipated Freud's theory of psychopathology by declaring that if the instincts do not express themselves in the eternal world, they will "turn inwards." However, Nietzsche's prescription for health through the liberation of the passions and artistic action has not been given any serious attention by the dominant psychologies of the twentieth century.

IMAGERY

The creative arts therapies are defined by their introduction of imagery and sensory communication into psychotherapy. The image is multi-sensory and is not limited to visual forms. In the creative arts therapies, we dialogue with, act out, and become the image. We do not simply interpret sensory imagery with analytic language as psychology has done. The image is the form of consciousness as it emerges from the process of imagination. Imagery takes many forms and the senses cannot be separated from one another. This total sensory use of imagery within the creative arts therapies allows the many forms and varieties of the psyche to emerge in the psychotherapeutic process.

Just as art and life are completely integrated in the creative arts therapies, so, too, are concepts of image, symbol and perception. Philosophical, psychological, theological and artistic studies of symbology have generated numerous definitions of symbol, sign and image which are at times supportive of one another and often contradictory. Symbol, image and perception are focal points of consciousness that may exist in and of themselves, and suggest something beyond. They emerge from both individuals and universal phenomena. Generally, concepts defining symbolism refer to something beyond the specific physical form which serves as a vehicle for representation. Symbols are further encumbered by stereotypic and fixed interpretations of forms that have histories within a particular culture. These preconceptions make it difficult to experience the particular structural and emotional qualities of a form that distinguish it from similar structures. Within a therapeutic and artistic context, sensitivity to the particular is necessary. The investigation of personal motives and associations to form requires that concepts of universality be sensitive to the individual creative process.

James Hillman describes symbols as "abstractions from images," involving a "conscious" process of seeing the image as a symbol. He feels that when a symbol is thoroughly stereotyped, it loses its imagistic qualities. Hillman, like the artist, prefers to concentrate on the image itself, because he wants "to inquire by sticking to the actual phenomena" (Hillman, 1977). If the image is perceived as a representation of something beyond itself, then it loses power. The poetic consciousness realizes that the universal exists in the particular.

Images transmit feelings and act as focal points for energy. The image is a tangible and constant receptacle for the feeling with which it is associated. Emotions are thus evoked and focused when a person reenters a relationship with a familiar image. Associations to a particular image may also change and this versatility accounts for the power of imagery. As Yeats said, a single image can lead the soul from entanglements and "unmeaning circumstance" into "a ceaseless reverie, in some chapel of the star of infinite desire" (Yeats, 1962).

Yeats believed that if we are able to focus completely on a thought in imaginary visions, then this idea will realize "itself in the circumstances of life." A fundamental purpose of his life was the restoration of the unity of religion and art. He feared fragmentation and emotional chaos and committed himself to the revitalization of imagery and ritual, which give form and direction to what he described as "undifferentiated energy."

The power of images in therapy is directly related to their ability to concentrate attention and energy which is directed toward the desired transformation of emotion. The image is both a collector and transmitter of energy. Rudolf Arnheim's gestalt psychology of visual perception demonstrates how formal qualities determine expressiveness. In this respect the particular structure of an image will affect its emotional power. Expression is determined by the structural forms of imagination and art making.

My experience has repeatedly shown that when people are freely engaged in the creation of personal healing forms, their imagery parallels ancient patterns. The positive evocations and psychic stimulations of imagery have been lost within the clutter and confusion of contemporary mass culture. We are surrounded by a multiplicity of forms seeking attention. The dispersion of power results in a fragmentation of the life force. Within the value systems of art, the multiplicity of belief characterizing contemporary culture does not have to be viewed negatively. Each belief and psychological system is a creation, attempting to provide a sense of purpose. Individual forms may differ, but the process of creation is constant from culture to culture and person to person.

The idea of the *sacrament* is particularly useful for those who wish to engage the powers of imagery in therapy. Sacramental perception can be defined as the creation of *sensible signs* and physical forms which allow the person to identify with, and establish a feeling of communion with, spiritual forces. The power of the sacrament depends to a large extent on its ability to express the mysteries and qualities of experiences not accessible to conventional communication.

CORRESPONDENCE

Healing practices in all cultures are unified by their use of the principle of correspondence. Paracelsus in the early sixteenth century determined that every malady contains its resolution and that nature contains all cures. Nature simply had to be carefully observed and studied in order to have its remedies become manifest. According to Paracelsus, "the outer reveals the inner" and "the similar is cured by the similar" (Paracelsus in Jacobi, 1969). Paracelsus' beliefs are consistent with techniques of shamans who perform a particular physical enactment with the goal of provoking a corresponding inner action. I do not wish to attach undue significance to the duality of *inner and outer* which some might not accept as an accurate description of life process. The relationship between "inner and outer" is only one of many constructs that can be used to suggest the interdependence of different aspects of experience.

James George Frazer described sympathetic magic as based on the principle of correspondence. In keeping with Paracelsus, he spoke of how "like produces like" (Frazer, 1966). This law of correspondence provides the theoretical foundation for homeopathic medicine and imitative magic. Frazer recorded rituals of sympathetic magic and correspondence from throughout the world—the Mexican Indian woman who stroked the serpent so that she could weave elegant patterns corresponding to the intricate designs of the snake's skin; the Indian who ritualistically sacrificed an image of the cow, deer, dog or hen that he wished to possess; the use of heavy stones as charms against impulsiveness and instability; the transference of the powers of animal totems to human beings; the casting away of a stick or stone as a purging of illness; nailing evil to a tree; passing over a bridge or through an opening in a rock as a means of transformation; spiritual purification through the cleansing of the environment and the body; etc.

Correspondence, also described as the principle of reciprocation and relationship, is manifested in the healing rituals of the different Native American cultures where health is perceived as living in a proper relationship to the cycles and rhythms of nature. There is also a correspondence between the Native Americans and Paracelsus, who said that "the book of medicine is Nature itself." Illness to the Native American comes when the relationship between the person and nature loses its harmony, when something becomes dislocated from the rhythmic pattern of the whole. Ritual acts and the manipulation of physical objects do not in themselves heal—this is the misconception of the modern observer. The healing enactment is intended to serve as a suggestion, an external manifestation, of the proper correspondence between the person and na-

ture. The curative powers of the ceremony are attributed to divine assistance achieved through the immersion of the participants into a proper
relationship with the life-supporting and healing energies of nature. Ritual enactment also focuses the powers of the person's will, both in the
waking and dream life, on the desired unification with nature's rhythms.

The image has the power to stimulate an emotional reaction within a
person that corresponds to what is suggested by, or associated to, the
stimulus. Rudolf Arnheim and the Gestalt psychologists refer to the
principle of correspondence as *isomorphism*. They focus on how order
perceived in a visual configuration has a parallel effect on the emotions
of the viewer (Arnheim, 1954, 1971). In the mid nineteenth century,
Friedrich Theodor Vischer spoke of how spiritual feelings and images
correspond to actual vibrations within the nerves of the perceiver (Vischer, 1867). Navaho sandpainting rituals are based on principles of correspondence. The image drawn on sand is identified with the person in
need of help, and during the healing ceremony various parts of the sandpainting are touched which correspond to parts of the sick person's body
and soul. The sand painting absorbs the illness. Frazer described similar
rites for the "transference of evil" in *The Golden Bough*. During the ceremony the illness is symbolically absorbed into the sandpainting in a
manner which provides a metaphoric enactment of what must happen
within the person's body if it is to be purged of its malady.

The healing powers of the arts can be attributed to the principle of
correspondence. The same applies to the contemplation of nature. Perceptions of vast open spaces, majestic mountains, rugged fields, freshly
mowed grass, neatly stacked woodpiles, flowing brooks, steady waves,
wild fields, fresh snow, grey skies, empty rooms, rundown buildings,
etc., stimulate corresponding emotional states. Within nature religions,
the night of the full moon is the time for sacred rites because the shape of
the moon, its ripe fullness, evokes corresponding spiritual feelings. Confusing and aggressive images similarly have a corresponding effect on
consciousness. However, people may react differently to a particular
stimulus, depending on their past experience. For example, a person
may feel discomfort in response to imagery typically associated with
pleasure. Operationally, the therapist and client work together to understand the nature of personal correspondence reactions and to direct
them toward desired outcomes.

The healing image is empowered by a correspondence between itself
and the desired result. The mandala is a physical image of the balance,

harmony and unity that the perceiver wished to internalize. Meditation upon external unity helps to bring about a corresponding inner feeling. With placebos, the physical act of consuming a pill, drink or edible substance believed to have curative powers, will, as recent research demonstrates, often provoke a positive reaction in those who believe in the efficacy of the remedy. Pilgrimage and prayer also involve the process of performing a series of external, phsyical actions which stimulate corresponding inner reactions. Principles of correspondence have been increasingly used in contemporary cancer and stress therapies. The person seeking help meditates upon a personal image that is associated with well-being and positive transformation of the pathological condition. Intense and sustained concentration, together with belief in the healing powers of the image, will mobilize natural healing energies within the organism.

I have found that the more personal the image is, the greater its healing power will be. If there is no relationship to the context of the person's life together with individual taste and values, the image will be ineffective. The same applies to the aesthetic power of the image and the enactment process. A bland, unimaginative and perfunctory enactment will not mobilize as much transformative energy within the person as will the aesthetically provoking use of imagery. There is a correspondence between the external remedy and the internal reaction.

IMAGE IN ACTION

In every historical epoch, healers have been concerned with diagnosis and focusing on tangible causes for illness. The specific focus concentrates energy on desired healing transformations. The healer reads signs from the body and the person's imagery as expressed in dreams, language and other forms and gives a tangible and specific diagnosis. This focus makes the illness accessible for transformation and offers the person something to direct healing energy toward.

Imagistic expressions of fragmentation, diffusion, stability, sensuality, aggression or transcendence will inevitably bring about a corresponding response when the perceiver is open and susceptible to external influence. Learning how to influence, direct, support and interpret this process of imagistic correspondence is fundamental to the training of the therapist. Diagnosis and therapeutic action are interchangeable. Through the principle of correspondence the therapist and client discover how the external expression communicates inner feelings while simultaneously using the image or external form as a guide for action and the focusing of energy.

Basic operational principles for the therapeutic use of imagery include respect for the image and its particular form. In our training groups, we stay close to the actual physical structure of the image and contemplate its qualities as opposed to simply perceiving the image as a representation of something that is not present. The image is a form of life unto itself. We also caution against hasty interpretations and the need to come up with "the correct" interpretation of an image. Every image can be interpreted in different ways, with each meaning contributing something to understanding. Group response reveals that the image characteristically suggests varied forms of meaning as opposed to singular interpretations attached to conventional psychotherapeutic approaches to dreams and artworks. Within our training groups, each person offers a response to the image which helps to clarify the original intent of the expression. Dogmatic or authoritarian responses impose the opinions of others and replace the process of imagistic dialogue, drama and revelation with static and fixed positions imposed from without. Within training groups, people offering their artwork and imagery for response from others learn what *feels right* and apply this understanding of the process of communication to their work with clients.

Pathological approaches to interpretation in therapy tend to diminish in relation to the therapist's personal involvement in the process. Ongoing personal artistic and imagistic expression helps therapists to be more sensitive to the importance of sequence and serial representation. Pictures, actions, sounds and statements are perceived in relation to what comes before or after, and the more general environment. The image is always in process, within a context that is changing. Separation from the environment of creation stops the process of the image and places it into a context that is often contrary to its original intent. Sequential expression allows for the amplification and diminishment of an image together with repetition and change. Mysterious and ambiguous forms often reveal their meaning and value through a sequence of images. Although patterns and styles may emerge together with refinement and clarification, the contrary may also occur.

When approaching the imagery of artworks, dreams and visualizations, every part and quality is given value as an independent element within the whole. What appears least significant at first may take on a key position within the overall drama of the image. The principle of reversal applies here in that it is often helpful to consider the contrary of every position. Hierarchical perspective in a picture may in fact reveal that the more dominant and larger qualities hold the greatest significance, but the reverse may also be true. Imposing size, formal placement, color and action may serve the purpose of concealment. As many perspectives as possible are taken when we approach the image. Different images within a dream, artwork or visualization can be likened to individual actors within a play where "minor" roles express pieces of information necessary to understand actions of the more "major" players and the message of the drama. The interpretation of imagery in therapy can be compared to scholarly interpretations in literature, typically characterized by a multiplicity of viewpoints and opinions. This acknowledgement of multiplicity can be helpful in guiding therapeutic responses to art.

A single image may have different meanings, with contradictions and varieties of interpretation revealing the content of the inner drama. It is best to approach the image with an open consciousness and with as little theoretical bias as possible. Every thesis contains its antithesis and images are uniquely capable of speaking in illogical and unusual patterns. They express an ancient, pre-verbal language, the wonders of which still challenge intellect and imagination.

The artistic approach to imagery not only allows for amplification and clarification of meaning through sequential expressions but also enables people to respond artistically to the imagery of another. Rather than responding exclusively through verbal modes, people carry on dialogues through imagery. Image stimulates image within a context where sensory forms are perceived as primary communication. When a person responds sensitively to another's image through a personal artistic statement, there is a sense of affirmation and understanding that arouses a dimension of communication not possible through the verbal response. The image to image dialogue between people establishes an equality of communication. Validation is offered in a physical form which also corresponds to the language of the original feeling. The artistic response reinforces the creative process and the value of the image as an entity unto itself.

Validation increases motivation to continue and to intensify the process of discovery. The dominance of verbal expression will often do the reverse, devaluing the image as a primary form of communication. With most people, the language of the image tends to be less familiar and therefore effort is needed to maintain concentration. Because we are so accustomed to the verbal response, we tend to talk too much and this takes us away from the emotion of the image. Spoken language is of course vital and necessary in imagistic dialogue. However, caution is advised in that verbal analysis can easily block and misinterpret the language of imagery.

The image needs breathing space and room to grow. It benefits from support and validation as a primary mode of communication with a language and expressiveness that is complete within itself.

RHYTHM AND AESTHETICS

I know what the cure is: it is to give up, to relinquish, to surrender, so that our little hearts may beat in unison with the great heart of the world.

Henry Miller

My colleague Paolo Knill began an experimental course that we were teaching by talking to the group about *submission*. We were going to spend the three-hour session finding our rhythm, staying with it and allowing the rhythm to become a group pulse. The major obstacle would be our personal resistance, and we were asked to submit to the rhythmic sensations within us and nature. We were to begin with our voices and movement and then use percussive instruments, open ourselves and engage rhythm. Submission was an emotionally charged concept, especially for those who were trying to move out from under personal histories of submissiveness and the restraint of their power. Paolo was, however, asking us to submit to our power, the biological and spiritual rhythmic force inside and all about us.

Opening to rhythm and being able to perceive its healing powers are fundamental abilities of the shaman, whose discipline allows for the engagement of the transcendent forces of rhythmic repetition. We have become progressively estranged from the simple teachings of cultures which define health as living in synchrony with the rhythms of nature.

When the rhythmic flow is interrupted or blocked, the organism experiences tension, depression and the loss of vitality. The tension created by this blockage is important in its own right since it becomes the fuel for future transformations. There is an ebb and flow in the maintenance and loss of rhythm. Acute emotional disturbance results when the person can no longer transform tension and becomes overwhelmed. It is as though a swimmer cannot continue to flow in relation to the rhythm of waves and begins to flounder, to lose direction, to fight against a superior force, sink, and ultimately be in need of help.

I have never been content with definitions of psychosis emphasizing how the person "loses touch with reality." Descriptions of this kind presuppose that there is a common agreement as to the nature of "reality." I perceive severe emotional disorders as resulting from a fragmentation of essential life rhythms. Traditional notions of psychosis as a fragmentation of personality can be integrated within the broader perspective of rhythm, since personality is only an image of the way in which we structure our individual lives in relation to the forces of nature.

Psychosis is increasingly prevalent because society as a whole progressively alienates itself from the logic of the senses. Within this schema, psychosis and severe mental disturbance are viewed as an acute loss of synchrony with the life rhythm. The individual loses the ability to act as a rhythmic whole in relation to the self, others and the environment. The power to transmit and relate to feelings requires a definite rhythmic flow and perceptual focus. In the case of psychosis, these rhythmic and perceptual powers are impaired and can no longer sustain themselves in relation to the multiplicity of sensation and values that permeate life. The individual thus becomes a chaos of emotions, and the rigid bodily rhythms that one sees during psychosis are attempts to hold this *massa confusa* together.

Health involves an ability to move with the changing qualities of each day. The life rhythm is never static or completely constant. It is always changing within the moment to moment context of successive relationships in time and place, and it is capable of making transitions between emotional peaks and depressions, rather than being destroyed by them.

Emotional well-being depends on the ability to become synchronous with nature's rhythms as they exist in ourselves, interpersonal relationships and the environment. During psychosis this synchrony is radically disrupted. The severely disturbed person characteristically shows a lack of synchrony between various body parts and movement is fragmented. When two people or groups of people are relating spontaneously to one another, there is a synchrony, often unconscious, in their movement. They feel the presence of the other and establish communion. The same applies to our relationship to nature. Just as rhythmic fragmentation characterizes psychosis, rhythmic synchrony characterizes health. The deepest inner movements are often inspired by the simplest artistic structure.

———————

Rhythm is based on interaction with the environment and demands that relationships be reciprocal. Aesthetic perception is similarly a principle of health, since it concerns how things relate to and complement one another in experience. Aesthetic behavior includes conscious and unconscious judgments of how to move through time and space, how to relate to specific objects and sensory stimuli in the environment, how to synthesize parts into synchronous relationships directed toward purposeful action, how to change direction in response to alterations of environmental structure, how to achieve satisfaction within a given situation, the appreciation of perceptual experience, and all other aspects of reciprocal relationships between individuals and environment. These principles are integral components of health, since they are so closely related to adaptation and the transformation of environment. Emotional disturbance involves a disruption of environmental rhythms and communications. Ecology, defined as the scientific study of how organisms establish interdependent relationships with their environment, provides a conceptual structure for viewing "disturbed" behavior that is needed in psychology.

Ecology reveals how the individual lives rhythmically and interdependently with all of nature. It is a modern scientific and spiritual perspective based on the ancient philosophical position that everything in this world is related and no element of life exists in complete isolation. By simply living in time and space, we relate to the elements of the immediate environment. Concepts of individuality and the self are of little use without the ecological perspective. Gestalt psychology is an expression of this wholistic tradition in declaring the whole to be more than a sum of its constituent parts. The whole influences and even determines the identity of the part, and the reverse can also occur.

Aesthetic approaches to health are wholistic and practical, dealing with immediate perceptions and actions within a given environment. All aspects of behavior are included together with the inevitable multiplicity of viewpoints present within human relations. "Reality" is never "one dimensional" or rigidly fixed. The aesthetic attitude appreciates and respects this condition and perceives life as relationship, change, adaptation and creation. The vastness of behavior disorders today can be seen as rising in proportion to the person's lack of purposefulness within a world of increasing stimulation and conflict. Aesthetic perception and creative action are healthy resolutions to stressful disorder. They bring about a rhythmic relationship between the individual and the environment. The aesthetic consciousness is what distinguishes life-enhancing cooperation with the energies of nature from psychotic diffusion. As the scope of human knowledge, experience and data expands, there has been increasing fragmentation within individuals unable to find themselves within the multiplicity. The healthiest response available to us is an appreciation of the immediate qualities of experience. Personal stability is characterized by an ability to accept the multiplicity of values in the world while maintaining the personal power to give value. From the treatment of psychosis to minor ailments, therapy can be approached aesthetically and with a desire for furthering reciprocal and rhythmic relations with the energies of nature, which can work for, or against, the person.

Creative adaptation emerges from every tradition as the principle mode of healing. The focus of art complements ecstatic release with contemplation and form. Through concentration on a particular rhythm, or particle of life, a sense of value and relatedness is felt which can spread to all aspects of a person's being.

REFERENCES

Arnheim, Rudolf: *Art and Visual Perception*. Berkeley and Los Angeles, U of Cal Pr, 1954.

Arnheim, Rudolf: *Visual Thinking*. Berkeley and Los Angeles, U of Cal Pr, 1971.

Cobb, Edith: *The Ecology of Imagination in Childhood*. New York, Columbia Univ Pr, 1977.

Ferrini, Vincent: Private conversation. Gloucester, Massachusetts, 1983.

Frazer, James George: *The Golden Bough, The Magic Art and The Evolution of Kings, Vol. 1.* New York, Macmillan, 1966.

Gaskell, G.A.: *Dictionary of all Scriptures and Myths.* New York, Julian, 1960.

Gonen, Ilan: Private conversation. Ramat Hasharon, Israel, 1983.

Grotowski, Jerzy: *Toward a Poor Theatre.* New York, Simon and Schuster, 1968.

Hillman, James: *Archetypal Psychology: A Brief Account.* Dallas, Texas, Spring, 1983.

Hillman, James: *Suicide and the Soul.* Dallas, Texas, Spring, 1983.

Hillman, James: *The Myth of Analysis: Three Essays in Archetypal Psychology.* New York, Harper and Row, 1978.

Hillman, James: *Re-Visioning Psychology.* New York, Harper and Row, 1977.

Hillman, James: An inquiry into image. *Spring,* 62-68, 1977.

Jacobi, Jolande (Ed.): *Paracelsus, Selected Writings.* Princeton, N.J., Princeton Univ Pr, 1969.

Jung, C.G.: *Psychology and Alchemy.* Princeton, N.J., Princeton Univ Pr, 1977.

Krause, Eckhard: Private conversation. Bad Bevensen, BRD, 1983.

Levine, Stephen: Merleau-Ponty's Philosophy of Art. *Man and world,* 2:3, 438-452, 1969.

Lieberman, E. James: *Acts of Will: The Life and Work of Otto Rank.* New York, Free Pr, 1985.

Middleton, Christopher (Ed. and Trans.): *Selected Letters of Friedrich Nietzsche.* Chicago, Univ of Chiago Pr, 1969.

Nietzsche, Friedrich: *The Geneology of Morals,* Ascetic Ideals, Sect. 7. New York, Doubleday, 1956.

Plato, *The Republic,* X, 601 and 603.

Papini, Giovanni: A visit to Freud. *Colosseum,* 1934. Reprinted in *Rev. Evistential Psychology and Psychiatry,* 9, 130-134, 1969.

Sartre, Jean Paul: *Essays in Existentialism.* Secaucus, N.J., Citadel Pr, 1977.

Stahre, Birgitta: Private conversation. Gothenburg, Sweden, 1982.

Stanislavski, Constantin: *An Actor Prepares.* New York, Theatre Arts, 1976.

Thoreau, H. in Volkman, A. (Ed.): *Thoreau on Man and Nature.* Mount Vernon, N.Y., Peter Pauper, 1960.

Vischer, Friedrich Theodor: *Kritik Meiner Aesthetik in Kritische Gange.* Stuttgart, 1867.

Yeats, W.B.: *Essays and Introductions.* London, Macmillan, 1962.

9. STUDENTS

PROFILES of student populations in the creative arts therapies are significantly affected by the educational guidelines of national professional associations. Music therapy students involved with entry level professional training are considerably younger than students in other disciplines because of the music therapy specialization's orientation to bachelor's degree education. Music therapy undergraduate education patterns directly affect the profile of the graduate student population, the majority of whom appear to be graduates of baccalaureate level music therapy programs. The creation of equivalency programs for those who do not have undergraduate training in music therapy, and an increasing willingness of master's programs to develop training experiences for people without music therapy undergraduate training, will ultimately diversify the population of music therapy students. Diversification of this kind, together with the encouragement of more comprehensive undergraduate liberal arts education, is strongly recommended for music therapists.

Art therapy has the second largest concentration of undergraduate students, following music therapy, but baccalaureate studies in art therapy are preparatory to graduate training. Graduates of undergraduate art therapy programs make up a small number of the students enrolled in master's degree programs in art therapy. The majority of students in both art therapy and dance therapy and integrated arts therapy master's degree programs do not apply directly from college. A number of dance therapy graduate programs state that they desire to work with "mature" students who will bring adult life experience resources into their education.

The majority of psychodrama "students" are experienced professionals who have already earned graduate degrees in other mental health

234

disciplines and who maintain primary professional identities in these areas. Most psychodramatists earn their graduate degrees before becoming involved in psychodrama training. Graduate degree training programs in psychodrama educate a minority of the total population of psychodramatists. There are also significantly more men involved in psychodrama than any of the other creative arts therapy specializations.

MINORITY INVOLVEMENT

All of the creative arts therapies have minority group members who are making key contributions to the discipline. However, the specializations generally find themselves in the position of actively encouraging greater minority participation. Increases are sought in college and university faculties, student bodies and in the professional practice area. The profession appears to fall behind fields like social work and education in terms of attracting members of minority groups. Training programs, as well as national associations, appear to be consistently committed to increasing minority participation in the profession. It is the general consensus of creative arts therapy educators that potential minority students tend to select more conventional mental health professions.

GENDER

Over the course of the past fifteen years, I have worked directly with over 1,000 creative arts therapy students in the United States and other countries. On the basis of my experience and my observations of other educational settings, I can report the strong female versus male presence within the creative arts therapy profession, with psychodrama being an exception. Within the art therapy specialization, I have observed that there is a higher concentration of practicing male art therapists than male art therapy students. Many men now prominent in art therapy have received their education in more conventional disciplines and have subsequently applied interests in art to therapy. There appear to be many more men involved in art and music therapy than dance therapy.

It is not accurate to suggest that men tend to stay away from professions that favor free expression and the body. There are many men involved with other body oriented and primal therapies. The relatively small number of men involved in dance therapy can be partially attributed to the male presence in dance over the past fifty years in the United

States. At the present time, male involvement in the study of dance is increasing and it is likely that in the future the profile of dance therapy students will reflect these changes. There have been considerably more men involved in the study of art and music, and this possibly accounts for the larger number of men who practice art therapy and music therapy than dance therapy. Drama therapy, which is just beginning as a formal creative arts therapy specialization, appears to reflect the female majority pattern of the creative arts therapies, but there are a significant number of men involved.

Today women are a decisive majority in creative arts therapy training programs. For years I have been involved with formal and informal dialogues with both women and men on this issue. Many explanations for the imbalance have been presented. Sex differences have been discussed in terms of the history of women, and not men, in direct caretaking roles within the family and society. However, many assume that the creative arts therapies are caretaking and adjunctive professions and this seems to reinforce the problem. All of the people that I have spoken with agree that the primary reason for the low percentage of men involved in the creative arts therapies has to do with the general image of the profession, relatively low salaries and the tendency of men interested in mental health to go into the more established professions of psychology and psychiatry. The significantly larger numer of men involved in psychodrama can be perceived as related to the fact that psychodramatists generally receive their degrees in psychology, counseling, psychiatry, social work and other disciplines. As I have stated earlier, many of the male art therapists who are practicing today similarly received their degrees in other fields. I believe that the higher male involvement in psychodrama may be partially attributed to the fact that it is a systematic "method" of psychotherapy with its own operational theory.

What presents itself as a controversial and interesting issue is the determination as to whether or not the creative arts therapy profession will benefit from a more balanced female and male membership. Although some may feel that the gender of creative arts therapists is of little importance or that the increased involvement of men may not be particularly helpful, the vast majority of female and male students and professionals with whom I have discussed this topic strongly prefer a more balanced distribution. Both training groups and clinical programs reinforce the necessity for the involvement of both genders. Men, who have been in a minority position in my classes and training groups, have generally done quite well in respecting and assimilating into the female majority. However, groups consistently express the desire for a better distribution according to gender. Male faculty also commonly find themselves in a position where they are working with a group made up exclusively of women. These gender issues present challenges to students, faculty and the profession.

Many prominent female educators believe that the issues of salaries and upgrading the image of profession, which are perhaps minimizing male involvement, must be addressed. Making salaries comparable with other mental health disciplines is in the interest of everyone. Bachelor's level standards and an adjunctive image of the profession will not help in this effort. As the majority of creative arts therapy educators believe, the master's degree is only the beginning of professional training. The primary reason for raising standards cannot be the argument that this will attract men. Such a position insults the pioneering work of the female majority in the profession. If, however, more comprehensive, consistent and advanced training improves the profession as a whole for both women and men, then this will be a productive course of action. Simply stated, every effort must be given to creating an image of the creative arts therapies as a primary mental health discipline. This movement is already underway in the majority of creative arts therapy graduate training programs. There is, however, a need for more coordinated action between the different specializations and the creation of a common psychotherapeutic identity.

Raising standards, rather than hurting admissions to training programs, will help to attract people from more varied backgrounds into the profession. Graduate degree programs in the creative arts therapies have consistently found that raising credits has not resulted in a decline in qualified applicants. To the contrary, rigorous standards tend to elevate the image, desirabiilty and marketability of a profession.

INTERNATIONAL STUDENTS

I am the dean of a graduate creative arts therapy training program in an urban environment in New England that has attracted students from many countries. The majority of our international students have either come from western European countries or they have European cultural backgrounds. Over a ten-year period, we have observed how there is a more even distribution between male and female students from western European countries than within the American student community. Our European students have come primarily from the German-speaking cultures of Austria, Switzerland and West Germany, as well as other central and northern countries of western Europe. I have also discovered that there are consistently more men involved in the training groups that we conduct in Europe.

Israel is a fascinating country from the perspective of creative arts therapy statistics. I have been actively involved in educational program development and training in Israel and have found a notably high interest in the profession in that small country. I have often commented on how the percentage of people interested in the creative arts therapies in relation to the total population of Israel far exceeds any other country in the world. In contrast to Europe, the vast majority of Israeli creative arts therapy students are women. The average Israeli creative arts therapy student tends to be a mature woman who has been involved in a career in the arts, human services and in many cases raising a family. I have often suggested that the many unique characteristics of the creative arts therapy profession in Israel will make a rich subject for doctoral research.

AGE

On the basis of informal statistics that I have compiled with faculty colleagues over the past ten years, we estimate the average age of our American and European creative arts therapy graduate students to be approximately twenty-eight with a range from twenty to the late sixties. The Israeli average age, by contrast, appears to be in the late thirties.

Our experience in training creative arts therapists has not indicated that there is any conclusive evidence to suggest that older students make better therapists. Like other graduate programs, we initially felt a bias in favor of the more "mature" student. There are therapeutic roles that young people in their early twenties are not qualified for in terms of life experience. However, we strongly recommend that this fact not be used as a universal barrier to their admission to graduate school. There are just as many roles that the young person is qualified to fill as there are roles that are inappropriate. Age must not be used as an element of discrimination in selecting students. Competence and potential are recommended as principle criteria for assessment.

On the basis of my personal experience, I have found that every age group brings something valuable and unique to the educational and therapeutic context. It is unnecessary to exclude any age group from creative arts therapy training. Many young people graduating from college find themselves being told by graduate schools to go out and work in order to acquire professional experience, while potential employers are looking for people with graduate degrees.

PREVIOUS DEGREES

Our experience in graduate education has clearly indicated that the majority of students apply to master's degree programs with a bachelor's degree. Every year at least 10 percent to 20 percent of our applicants have earned master's degrees in related fields. We have also worked with a small group of post-doctoral students who desire professional training in the creative arts therapies.

PREREQUISITES FOR SUCCESS

It is important to note that our experience in direct training and our observations of the creative arts therapy profession, as a whole, offer no indication whatsoever that undergraduate training in the creative arts therapies has a significant positive effect on performance in graduate schools or later professional achievement. The career patterns of people in the early and present stages of the creative arts therapy profession indicate that students with exceptional artistic skills, sophisticated aesthetic sensitivities, and what may be defined as a "primary" life commitment to art are more apt to maintain long-term identities as creative arts therapists.

We have observed that artistic competence clearly affects the quality of professional work and the range of a therapist's skills in working with artistic expression. The creative arts therapist's personal identity as an artist does tend to influence the extent to which the arts act as *primary* modes of communication in therapy. High artistic standards are strongly recommended for the profession. However, technical skills should not be used as a sole criteria for acceptance into educational programs. Admissions standards can be flexible and can encourage the involvement of people in the profession who are beginning to develop themselves as artists. What seems to be most important is the person's aesthetic sensibility and commitment to art, as well as the ability to apply the creative process to therapy. Strict guidelines as to what degree of artistic competence is necessary to become involved in the creative arts therapies will present unnecessary obstacles to free access to multi-sensory and aesthetic expression in therapy and will discourage the participation of other mental health disciplines.

Success in creative arts therapy training and later professional work is equally dependent upon clinical sophistication and psychological knowledge. Our experience has revealed that having an undergraduate degree in psychology, a degree in the fine arts, or a combination of both, does not result in greater success. This combination of studies does, however, help in the preparation process, and coursework in these areas is advised. Competence can be achieved in different ways. Often a student will graduate from an undergraduate school with a psychology major limited to a particular theoretical orientation. The same applies to certain fine arts majors. I have discovered that a student with an undergraduate major in comparative religion and who has studied in the arts and psychology may be better prepared for graduate study than the person with a narrow behavioral science or fine arts education.

When reviewing applications for graduate study, I find it essential to focus primarily on the assessment of the person. Colleagues in creative arts therapy graduate education seem to agree on this priority. Rather than requiring prescribed coursework as prerequisites, we review competence in the fundamental areas of interpersonal skills, the arts, psychology, clinical experience, the humanities and, most importantly, potential to succeed as a creative arts therapist. The assessment of a student's potential requires flexibility, intuition and experience in training creative arts therapists. Certain evaluation skills can be developed only through many years of experience that allow the educator to anticipate what the student will encounter as the training process unfolds.

Undergraduate study in the creative arts therapies is appropriate for students who have made early choices in career direction. Practical training experiences and theoretical knowledge in the creative arts therapies help to build self-confidence and competence. We have observed how students who come to graduate school directly from college are able to make a considerably smoother transition if they have already been introduced to the creative arts therapies. Our experience has consistently revealed that depth of understanding in clinical work and human relations is strongly related to a broad liberal education and personal interests. Narrow specialization on both the undergraduate and graduate levels limits intellectual, artistic, interpersonal and cultural understanding, all of which are essential for excellence in creative arts therapy.

In 1985 the National Commission for Excellence in Teacher Education established by the American Association of Colleges for Teacher Education released a report entitled "A Call for Change in Teacher Education." The report is consistent with recent criticisms of medical education, in that it stresses the importance of the liberal arts in the training of professionals. The commission described teaching as "a complex human endeavor guided by knowledge that is both scientific and artistic" (NCETE, 1985) and declared that every element of teacher education is in need of improvement. A majority of the commission supported the expansion of teacher training programs from four to five years in order to allow for expanded liberal studies. Institutions of higher education were challenged to create learning environments that will attract the highest quality education students whether they be liberal arts majors or professionals desiring to change career directions. "We strongly affirm that those entering the teaching profession should have an academic concentration and genuine liberal education. In effect, those requirements are equivalent to a bachelor's degree" (Ibid.). A minimum of four years of liberal studies was recommended by the majority of the commission. Institutions of higher education, according to the study, are the appropriate place for the preparation of teachers because of their resources for integrated and comprehensive education. Colleges and universities, in a creative and supportive partnership with practical training sites, provide ideal conditions for professional education.

Although the report did not formally recommend the master's degree as the entry level credential for teachers, it came very close, perhaps not wanting to suddenly upset the basic structure of teacher education programs in over 1,200 American colleges and universities. "We particularly encourage those colleges and universities offering only a baccalaureate degree and those having graduate programs to explore mutually beneficial arrangements that will permit all highly qualified students desiring to become teachers to complete the best program possible" (Ibid.).

The text of this report on teacher education can be applied to the creative arts therapies. The principle argument for the liberal arts in undergraduate education is that they increase the number of excellent applications to creative arts therapy graduate programs. This is combined with my observation, as confirmed by colleagues, that highly focused undergraduate professional education does not generally result in better performance in graduate school or in professional work. The broadest possible admissions criteria for graduate school are encouraged. Graduates of bachelor's level training programs in the creative arts therapies as well as liberal arts graduates should be considered together. It is also recommended that undergraduate students be given the opportunity to choose between early professional preparation in conjunction with liberal studies and a complete liberal arts education. We have discovered that what students in undergraduate creative arts therapy programs gain in early professional education is sometimes lost in missed liberal studies. Nevertheless, it is in the best interest of the creative arts therapy profession to continue to offer students a variety of high-quality educational choices.

REFERENCES

National Commission for Excellence in Teacher Education: A call for change in teacher education. *The Chronicle of Higher Education*, March 6, 1985.

10. FACULTY

FIRST AND SECOND GENERATION FACULTY

FACULTY PROFILES in the creative arts therapy profession are varied. They tend to include two distinct groupings composed of what can be referred to as first and second generation creative arts therapists. The first generation includes pioneers in the profession who did not graduate from formal academic training programs in the arts and psychotherapy. Second generation educators are those who have graduated from degree programs in the creative arts therapies. First generation creative arts therapists are typically those who established graduate and undergraduate training programs. They are people who prepared themselves for their largely self-created positions in higher education through the clinical practice of the creative arts therapies. They developed training programs by either persuading colleges and universities to become involved or by responding to invitations by academic institutions interested in the profession. Second generation creative arts therapy educators have also become involved in the creation and spread of training programs. After graduating from a formal program and receiving post-graduate experience, they have gone to other regions and have become involved in the creation of new educational programs.

It is generally true that the majority of creative arts therapy educators involved in establishing programs were relatively inexperienced in higher education teaching and administrative roles. Exceptions to this general principle are a substantial number of first generation creative arts therapy educators who came to the profession through the arts in education. This group is comprised of arts educators (for the most part, holders of doctoral degrees) who were teaching arts education on the graduate and undergraduate levels. These arts education faculty mem-

243

bers then changed their academic and administrative orientations to include the creative arts therapies. This group is made up of both first and second generation creative arts therapy educators. Many second generation educators with previous backgrounds in the arts and education returned to master's level training programs to become educated in the creative arts therapies. The Lesley College Graduate School has established a special post-doctoral fellows program for university faculty who wish to receive training in the creative arts therapies. The post-doctoral program recognizes the unique educational status of the fellows while also engaging them in training experiences required of all master's students. American Art Therapy Association professional registration standards have made special provisions for holders of doctoral degrees who return to school for graduate study in the creative arts therapies.

In addition to experienced faculty in the arts in education, professors of clinical psychology, fine arts, medicine and other disciplines have expanded their roles to include a professional identity as a creative arts therapist and have been influential in establishing training programs within institutions of higher education. The experience of this group of higher education veterans has been helpful to the development of creative arts therapy training, in that they have been able to share their expertise in educational issues with less experienced colleagues.

The vitality and innovative characteristics of educational programs in the creative arts therapies can be attributed to the absence of conventional academic thinking on the part of pioneering educators who were involved in the creation of the first training programs. This group generally came to higher education directly from intensive field experience. Many educators continue to maintain a clinical practice in addition to their educational roles.

As a result of this practical dimension, faculty and educational programs in the creative arts therapy field tend to be action oriented and directed toward the training of practitioners within an environment of close supervision. The newness of the profession has also encouraged an educational atmosphere which values peer sharing and cooperation among students and faculty. The spirit in creative arts therapy training programs has continued to be idealistic and committed to social service. All programs share a common ideology calling for greater public and professional awareness of the healing powers of the arts. There is a distinct growth mentality within the profession and these values are conveyed through educational programs. Faculty therefore tend to be uniformly characterized by personal inclinations for innovation and development.

Virtually every faculty person involved in the creation of an educational program has had to be involved in establishing and communicating a rationale for the training program within the academic and professional community. These faculty members have also had to work, for the most part, in isolation and with little external support for their work. They have had to demonstrate the validity of the profession and be articulate enough to persuade institutions to become involved. These job-related demands are not as strong for second generation creative arts therapy educators who are filling established positions within higher education. The profession is in this respect becoming more regularized in relation to older academic disciplines. It would appear that the majority of faculty being hired today are graduates of formal training programs in the creative arts therapies. It is predicted that this trend will grow even more uniform in the future.

First generation creative arts therapy educators make up a strikingly varied group. They include people with professional training in the arts, education, the arts in education, clinical psychology, religion, medicine and other fields. They are typically people who developed a vision of the professional identity of the creative arts therapist and then directed their careers toward the realization of this goal. There are leading education pioneers who did not, or do not, hold graduate or even bachelor's degrees. They so thoroughly distinguished themselves through clinical practice and scholarly achievements that universities admitted them to the academic community. In this respect, the early stages of creative arts therapy education paralleled standards of fine arts education where distinguished masters without academic degrees are admitted to higher education faculties. As the profession matures and professional associations establish guild standards, this variety within the faculty community is in progressive decline. The trend is not only a result of the way in which professional associations produce uniform standards but also because opportunities for pioneering work by non-credentialed people within clinical practice are being eliminated.

The majority of first generation educators did not hold doctoral degrees when they began their work within institutions of higher education. A large percentage of this group has subsequently gone on to earn doctorates while on the job. They have respected the need to hold a doctoral degree within institutions of higher education. At the present time the doctorate is not required, but rather recommended, by most institutions of higher education hiring creative arts therapy educators. Individual schools do require the doctorate. It is not possible to require the doctorate for all faculty positions because of the scarcity of qualified people. Institutions often find themselves receiving applications from holders of doctoral degrees with little clinical and leadership experience in the creative arts therapy field and correctly lean toward hiring the more experienced leader in the profession who does not have an advanced degree.

The professional creative arts therapy community will generally have more respect for programs hiring faculty with strong clinical, scholarly and professional leadership experience. Colleges and universities which have eschewed these priorities in favor of the doctorate have encountered many difficulties in achieving quality education. Students typically show more respect for, and motivation to study with, the experienced professional. Experienced arts educators, clinical psychologists and other faculty who hold doctorates, and who have attempted to change their professional identity to the creative arts therapies, have similarly encountered difficulty in their credibility as educators because of their lack of comprehensive experience. It is strongly recommended that all faculty from related disciplines desiring to adopt the creative arts therapy profession become fully involved in personal training and supervised clinical experience before attempting to teach.

Increasing the amount of faculty in the creative arts therapies who hold doctorates is also hampered by the present lack of opportunities for doctoral study. Many faculty have earned doctorates in related fields of psychology, counseling and education or interdisciplinary studies programs. Many arts therapy educators have, as mentioned previously, earned doctorates in the Union Graduate School of the Union for Experimental Colleges and Universities which provides the opportunity for self-designed Ph.D. study in the arts and psychotherapy. Music therapy offers a selection of programs for doctoral study and, because of its relatively older professional status, involves a higher percentage of second generation faculty members in training programs.

Psychodrama is unique among the creative arts therapies, in that most training, as mentioned previously, takes place in private institutes outside higher education. Psychodrama trainers are therefore not under similar academic pressures to hold advanced degrees. Virtually all psychodrama trainers are in the second generation category because, unlike the other specializations, training in the early years of pscyhodrama was focused almost exclusively on J.L. Moreno and his associates. Because psychodrama is a method almost exclusively formulated by a single person, Moreno himself may be the only first generation educator. The other creative arts therapies have been developed and invented by many different people around the world. First generation educators are still coming into prominence in regions where the profession has not been developed. This variety of origins is considered to be a desirable quality emphasizing universal elements of the creative arts therapy experience that unify all practitioners as well as differences. It is recommended that future faculty standards continue to foster variety. Professional associations have typically taken on the role of promoting uniformity and standardization.

Faculty in virtually all programs are comprised of a combination of creative arts therapists together with professors from other disciplines. Creative arts therapists generally supervise field placements, advise students and teach courses in their areas of expertise. Psychologists, psychiatrists and other mental health professionals might teach courses in related clinical and psychological subjects or research methodology. Graduate level, as opposed to undergraduate, programs tend to give creative arts therapy faculty responsibility for the student's entire educational program.

REGULAR AND PART-TIME FACULTY

At the present time, faculty in the creative arts therapies are for the most part focused on teaching, supervision and the development of the profession. Research and scholarship, though valued by virtually all training programs, are a major priority in few. This trend will change with the increasing development of doctoral education.

If there is a typical profile of the creative arts therapy faculty member, it might include the following traits: teaching responsibilities combined with program administration and supervision; ongoing praticum site development and job placement for graduates; admissions responsibility and involvement in program development; cooperation with other departments and faculty within the college or university; service on school committees; articulation of the goals of the training program to academic administrators; supervision and coordination of adjunct faculty; part-time scholarship and research; active involvement in one or more national associations in the creative arts therapies; and often the maintenance of a clinical practice. Some faculty are able to also maintain careers as professional artists while others are working on doctorates.

This type of schedule, characteristic of the creation and development of an emerging profession, often results in a high degree of faculty and administrative burnout. Sabbaticals are necessary together with creative staffing arrangements and other forms of support to faculty which encourage the ongoing regeneration of energy.

Faculty in the creative arts therapies often find themselves involved in more than one academic department within the college or university. Program identity is also complicated by the use of adjunct faculty by many academic programs. All of these characteristics can serve as strengths for the program. More than one departmental affiliation for the faculty member can further interdisciplinary cooperation and communication within the institution. Program respect within an institution of higher education typically corresponds to the reputation and credibility of individual faculty members. If the faculty member is not fully integrated into the academic community, the image of the program within the school will suffer.

Adjunct faculty can be a vital resource to the training program. Qualified adjuncts tend to be highly motivated and dedicated teachers who draw on their present work experiences. The adjunct complements the teaching of full-time faculty with a practitioner perspective, necessary in professional education. Regular and clear communications are essential between adjuncts and regular faculty in order to avoid the fragmentation of the training program.

A 1984 report on part-time faculty in higher education describes a significant increase in reliance on adjuncts over the past thirty years and predicts further expansion in the future (Gappa, 1984). Part-time faculty in the creative arts therapies are typically employed in occupations related to the subject matter of their teaching. Their motives for teaching include the desire for personal development, needs for professional and intellectual stimulation and the desire to contribute to the profession. Advocates for part-time faculty feel that their contributions to higher education are not adequately recognized by institutions which rely heavily on them while not giving proper attention to their work and their essential teaching status within the academic community. Colleges continue to perceive "the faculty" in traditional collegial terms while an ever-increasing number of courses is being taught by "adjuncts." The term adjunct is itself an expression of the way in which these faculty are perceived by institutions of higher education, suggesting a dependent, subordinate and nonessential relationship.

> More than a quarter million part-time faculty are employed in American colleges and universities (NCES 1980). A reasonable guess is that they carry 15 percent of the total college-level teaching load. Most part-timers are poorly paid, have marginal job security at best, and get little institutional support for their teaching efforts. Nearly all to some extent resent the uncollegial treatment they receive and are frustrated by the impediments to good teaching performance they must put up with. But on the balance, they are sufficiently satisfied to continue. Some teach more for the prestige it provides in relation to their full-time careeers than for the money. Few rely wholly on part-time teaching for their livelihoods (Gappa, 1984).

In addition to their orientation to practice, one of the major strengths of part-time faculty is the fact that they are not economically dependent on the academic institution. Part-time faculty in the creative arts therapies tend to be well integrated into training programs and receive considerable respect from both students and full-time faculty. This positive attitude toward part-time faculty is largely a result of the strong commitment in the profession to clinical practice as the major focus of education. These conditions are not always present in other academic disciplines where the status of part-time faculty is not as high.

The part-time faculty member can serve as a continuing model of the teacher/practitioner which will hopefully continue as the ideal for all creative arts therapy faculty. As the profession becomes more established within academic communities, an additional effort may have to be made to encourage faculty to maintain their identities as practitioners. Scholarship and active involvement in personal artistic expression are equally important if the faculty member is to sustain the optimum skill level for full performance in the role of educating creative arts therapists.

THE INFLUENCE OF NATIONAL PROFESSIONAL ASSOCIATIONS

Recent reports on reform in higher education, published by the National Endowment for the Humanities and the Study Group on the Conditions of Excellence in American Higher Education, were sharply critical of excessive specialization in the curriculum of American colleges and universities. The reports conclude that the quality of learning is primarily influenced by effective teaching and contact with faculty who are charged with the responsibility for standards of excellence.

The report of The Study Group on the Conditions of Excellence in American Higher Education was critical of accreditation standards established by professional associations.

> Accreditation standards for undergraduate professional programs often stand as barriers to the broad understanding we associate with liberal learning. For example, the guidelines of one professional accrediting association confine one-half to two-thirds of a student's baccalaureate program to courses in two areas. Another association prescribes approximately 70 per cent of a student's total program and confines that percentage wholly to two subject areas. And according to the standards of yet another association, the bachelor's degree program should involve as much as 80 per cent of a student's work in the professional field.
>
> Specialization may be a virtue for some students. But as ever more narrow programs are created, they become isolated from one another, and many students end up with fragmented and limited knowledge. While depth of study in any area has great value, the guidelines laid down by many professional accrediting bodies distort students' expectations and close off their future options. The result is that the college curriculum has become excessively vocational in its orientation, and the bachelor's degree has lost its potential to foster the shared values and knowledge that bind us together as a society (Mortimer et al., 1984, p. 36).

The professional association is typically more interested in promoting specialized education within the discipline than it is concerned with comprehensive education. The responsibility for upholding standards of comprehensive education rests with institutions of higher education. However, few colleges and universities are interested in challenging the professional associations which ultimately approve or do not approve their programs and in so doing affect their marketability. These factors therefore create the excessive vocationalism and over-specializaton described by The Study Group on the Conditions of Excellence in American Higher Education.

If creative arts therapy education develops according to its present course, with certain national professional associations taking an expanding interest in prescribing a highly specialized curriculum, then faculty will find themselves increasingly involved in teaching standard courses year after year as stipulated by the national association charged with program approval. Not only faculty but college administrators will have less autonomy and power to create curriculum. Narrow specialization will take on even more influence and universities will lose their ability to shape curriculum and faculty standards in their own academic and economic interests. There is at present a large imbalance in responsibility for creating curriculum, with some national professional associations making prescriptions to university faculty and administrators who follow these directives. Institutions of higher education tend to feel that the learned society knows better, since all of professional training has become so thoroughly specialized that the administration of a college or university must rely on outside authorities for guidance. Many colleges and universities are abandoning the classical commitment to freedom of learning and freedom of teaching and are becoming vocational training institutes with standards controlled by outside professional associations. The institutions of higher education are not necessarily responsible for these conditions. They often find that unless they go along with these trends, they cannot compete for students who are growing increasingly concerned about specific educational criteria for employment as prescribed by national professional associations. Through their control of the professions and jobs, the national professional associations in turn control institutions of higher education and faculty.

Professional associations do of course have many necessary and vital functions in relation to educational standards. However, today there is an extreme imbalance of power in those situations where professional associations prescribe curriculum and faculty credentialing standards to colleges and universities.

William Bennet, when serving as Chairman of The National Endowment for the Humanities, called on the faculty and leaders of American colleges and universities to avoid the creation of "isolated disciplinary packages" which narrow rather than expand knowledge and competence. He asked for the support of inspired and passionate teaching dealing with "the interrelatedness of great works, ideas and minds."

> When one reads thoroughly in the works by Darwin, Marx and Freud, what one finds most impressive is not the competence they show in the studies we associate them with, though that is of course impressive, but the range of what they knew, the staggering breadth of the reading which they had made their own and without which, one comes to understand, they could never have achieved the insights in their own areas that we honor them for. Today, it seems to me, we are still moving mostly in the opposite direction, despite here and there a reassuring revolt. We are narrowing, but not enlarging our

horizons. We are shucking, not assuming our responsibilites. And we communicate with fewer and fewer because it is easier to jabber in a jargon than to explain a complicated matter in . . . real language . . . . How long can a democratic nation afford to support a narcissistic minority so transfixed by its own image (Bennet, 1984, p. 19)?

Bennet advocates academic diversity, breadth and creativity in the training of professionals. He describes how the National Endowment for the Humanities Study Group on the State of Learning in the Humanities in Higher Education stated that:

> No single curriculum should be appropriate in all places. The study group recognizes the diverse nature of higher education under whose umbrella are institutions with different histories, philosophies, educational purposes, student body characteristics, and religious and cultural traditions. Each institution must decide for itself what it considers an educated person to be and what knowledge that person should possess . . . the choices a college or university makes for its common curriculum should be rooted firmly in its institutional identity and educational purpose (Bennet, 1984, p. 17).

Institutional and faculty diversity and freedom to design curriculum suited to the mission of a particular school are not priorities for many of the national associations in the creative arts therapies. The organizations vary as to the degree of autonomy given to programs and faculty. The situation that exists today gives virtual dominance to the national professional associations which not only stipulate a particular curriculum that is to be replicated at different schools, but certain associations also require that courses be taught by faculty registered with the association. The American Art Therapy Association has departed from these policies and now, instead of requiring that courses be taught by a "registered art therapist," requires that they be taught by a "professionally qualified art therapist." The practice of requiring that courses be taught by a person registered by the same association which constructs standards for training is potentially in violation of anti-trust laws while also establishing narrow guild interests as the priority in faculty staffing. The American Art Therapy Association has stated that faculty qualifications are not necessarily tied to registration with a particular association. Other associations still require that faculty teaching in programs that they approve have specific registrations and certifications. The associations are at the present time moving to separate professional credentialing from membership in their guilds because of the legal probems with such practices. However, the creation of separately incorporated credentialing groups does little to change the substance of association control.

Education in the creative arts therapies is a multi-million dollar a year industry. Because educational programs have such a strong vested interest in the policies of national associations, educators who make up a small percentage of the membership of these organizations tend to be actively involved in association affairs. They are supported in these roles by their academic institutions and are often given office support and assistance for association business which is recognized as vitally connected to educational business. This contrasts to the working therapist who does not have these resources and who does not tend to have a comparable economic interest in the policies of national associations.

Educational programs have made major contributions to the definition and legitimization of the creative arts therapy profession. However, as with all positive developments in human behavior, the emphasis on education in our professional associations can have its negative dimensions. My chief concern has been that those who desire to make professional registration dependent upon circumscribed educational experiences at particular schools are often the people who benefit most from these regulations, both financially and in professional influence. Educators will argue that they are in the best position to formulate training procedures, yet it must be understood that they have a strong vested interest. Historically, constituents have been easily influenced by leaders who argue for clear, specific and consistent training standards which appease the membership's concern for "quality" while also reinforcing the business of those programs which offer "approved" training processes.

It is recommended that national associations in the creative arts therapies move away from single standard approval processes and encourage experimentation, creativity and autonomy within college and university faculties. Interdepartmental affiliations, as well as cooperation between the different creative arts therapies, needs to be encouraged. Narrow professional vested interests are to be discouraged in favor of incentives for collaboration with other creative arts therapy specializations. Present association educational standards do the reverse, supporting isolation. This problem will be compounded in the future when an increasingly large number of faculty members will be graduates of these specialized programs. First generation faculty bring the benefits of diversity in their personal educational backgrounds. Values of narrow specialization will shrink the intellectual, artistic and clinical boundaries of the profession together with growth opportunities for faculty and students.

At the present time the different creative arts therapy associations are working closer with one another than ever before on issues of job development, third-party payments and governmental regulations. It has become clear that in these areas, cooperation is much more in their mutual interest than separation. It is time for the associations to become similarly enlightened on issues of clinical and educational cooperation. Professional associations are in essence collectives of many professionals with varied backgrounds and interests. It is the members who ultimately control their destiny. It is recommended that all professional members of creative arts therapy associations become actively committed to educational values which support diversity and methods of training that will engage the complexities of clinical practice in the contemporary mental health profession. Members of national professional associations should encourage innovation and creativity in education rather than simply following conventional guidelines which give little attention to different ways of learning.

A CHALLENGE TO FACULTY

Excessive specialization and vocationalism in the undergraduate and graduate curriculum have been widely criticized in higher education studies. "Many critics suggest that until departmental walls are removed or at least made semipermeable, wide-scale systematic reform will be impossible, and the students' pleas for a recognition of the interconnections of knowledge will go unheeded" (Heiss, 1970, p. 66).

A committee of the Association of American Colleges concluded from a 1984 study that vocationalism and the one-sided commitment of faculty to their disciplines rather than to the total educational process is undermining the college curriculum. The committee report mentions how well-intentioned faculty curriculum committees suffer from "chronic paralysis" because of the prescriptions of specialized accrediting groups and professional societies (AAC, 1984). "Excessive structure," "overprescription of training" and "narrowness" are cited as the problematic features of the contemporary trends in higher education.

Faculty are being charged with the responsibility for the revitalization of the curriculum. They must respect the suggestions of external agencies and associations but never abandon their personal values and their responsibility to the total educational process. Faculty creativity, curriculum innovation and commitment to excellence in teaching cannot be contained and directed by external groups intent upon promoting their specific interests. The principle argument in support of the present over-specialization present in American higher education is that highly concentrated studies in a particular discipline are necessary in order to achieve "depth" in learning. This attitude toward academic and professional excellence would have us believe that depth is experienced by moving exclusively in a single direction throughout a program of studies. Intellectual, artistic and clinical depth is not experienced in this way. Depth of understanding has more to do with diversity and the interdependence of different sources of knowledge. Narrowly defined prerequisites for graduate study are often an expression of the bias of the particular discipline or school.

> For our purposes a course of study has depth if it in fact offers a complex structure of knowledge. The comprehension of this structure — a decent understanding and control of it — is what we mean by a study in depth . . . [which] requires multiple dimension; it cannot be reached merely by cumulative exposure to more and more of a specified subject matter . . . . A course of study that offers depth will almost invariably exhibit certain features. It will have a central core of method and theory that serves as an introduction to the explanatory power of the discipline, provides a basis for subsequent work, and unites all students who join in the study in a shared understanding of its character and aims. It will force students to experience the range of topics that the discipline addresses and the variety of analytic tools that it uses . . . . It will provide a means — a project or thesis — by which the student's final mastery of its complexity, however modest or provisional, may be demonstrated . . . . Depth requires sequential learning, building on blocks of knowledge that lead to more sophisticated understanding and encourage leaps of the imagination and efforts at synthesis (Ibid.).

American education from the primary grades through the doctorate separates the different aspects of the curriculum from one another. Little emphasis is placed on the integration of varied sources of knowledge. The perspective of individual disciplines is projected onto knowledge and the educational process. Subjects are studied in isolation from one another. This epistemology contrasts to a more wholistic approach to knowledge which respects all sources of learning and places emphasis on the need of the individual to understand and integrate varied resources. Over-specialization in education is now proceeding to such extreme limits within higher education that those who hold the system as a whole in trust are proclaiming a crisis. The Association of American Colleges' report on *Integrity in the College Curriculum* mentions the problems of over-prescribed studies in premedical education. Since many sectors of the creative arts therapy profession have emulated the educational standards of the medical profession, this criticism should be carefully considered.

> It is time to wean faculties away from the excess that now characterizes the science requirements for premedical students. The medical schools must be encouraged to pay attention to the forceful critics who have risen from within their ranks. Doctors should have the benefit of the course of study we propose. There is no valid reason why physicians should be denied the educational advantages that will be enjoyed by lawyers, businessmen, artists, and all the others for whom the curriculum will be a liberating experience (Ibid.).

Faculty members serve as role models within the academic community. If they are dedicated to narrowly defined studies, these values will be projected throughout the college or university. The expansion of the scope of scholarship, commitment to the interdependence of different sources of knowledge, and the restoration of the primacy of personal integration as essential values in higher education must begin with the actions of the faculty. As a relatively new profession, the creative arts therapies are not overly restricted by the past. We are in an exceptionally good position to promote the values of interdisciplinary cooperation, the integration of varied sources of knowledge and a course of studies which synthesizes the many academic, artistic and clinical disciplines which contribute to the profession.

The creative arts therapy profession is also fortunate to be new enough that faculty throughout the country are committed to the importance of excellence in teaching and clinical practice. It is strongly recommended that as the profession grows, this commitment to teaching should be maintained. Research will ideally emerge from, and ultimately enrich, practice.

REFERENCES

Association of American Colleges: Integrity in the college curriculum, the report of the project on redefining the meaning and purpose of baccalaureate degrees. *The Chronicle of Higher Education.* February 13, 1985.
Bennet, William: To reclaim a legacy, text of the report on humanities in education based on findings of the National Endowment for the Humanities study group on the state of learning in the humanities in higher education. *The Chronicle of*

Higher Education. November 28, 1984.

Gappa, Judith: Part-time faculty: higher education at a crossroads. *ASHE-ERIC Higher Education Research Reports Executive Summary*, Report No. 3, 1984.

Heiss, Ann: *Challenges to Graduate Schools*. San Francisco, Jossey-Bass, 1970.

Mortimer, K., Astin, A., Blake, J.H., Bowen, H., Gamson, Z., Hodginkson, H.L. and Lee, B.: Involvement in learning: realizing the potential of American higher education, the report of the study group on the conditions of excellence in American higher education. *The Chronicle of Higher Education*, October 234, 1984.

National Center for Education Statistics. *Digest of Education Statistics*, 1980.

11. DIALOGUE WITH EDUCATORS

THE METHOD

A S KEY ISSUES emerged from my preliminary research on higher education in the creative arts therapies, it became clear that it was necessary to dialogue with colleagues and receive their opinons. Interviews were conducted in person and by telephone. I attempted to involve a representative sample of the different points of view that exist within the creative arts therapies. The majority of the people that I interviewed are senior educators and pioneers in the development of educational programs in the creative arts therapies. In this chapter, I will summarize and interpret the interviews in a narrative form focusing on the principle themes that emerged. I am grateful to the educators for their enthusiastic and thoughtful cooperation. Their accessibility and consistent commitment to the development of the profession was impressive. The interview process allowed me to directly experience the vitality and intelligent articulation that is taking place in varied sectors of creative arts therapy higher education.

The dialogues with educators demonstrated the stability and depth of the profession and the excellent resources that exist within higher education. I found the educators to be capable of integrating the arts, psychology, clinical practice and the more general principles of culture and the humanities with sophisticated clinical insights. The interviews with educators convinced me that the creative arts therapy profession is capable of achieving the highest educational ideals proposed in this study. I consistently found myself challenged by the educators and believe that we will ultimately reach far beyond the limits of this book. Every educator appeared to be dedicated to the continuous improvement of educational standards. There were few who were content with where we are now.

The limits on educational excellence are simply a result of the continuous evolution of the profession. There appears to be a consensus that we are an emerging discipline with extraordinary potential.

The fact that this is a comparative study in creative arts therapy education required me to give considerable attention to creative arts therapy specializations and points of view that I had not been previously engaged with on a national level. I had to reach out and speak to people outside of my previous frame of reference and conceptual circle. I discovered that a number of the people that I talked to were equally unaware of what colleagues in other creative arts therapies specializations, and even those within their own specializations, were involved with. The interview process supported the position that the creative arts therapies are one profession. There was a consistent grasp of the common elements of creativity in therapy in every interview. I found that all of the educators were committed to the same core principles. Differences between the educators appeared to have much more to do with theoretical orientation than media. The dialogues made me realize how creative arts therapy educators can benefit by becoming more involved with one another. A number of the educators described how they have no contact with colleagues outside of their specializations. The issues and concerns that we have within higher education are interchangeable.

I wish to acknowledge the contributions of the following educators:

Gladys Agell, Associate Professor of Art Therapy and Director of the Graduate Art Therapy Program, Vermont College of Norwich University. President of the American Art Therapy Association and former Chair of the AATA Education Committee.

Dr. Gary Barlow, Professor of Art Therapy and Art Education, Coordinator of the Art Therapy Graduate Program, Wright State University. Chair of the Education Committee of the American Art Therapy Association; former Chair of AATA Research Committee; and Editor of *Art Therapy*.

Dr. Penny Bernstein, Dance and Expressive Therapy Faculty, Lesley College Graduate School. Founder and former director, Antioch New England Dance-Movement Therapy Graduate Program.

Dr. Kenneth Bruscia, Professor of Music Therapy and Coordinator of Music Therapy, Temple University. Chairman of the National Coalition of Arts Therapy Associations and former President of the American Association for Music Therapy.

Dale Richard Buchanan, Chief of the Psychodrama Section, St. Elizabeth's Hospital. Vice President of the American Society of Group Psychotherapy and Psychodrama; past member of the American Board of Examiners in Psychodrama, Sociometry and Group Psychotherapy.

Norma Canner, Associate Professor of Dance Therapy and Expressive Therapy, Lesley College Graduate School.

Dr. Mara Capy, Director of the Dance-Movement Therapy Graduate Program, Antioch New England.

Bob Fleshman, Assistant Professor and former Head of the Drama Therapy Program, Loyola University, New Orleans. Former member of the Board of Directors of the National Association for Drama Therapy.

Dr. Alicia Gibbons, Associate Professor and Director of the Music Therapy Program, University of Kansas. President of the National Association for Music Therapy.

Dr. Eleanor Irwin, Assistant Professor of Psychiatry, University of Pittsburg. Former Chair of Standards and Ethics Committee, National Association for Drama Therapy.

Dr. Paolo Knill, Professor of Expressive Therapy, Lesley College Graduate School. Former President of the Swiss Association for Music Therapy and Chairman of the International Association for Artist-Therapists.

Helen Landgarten, Professor and Chairperson of the Department of Clinical Art Therapy, Loyola Marymount University, Los Angeles. Board Member of the American Art Therapy Association.

Dr. Myra Levick, Professor in the Department of Mental Health Sciences and founder of the Creative Arts in Therapy Graduate Program, Hahnemann University. Former President of the American Art Therapy Association; AATA Honorary Life Member; Former Chair of Education, AATA.

Dr. Vija Lusebrink, Associate Professor of Expressive Therapies, University of Louisville. Former member of the Professional Standards Committee of the American Art Therapy Association.

Dr. Howard McConeghey, Professor of Art Education and Art Therapy and Director of the Graduate Art Therapy Program, University of New Mexico.

Mark Rider, Associate Professor of Music and Coordinator of the Music Therapy Program, Eastern Montana College.

Dr. Arthur Robbins, Professor of Art Therapy and former Director of the Creative Arts Therapy Graduate Program, Pratt Institute.

Peter Rowan, Associate Professor of Psychodrama and Expressive Therapy, Lesley College Graduate School. President of the American Society of Group Psychotherapy and Psychodrama; Past Chairman, American Board of Examiners in Group Psychotherapy, Psychodrama and Sociometry.

Dr. Claire Schmais, Professor and Coordinator of the Dance-Movement Therapy Master's Program, Hunter College.

Dr. Lewis Shupe, Professor of Art Therapy and Communications, Wright State University. Former Chair of the Education and Training Board of the American Art Therapy Association.

Dr. Harriet Wadeson, Associate Professor and Director of the Art Therapy Graduate Program, University of Illinois at Chicago. Former Director of the Art Therapy Graduate Program at the University of Houston/Clearlake. Publications Chair, American Art Therapy Association.

BACCALAUREATE LEVEL TRAINING

In general, there was consistent agreement amongst educators with regard to many of the fundamental issues of higher education in the creative arts therapies. This was surprising, since I anticipated that there would be significant differences of educational philosophy and method. The only exception to this pattern of consensus was the issue of undergraduate professional level training in music therapy. Before initiating this study, I was aware of the fact that many creative arts therapists felt that the bachelor's degree standards of music therapy were reinforcing the adjunctive and lower level image of the profession. Because of this previous knowledge, I attempted to give careful consideration to music therapy educational standards and procedures. When speaking to music therapy educators, I tried to empathize with and respect their positions while also presenting the criticisms that are typically directed at bachelor's level therapeutic training programs.

The music therapy educators that I spoke with articulated the general position of the specialization with regard to bachelor's level standards. Some feel that bachelor's level professional training will have validity as long as they continue to see positive results. An educator spoke of how all training is a matter of "degree," progressing from lower to higher levels. In response to the criticism that psychotherapists cannot be trained at the bachelor's level, the music therapists tend to agree. One educator said that they are training "music therapists" at the undergraduate level. However, as a whole the music therapy educators supported advanced graduate training.

A music therapy educator described how there is an "enormous difference between our B.A. and M.A. students. The bachelor's graduate is prepared for educational, adjunctive and activities therapy work where the master's student trains toward psychotherapeutic and primary therapeutic responsibilities. At the undergraduate level, students are hesitant and not prepared for verbal integration in therapy. Psychotherapeutic training cannot take place at the bachelor's level. With master's students, we can also operate on different theoretical streams. We do not do this with undergraduates. On the bachelor's level we need a B.A. model rather than a B.M. (bachelor's of music), because there are so many things that have to be studied other than music. I believe that you do need a master's degree to practice music therapy, but that training does begin at the B.A. level. A major danger of undergraduate standards is their tendency to reinforce undergraduate level clinical proficiencies which can produce denial that other levels of proficiency exist and are necessary. What music therapists present as their competencies, and the same applies to the other creative arts therapies, can conceal what they are not capable of doing. Not enough music therapists are coming back for graduate study."

Another music therapy educator spoke of how life experience tends to be the major distinction between undergraduate and graduate students. This person felt that the "best" undergraduate music therapy students can be matched with the "best" graduate students. It was recommended that the education of undergraduate music therapy students be approached through a "problem-solving" model supporting "action" in therapy. Distinctions should also be made between undergraduate level and graduate music therapy skills and client populations.

The music therapy educators openly addressed issues of quality in education and spoke of the problems connected with some undergraduate programs that offer a small number of music therapy courses taught by a single person. It was felt that the best way to assess quality is through the evaluation of the individual rather than through narrow educational prescriptions. It is hoped that high standards for the assessment of the individual will help to raise educational standards. It appears that music therapy educators working within a graduate context support the evolution to graduate level standards. They feel that these changes should be made as a free choice on the part of colleges and universities as well as their faculty members. It will ultimately be the marketplace that provides the incentive for change both in terms of the professional's desire for training and the employer's demand for more advanced skills.

Music therapy educators also spoke openly about the need to strengthen humanities and comprehensive education standards on the undergraduate level. One of the educators described how the need for undergraduate programs to be approved by the National Associaton of Schools of Music supports the strength of the music therapy specializaton which tends to rest in high artistic standards, but also reinforces the weakness of rigid course requirements and the necessity of staying within the format of a music department. Many of the most articulate leaders in the contemporary music therapy profession appear to have strong personal backgrounds in the humanities. NASM requirements, however, make it difficult for the average music therapy program to address quality education in both the humanities and the clinical practice of music therapy. It was felt by one of the educators that certain required music courses are not as necessary for training music therapists as additional clinical courses and that music therapy educational programs created outside of the music department context have considerably more freedom to address the core training needs of the music therapist.

The music therapy educators presented an expanding and vital image of their specialization. In addition to challenging the artistic standards of the other creative arts therapies, the music therapists were confident that their field is rapidly increasing its internal theoretical depth and variety. The "behavioral psychology" orientations of the past continue but are today complemented by diversified and interdisciplinary approaches to the use of music in therapy. Psychotherapeutic orientations to music therapy are being perfected as well as approaches to the depth psychology of music. One educator described how certain music therapists who work with behavioral methods will inevitably resist more psychodynamic approaches because "behavioral methods are easier to learn." However, I received the impression from the educators that psychodynamic principles will be much more prominent in the future of music therapy. We discussed the relative absence of music therapy literature dealing with psychotherapeutic principles. One educator described how this is partially due to the "pre-mature" emphasis on quantitative and "hard" research in many music therapy undergraduate and master's programs. "Graduate programs need to place more emphasis on the integration of theory and practice. We need to develop stronger clinicians and not place the major emphasis of master's degree programs on research, which limits opportunities for clinical training. Psychotherapeutically oriented music therapists do not publish within the mainstream of music therapy literature because of the historical orientation to behavioral methods. There are music therapists working with depth psychological principles and there will be continued future growth in psychotherapeutic approaches to music therapy."

Art therapy, dance therapy, drama therapy and psychodrama educators were unanimously and fervently against entry level professional training in the creative arts therapies at the undergraduate level. However, most were in agreement with the position of one of the music therapy educators who stated that professional training can *begin* at the undergraduate level. Pre-professional training at the undergraduate level, in the opinion of the educators, should under no circumstances interfere with and limit opportunities for liberal and comprehensive education. All of the art therapy, dance therapy and psychodrama educators spoke of how the creative arts therapy profession must encourage advanced degrees and clinical sophistication in order "to be taken seriously." Licensure was discussed as the "cutting edge" of the profession's future, in that licensing boards will require consistent standards of all specializations. Educators repeatedly described how it is not possible to even approach "complete" professional educational at the undergraduate level. They spoke of how baccalaureate training experiences can focus on preparation for in-depth graduate study. "Undergraduate programs can train students in materials and instruments of expression while also introducing them to the varieties of knowledge outside a single professional discipline." Without prerequisite graduate education and advanced training standards, a specialization will not begin to explore its range and depth.

Educators described how it is only in recent years that increasing numbers of creative arts therapists are working as primary therapists in clinical programs and private practice. Educational standards therefore need to be raised in order to keep pace with the demands of clinical practice. Expanding opportunities for the development of the creative arts therapies are, in this respect, creating the need for more advanced educational programs. Psychodrama educators described how they can train "good psychodrama technicians" with undergraduate degrees, but that these people do not generally have adequate psychotherapeutic skills.

Educators were divided over whether or not bachelor's level graduates can fill certain clinical positions. Some felt that the graduate of the baccalaureate program can serve in educational, adjunctive and activity oriented positions where their major responsibilites are "supportive." Others believe that all forms of therapeutic work, whether with the emotionally troubled, mentally handicapped or physically handicapped, should require at least a master's degree. It was stated that even if we deal only with "behavior," advanced psychological skills are necessary. Every educator in art therapy, dance therapy, drama therapy and psychodrama expressed how master's level education is only the beginning and that all members of the profession must be involved in lifelong training. It was generally felt that it is unwise to attempt to "crowd it all into undergraduate education" experiences which do not generally allow for reflection on more complex theoretical issues and the development of advanced clinical skills.

An educator involved in undergraduate training in the creative arts therapies expressed personal frustration with the "severe limitations" on training programs at that level and how "baccalaureate students are not adequately prepared for therapy." Educators described how there are exceptions and that gifted therapists will sometimes emerge from undergraduate programs, but that educational standards cannot be constructed around these exceptional cases.

Many educators spoke of how bachelor's level standards will ultimately limit the potential of the profession. Strong opinions were expressed. One educator said that bachelor's level professional education in the creative arts therapies is "abominable" and supportive of the "handmaiden" image of the profession while also undercutting the vital liberal and cultural education necessities of undergraduate education. Others described how master's level training must "definitely" be required. One educator described how the bachelor's level standards that exist in certain parts of the creative arts therapy profession are "a fact of life that will continue regardless of our feelings" and that the marketplace will ultimately resolve the issue. Another educator felt that vested interests make it clear that an element, or force, from outside the profession will have to resolve the issue. I believe that advanced standards will be supported through a better articulation of master's level and post-master's educational priorities as opposed to giving excessive attention to a critique of bachelor's level education. We should evaluate ourselves and go further with quality within our individual areas of expertise and advance the interests of education through example, cooperation and inspiration.

In summary, it clearly appears from my discussions with educators that we are not far apart "in spirit" and in terms of the high standards we are all aspiring toward. For example, every educator that I spoke with was passionately committed to liberal and cultural education at the undergraduate level. Because of their educational history and present standards, music therapists simply have more to contend with in terms of supporting comprehensive education. Music therapy educators are correct, in that they have much to offer the other creative arts therapies as a result of their longer history in higher education. I am confident from my interviews with educators that we are all working toward higher educational standards and that the only course to take at the present time is one of mutual support and honest discussion of the strengths and weakenesses of every training model. All of the specializations are only beginning to reach toward their professional potential. Each specialization has its unique educational and professional history that must be recognized and respected. However, the time has come for the definition and celebration of the essence that is shared by all of the creative arts therapies.

THE PRESCRIPTION OF CURRICULUM

Educators from every creative arts therapy specialization were in general agreement on the importance of avoiding excessive curriculum prescriptiveness on the part of national professional associations. All educators felt that there is a central core of knowledge and competence that every specialization must support. They spoke of the dangers involved with narrow interpretations of these core principles which restrict the development of the profession and responsiveness to the changing social context. An art therapy educator described how the best prescription will encourage freedom, student choice and the development of varied programs. The educator supported as little regulation as possible so that the field can develop depth through the process of free inquiry and choice. "People with diversified backgrounds and interests can only arrive at agreement on the most basic structural universals that are shared by all." There was a consensus among the educators that "variety is healthy." Core studies must also be interpreted broadly.

A number of educators clearly stated that the national association should be concerned with high standards but not through specific prescription which ultimately limits education and produces "mechanistic standardization." Educators seemed to agree that the association's role is the development of "broad and open" standards of excellence. As soon as a particular group attempts to impose its philosophy or method on the profession, there will be conflict and energy wasted on simply protecting a point of view.

Educators spoke of how freedom does not necessarily produce anarchy. The older associations have discovered that prescriptive educational guidelines do not improve quality. Ultimately, the job marketplace, the survival of an educational program, the stability of the college or university, the performance of graduates and faculty, free intellectual inquiry, innovation and the constant pursuit of higher standards are the best indicators of success. The profession must begin to move toward these "real" evaluations of quality as opposed to the present tendency to determine whether or not a program fits a national association curriculum prescription. All of the educators seemed to be in agreement with a music therapy faculty member who said that high standards must be achieved through "inspiration rather than prescription."

It was generally felt that prescription "kills creativity . . . and leaves little room for growth . . . . You learn your thing and never go beyond." Educators addressed how the need for prescription is a serious problem in professional education. Some students want to be "fed" and have been exposed to educational methods where personal and programmatic experimentation and discovery are not encouraged. Schools are often driven by feelings of safety and security that are associated with "rigorously prescribed" training guidelines. Another educator described how the national association should only be concerned with defining competence and allowing people to achieve this objective in different ways. "Prescription stops research, experimentation and the development of new materials, courses and programs. Faculty should teach from the basis of their research, experimentation and experience rather than within a curriculum established by a national association."

The creative arts therapy profession has legitimate concerns with educational quality and the need for all educational programs to meet minimal standards. However, the history of higher education does not offer evidence that quality is heightened through a prescribed curriculum. The concerns and fears that professions have about quality typically produce "over-regulation" in higher educaton which ultimately plays right into what one educator described as the politics of "turf." Quality has much more to do with the performance of people and institutions. An educator described how association education guidelines "must support innovation rather than be threatened by it."

The psychodrama educators related the dangers of an overly prescribed curriculum to the core philosophy of the psychodramatic process. They spoke of how beliefs in spontaneity and creativity necessitate allowing the training model to be "a product of the interaction" between faculty and students. Psychodrama educators agree with their colleagues in the other creative arts therapies that there are core competencies but that this should not lead to "a stamping machine mentality." Within psychodrama there appears to be agreement that minimal prescriptions should be made only to guarantee a "common base . . . the majority has to be inspiration." A psychodrama educator described how certain professional "types believe that there is a single way to educate a person and that this should be prescribed. The more intuitive educator believes that the way is always evolving and there are no guideposts."

Psychodrama educators described their experience with the implementation of examination procedures which involve both written and action components. The written exam was described "as an attempt to embrace academia" which psychodrama has isolated itself from through its private institute educational model. I was told that "there is some validity to the written exam but the action assessment is far more important." An educator experienced with all forms of psychodrama training stated that the action exam is complete unto itself and can present everything that a written exam will reveal and more. "Action is the crucible" in psychodrama education. Psychodramatists were sharply critical of the prescription mentality as "an expression of narrow-minded people who cannot understand the dynamic and total process of education in the creative arts therapies." They describe how a strength of their apprenticeship model of training is the fact that people working within this context "refuse to be told what to teach, whereas academia is much more open to prescription."

TECHNIQUE AND THEORY

Educators in all of the creative arts therapy specializations agree on the need for the profession to create theory which articulates the process of our work. There was strong support for the creation of theory that places primary emphasis on the language of art. Educators described how the profession is not a subdivision of psychology. "We see things differently; we have a different philosophy and language." I was surprised to hear educators speaking passionately and precisely about the necessity of articulating what happens within the creative arts therapy process. Rather than interpreting artistic expression from the perspective of stereotypic psychological theories, creative arts therapists and students, according to an art therapy educator, need to be able to observe what is taking place when a person enters into a relationship with art materials and other people. They must be able to conceptualize and express what is taking place within the relationship. The art therapy educator spoke of how conventional psychological theories often serve as a "mask, hiding the person's inability to look into and explain what is happening with the material."

Dance therapy educators also stressed the importance of thinking within the context of the art medium as opposed to analyzing artistic expression with psychological constructs that do not originate in art. Interpretations of this kind place art in a secondary role and the psychological theory in the dominant position. Dance therapists spoke of how movement cannot be a secondary response within the dance therapy relationship. The body is the primary mode of communication. The therapist has to "own the dance" and use it as an "instantaneous response." Explanations of what is taking place within the dance therapy relationship must therefore be articulated in clinical language which expresses the movement dimension.

Educators spoke of how we have to take a fresh look at the different forms of artistic expression and empirically observe different media and the way in which they affect people. We must determine whether we have theories of our own or whether we attach ourselves to other disciplines such as psychiatry and psychology. Our interdependence with psychology should not interfere with our creativity and exploration of our art media. An educator described how the creative arts therapies translate many of the theories of psychology through the artistic process.

Prior to my interviews with these educators, I did not believe that there was strong support for the creation of theoretical structures that place primary emphasis on the language and context of art. I had thought that educators were more closely associated with conventional psychological theories. As higher education within the creative arts therapies matures and individual programs develop a history of their own, distinct from psychiatry and psychology, there seems to be a growing sensitivity to the necessity for theory indigenous to art and the creative arts therapy profession. Educators expressed their strongest opinions on the issue and consistently labeled theoretical development as "imperative" for the profession. They expressed the need for research to substantiate and clarify what we are doing. One educator described the history of research in the creative arts therapies as beginning with descriptive and concrete materials such as case studies which tell the story of what we are doing. Now there is a need to evaluate, compare, find universals and differences and establish theories.

Psychodrama educators said that their specialization must strengthen its research activities. "The apprenticeship model has been highly effective as a mode of practical training but the exclusive association of psychodrama with non-academic institutes has limited its theoretical resources." Psychodramatists describe how the theoretical basis established by J.L. Moreno keeps some people at a distance because involvement in psychodrama is considered to be acceptance of Moreno, who for many is a strikingly controversial person. Psychodramatists also know that the specificity of their theories and methods is a source of significant strength and clinical definition. They are in this respect well aware of the power of theory which emerges directly from action. The psychodrama educators feel that it is essential at this time to continue to expand their theoretical foundations.

Theory creation within the creative arts therapies does not have to negate contributions by other psychological disciplines but can rather build upon them. The difference will lie in the fact that the new theory will come directly from body language, imagery, sound and dramatic enactment. The media will be interpreted within art-based theories rather than from an outside perspective. An educator expressed how the creative arts therapies are to be defined in relation to the totality of art media within the profession as opposed to a single theory and a specific approach to media. In order to maintain the vitality of the profession, we must stay open to diverse ways of using media. Theory must evolve directly from the engagement with media as an attempt to define and guide action. The profession will weaken its artistic mission if action and the interpretation of action are limited by theory. Teaching must maintain the experimental ideals of the scientist's laboratory and the artist's studio. Education is an ongoing process of research and personal inquiry.

Educators were in complete agreement with regard to the problems of teaching techniques before students have worked through their personal beliefs, values and interpersonal capabilities. A colleague, who was not interviewed during this study, describes the problem in terms of a student who appeared for graduate study declaring that "There is nothing wrong with getting to know myself but I came here to be a therapist." Experienced educators know that the "how to do it" approach does not work in the training of therapists. As an art therapy educator said to me, "technique is a way of getting to process." It is not technique but, rather, process that is the primary objective of therapeutic training. However, the two are totally interdependent. Rather than perceiving technique as a series of highly controlled exercises, I see it as an essential element of personal style. What works for one person cannot be simply adopted by another. Therefore, the core curriculum of the creative arts therapies focuses on personal style and technique as guided by certain universally accepted principles.

An art therapy educator described how the primary objective of training is helping students to develop a philosophical understanding of what they are doing. Techniques cannot be taught as "a bag of tricks." Students must understand what they are doing and why certain things are necessary. "I do not think you can teach procedures which ultimately lead to emerging techniques without first understanding the self and the philosophical base of who you are at that time and where you are going. Too many educational experiences are directed toward technique without philosophy and personal introspection." Creative arts therapy educators consistently say that they resist teaching techniques that students eagerly write down, but rather teach the nuances of therapy by helping the person "just to be."

In general, the response of educators to the necessity of developing an artistic theory of mental health was "I could not agree with you more." The educators spoke passionately and consistently about the need to avoid training strategies based exclusively on the acquisition of techniques. A drama therapy educator said that, "When it comes to working with live people, we discover that the boundaries we create are false. The boundaries are created for our benefit, to make us feel secure and confident. If you are really in tune with the people that you are working with, you will be able to follow them wherever the process happens to take you. This way of working contrasts to directing people through techniques. It takes comfort and security with oneself and clinical knowledge to be able to follow the person. This dynamic interplay between the therapist and client contrasts to technique oriented therapy where there is excessive leading. Therapy is based more on interaction than directive technique."

Another drama therapy educator described how the absence of unifying theory can limit the potential of the profession. Theory can in this respect provide focus, power, identity and a sense of purpose. The educator described how the ability of drama therapy to integrate so many different aspects of life and expression also creates problems of identity. "The main problem of drama therapy is that it combines so many areas and all of the arts and thus becomes a profession of mixed art forms. This multiplicity corresponds to life. I have trouble separating psychodrama from drama therapy even though I understand the difference in technique. I know what is not psychodrama but sometimes I do not know what is drama therapy. At this point drama therapy has to create something which holds all of the elements of the arts together. Psychodrama has been able to do this through an integrating theory and philosophy of what therapy — and life — are. In drama therapy we need depth to hold it all together."

In my opinion drama therapy has an unusual opportunity to be inclusive of varied approaches to the arts and psychotherapy that do not fit into single-modality specializations. The ability to integrate variety, multi-dimensional expression and an aesthetic orientation that includes all of life can give definition and strength to the new specialization of drama therapy which might consider adopting Wagner's concept of *gesamtkunstwerk*, advocating an integrated approach to all of the arts. Theater can serve as a single art form and professional identification for integrated creative arts therapists. Since all psychotherapy is based on principles of enactment and storytelling, drama therapy might build upon these core elements, expanding their possibilities for expression within the therapeutic process. Because theater includes so many different media of expression, it is in need of theory to give it definition. By contrast, the other creative arts therapies receive considerable definition through the media alone.

Educators saw the creation of an artistic theory of therapy as essential to the survival of the profession since continuity is as much dependent upon ideas as upon action. "Aesthetics and artistic sensibility have to be applied to psychodynamics and therapy. We need to develop a theoretical framework that is consistent with our work. These concepts will help us to be a clear and separate discipline. We will make it or not on the basis of having a theory and technique that is ours alone and not a potpourri. Although our theory may evolve from others, ultimately it becomes unique, distinct and articulated in our language."

WHAT EDUCATORS STRUGGLE WITH

This book began as a result of my personal documentation of what I found most difficult and challenging in the work of training creative arts therapists. My conflicts and struggles have in turn provided by deepest insights into the nature of the profession and the educational process. In speaking to my colleagues, I discovered that their experience generally paralleled my own.

The interviews with faculty members supported the importance of "opening" in psychotherapeutic work and in relationships to students. A dance therapy educator said to me that: "The most difficult thing is to stay open in terms of my own process when working with students. The field deals with dynamics and you cannot do this without evoking feelings. It is exhausting. I am on the line all of the time, personally and professionally. I know some of the answers, but not all. Students and faculty are in the process together. Any person who claims to have all of the answers should get out of the field. It is a constant process of self-investigation, of self-learning, of balancing the inner and the outer, and distinguishing what has to do with the system and what has to do with me. It is tiring to keep examining and looking over these things."

An art therapy educator described how difficult it is at times to know how much the art experience will do on its own without intervention by the therapist. The art of "standing back" and allowing the artistic process to work was distinguished from "stepping in." The same educator described how difficult it can be to deal with prescriptiveness in a profession that focuses on art. "Great art is not produced through prescription. Each artwork is a different struggle. I never know how it will turn out until it is finished. This principle applies to therapy as opposed to the belief that a certain kind of activity is to be done with a particular type of diagnosis." Another educator spoke of how the art process is not always healing and described the therapist as "the guide who helps the person to tie things together. Art is the binding factor. This is quite different from taking art to a verbally oriented therapist."

Experienced and successful educators in the creative arts therapies consistently supported the need to operate according to aesthetic and intuitive principles in both therapy and training. Their conflicts often came from dealing with expectations from students that the educational process would be "clear-cut," definitive and free of ambiguity. It is perhaps true that as educators we have a good portion of the demanding and concrete student within ourselves and evaluate our personal performance according to the need for tangible operational principles. It seems that an essential element for success in faculty performance involves the recognition and acceptance of how training in the arts and therapy takes place. The faculty member needs to be able to interpret the process to students and be capable of helping them to understand the necessity for aesthetic and intuitive judgments, together with the development of a personal style of operation. We must also be able to understand the complexities of our personal performance as educators.

It is necessary to learn how to appease the harsh critics within ourselves so that our personal doubts do not undermine the basic self-confidence needed to perform competently. A dance therapy educator spoke to me about how the educator has to be "grounded" in the self in order to help students do the same. "It does go wrong for me when I am not resolved in my own issues. I begin to struggle with myself, become resentful, angry and incapable of healthy communication that is essential to being a good teacher and therapist. There have been times when I have not been the model I should have been. I am at my best when I work intuitively and spontaneously while also questioning what I am doing. I become part of a force that makes me grow. What wipes people out is the inability to take conflict, criticism and aggression and work with it. In dance terms I have to be grounded and show students that I will not disappear when attacked. I have to be there, waiting and not allowing anxiety to go wild." The teacher must help students to find their personal ways of working and not be afraid of engaging fears. The process of becoming a therapist is often painful and arduous but equally rewarding if successfully pursued.

Another educator said, "The hardest thing is the line between teaching and therapy. You cannot teach creative arts therapy approaches without people experiencing them. If you want to train primary therapists, you have to give them depth training. There are situations where someone gets deeply involved in the experience and I have to determine how much I will work with the human being in relation to what is good for the class as a whole. Decisions are made through instinct. Personal disturbance and pain take priority. If conflict emerges from something I present, I must work with it. However, I will try not to push a vulnerable person with rigid defenses. The classes involve learning contracts that are distinct from therapeutic relationships. I ask for volunteers and everyone works at their own level. Involvement of this kind is essential to learning. If a program does not engage this process then it cannot be training therapists."

A number of creative arts therapy educators described how they take courses themselves at other institutions in order to maintain a sensitivity to the student role and to make themselves more "vulnerable." Others spoke of the need to keep their "hands in the process of doing therapy in order to be honest and relevant."

Educators described the difficulties inherent in the role of being "nurturing and affirming" while at the same time being "analytical and critical." An art therapy educator described how the multi-sensory engagement with media in the creative arts therapies exposes faculty to their personal vulnerabilities. "I take the information in on many different levels, not just verbally. I respond to the art, client and student in terms of color, texture, movement and other visual elements. This engages me on a deeper personal level than talking. The art experience has an intensity that touches much closer to my most basic being. This is the power and also the fearful element of the medium. Art therapists often do verbal therapy because the art, or feeling part, becomes too threatening. The person needs great stamina and strength in order to be involved in this work; to go out and come back and rejuvenate. Some people can bring many things together and others cannot; they become overly distracted. It takes great mental capacity to know when I have reached my limits; to go beyond but get back; to know when I have reached the end of my capacity and must sleep. The sick or weak person may get into the magic garden but cannot get out. If I go beyond I must maintain a consciousness that will enable me to return."

Educators spoke with deep conviction about the necessity of recognizing that the student's personal emotions and life struggles, as well as those of faculty members, cannot be avoided in training therapists. What appears to emerge from their descriptions is the need to become aware of this factor and to develop a personal philosophy and style for engaging the material. An educator described the importance of not becoming so involved in the student's personal life that it is impossible to fulfill the faculty role. The line between faculty's therapeutic and educational roles with students was presented as being °fine" and delicate. "What is happening is very intense. Criticism tends to be amplified and heightened. It cannot help becoming a therapy-like process. This cannot be avoided. It is necessary for students and supervisors to speak about the dynamics of their relationships often. Supervisors sometimes stray and use their powers and their students to gratify their needs. Roles must be constantly clarified."

Faculty describe how it takes skill and experience to assist students when they become deeply involved in personal feelings while also maintaining the role of teacher. They spoke of how the faculty member must take on so many challenging roles while also being constantly exposed to personal and institutionalized forms of criticism and evaluation. The work clearly demands exceptional personal abilities and emotional determination and strength.

I discussed the problems of beginners who take on these difficult roles. If experienced and prominent educators find the work so challenging, it might be asked how a novice can survive and operate competently. A senior educator described how beginners "have to take risks; go slowly; be willing to fail and learn from it; trust their instincts; acknowledge their inexperience; and stay with the work. If a person gives up, it is gone. Those of us who are still at it have simply stayed with it. Educators have to continuously observe what they are learning and make it part of themselves." The principle error made by beginning as well as veteran educators is the creation of a facade of excessive control which hides personal insecurity. The master teacher is consistently the one who is able to learn from students and the context while acknowledging personal fallibility.

Prominent educators and program directors also have difficulties that are unique to their status. Directors told me that students often see them as "over-powerful" and are less likely to bring personal problems and errors of judgment to their attention. I have personally found that the director has to express an interest in the individual student and project an image of accessibility. I have consistently discovered that when I make myself available to students, they will generally respect my role and time. There is also enormous personal gratification attached to helping students. When I am deeply involved in the many demands of program development and leadership, I have to constantly remind myself that it is an interest in serving students and the learning process that brought me to higher education and not a desire for a career in administration. I have found that when I make myself inaccessible to students, I spend more time and energy defending my privacy and trying eventually to compensate for the interpersonal tension that my behavior may provoke. It is far more efficient, effective and personally rewarding to strive toward openness and hospitality. I have also found that "powerful" directors must express a personal "vulnerability" and humanness if students are to take them into their confidence. An experienced creative arts therapy program director said, "We cannot deny the emotional relationships that we have with our students. I have to understand how I relate to the student and how I am being perceived. I must also realize that I represent some object from the student's past. A psychiatrist once told me that I cannot be mother, teacher, therapist, etc. I disagree. I have to know when it is appropriate to be a mother and when it is not. The highly subjective nature of interpersonal work cannot be avoided."

A number of program directors described how they struggle with the institutional pressures of the schools that they work within. Educators varied in terms of their responses to this issue. Some have complete support and recognition within their institutions and others find the complexities of academic politics to be a "tremendous drain." Educators who left their roles as program directors spoke of how difficult it was to cope with institutional and national association politics. A program director in a liberal arts college described how discouraging it is when the school's administration does not understand the program. "The college values students who are high testers and who deal with the world rationally. Oftentimes these students find it difficult to get to the emotional self underneath their ideas. They can talk about therapy but have difficulty experiencing the process. A psychology faculty member in the college said to me, 'All of the people you want in your program are the ones we are trying to get out of psychology in the first year.' " This faculty member and others spoke of the struggle that often takes place in convincing both students and institutions that it is worth their while to open to the honest expression of feelings.

In describing the challenges and difficulties required to perfect the art of teaching, creative arts therapy educators reveal how their methods differ from conventional academic lectures and prepared presentations. "It is a constant challenge to work with what is presented to me by students and immediately bring it to clarity without going to an old response. Each class is a re-search for the ability to engage the immediate material. I try to present the theory that is emerging from that point in my life and career rather than the theories of the past . . . . I struggle with the lack of time. There are so many levels to engage as an artist, therapist, teacher and researcher."

I was pleased to see that many of the senior educators in the creative arts therapies spoke of the primacy of art in their work. A dance therapy program director said, "The more I work and the older I get, the more importance I attach to the core art process. Dance therapy has moved heavily toward theoretical inquiry which is necessary in the profession, but the art has much to say about the nature of healing and transformation. We have to keep the artist in ourselves going." Another experienced educator said, "I have been developing an enormous respect for art. You cannot throw art aside or use it as an instrument. I have been developing an almost religious feeling for its importance; an increasing respect and hunger for ART." An art therapy program director who has been active in national association affairs said, "It bothers me that I do not devote enough time to my personal art. We also do not give our students adequate opportunities for their personal artistic expression. We need to be more involved in the creative process. What worries me is that there are art therapists working who do not touch media and I fear that the understanding of what we are all about may get lost."

My interviews with creative arts therapy educators indicated that there is a stable core of training taking place throughout the country from which the vision of the profession may expand. The most encouraging message that I received from the educators is that creative arts therapy education needs to be focused on the person of the therapist. The collective experience of all of the educators indicated that, "What matters is the person of the therapist and we must therefore try to bring the highest quality people into the field. Numerous studies have shown that it is neither the technique nor the theory that makes for success in therapy."

The longer educators are involved in training therapists, the more they seem to realize that training programs are only an introduction to lifelong learning. The most significant quality of training would appear to be its role in building values and inspiring students to perfect themselves and their profession. An educator described how "The person of the therapist or student influences the training experience. I am concerned with the essentials of self-awareness and creativity in the broadest sense which override issues of particular curriculum content and technique. There is so much information that is necessary to the profession that cannot be covered in a two-year graduate program. The training program is the launching pad which enables the person to practice but should also provide the basis for lifelong learning. Experiential learning is crucial and stresses how the essence of training is the person of the therapist. A two-year master's program only begins to train good clinicians. Research should take place at the post-master's level. We need to create new modalities for research since the old behavioral science methods do no always apply."

Statements like this need to appear in the educational guidelines of national professional associations. In training therapists there must be a recognition that personal life history, style, interests, culture and values have a major impact on how therapeutic identity and skills will emerge. Guidelines for training need to recognize the process of human *emergence* and the manner in which the student's person influences and directs education. If curriculum prescriptions are to exist, it would be useful to address the core issues of training.

It is my belief that a vision of our profession can include excellence in the arts, clinical skills and human understanding. An educator described how, "It is crucial for us to work together in order to develop a solid concept of what the creative arts therapies are. We must learn to respect one another and what we can and cannot do." There is no doubt that there must be increased cooperation between the different creative arts therapy specializations if we are to achieve our shared potential. There is a need to advance the image of the profession in higher education and society. Funding for research in the field should begin to reach the minimal levels achieved by other health professions.

Studies of higher education in the creative arts therapies can become a discipline unto itself. Research into what is required to train creative arts therapists will in turn increase our understanding of clinical work. At the present time, we can take pride in all that has been achieved within the profession in terms of clinical practice and training. It is remarkable that programs have developed with dignity within an economic environment consisting almost exclusively of student tuitions and relatively low salaries for graduates. We have proven our ability to thrive within conditions of adversity. Now it is time to consolidate our gains; strengthen our place within higher education and the places where our graduates are employed; and continue to aspire to the highest limits of art, scholarship and healing. The creative arts therapies have demonstrated their ability to offer excellent training programs within institutions of higher education. The next major objective for the profession must be scholarship, research and the continued heightening of our image as a vital and necessary part of health services.

INDEX

281